Acquiring Enterprise Software: Beating the Vendors at Their Own Game

ISBN 0-13-085731-9

90000

9 780130 857316

Prentice Hall PTR
Enterprise Software Series

Thomas A. Curran, Series Editor

PeopleSoft HRMS Reporting

Bromwich

SAP™ R/3™ Business Blueprint:
Understanding Enterprise Supply Chain Management, Second Edition

Curran / Ladd

SAP™ R/3™ Reporting and eBusiness Intelligence

Curran / Ladd / Ladd

Acquiring Enterprise Software: Beating the Vendors at Their Own Game

Verville / Halingten

Acquiring Enterprise Software: Beating the Vendors at Their Own Game

Jacques Verville
Alannah Halingten

Prentice Hall PTR, Upper Saddle River, NJ 07458
www.phptr.com

Library of Congress Cataloging-in-Publication Data

Verville, Jacques C.

   Acquiring Enterprise software : beating the vendors at their own game / by Jacques C. Verville and Alannah Halingten.

   p. cm.

   ISBN 0-13-085731-9

   1. Application software--Purchasing. I. Halingten, Alannah. II. Title.

QA76.76.A65 V47 2000

658'.0553--dc21

                                         00-034668

Editorial/Production Supervision: *Laura Burgess*	Cover Design: *Nina Scuderi*
Acquisitions Editor: *Tim Moore*	Cover Design Direction: *Jerry Votta*
Editorial Assistant: *Julie Okulicz*	Art Director: *Gail Cocker-Bogusz*
Marketing Manager: *Bryan Gambrel*	Interior Series Design: *Meg VanArsdale*
Buyer: *Maura Goldstaub*	Interior Formatting: *Vanessa Moore*

© 2001 Jacques Verville and Alannah Halingten
Published by Prentice Hall PTR
Prentice-Hall, Inc.
Upper Saddle River, NJ 07458

Prentice Hall books are widely used by corporations and government agencies for training, marketing, and resale.
The publisher offers discounts on this book when ordered in bulk quantities. For more information, contact:
Corporate Sales Department, Prentice Hall PTR
One Lake Street
Upper Saddle River, NJ 07458
Phone: 800-382-3419; FAX: 201-236-7141 • E-mail: corpsales@prenhall.com

SAP is a registered trademark of SAP Aktiengesellschaft, Systems, Applications and Products in Data Processing, Neurottstrasse 16, 69190 Walldorf, Germany. BAAN is a trademark of BAAN Development B.V. PeopleSoft is a trademark of PeopleSoft, Inc. ORACLE is a trademark of ORACLE Corporation. Computron is a trademark of Computron Technologies Corporation. Hyperion is a trademark of Hyperion Software Operations, Inc. SQL Financials is a trademark of SQL Financials International, Inc. Lawson is a trademark of Lawson Associates, Inc. IBM is a trademark of International Business Machines Corporation. INTELSAT is a trademark of International Telecommunications Satellite Organization. INMARSAT is either a collective trademark or collective service mark of International Maritime Satellite Organization. UNIX is a trademark System Laboratories, Inc. Microsoft Windows 3.1/95/97/NT is a trademark of Microsoft Corporation. WordPerfect is a trademark of Satellite Software International. OS/2 is a trademark of International Business Machines Corporation. Gartner Group is a trademark of Gartner Group, Inc. Meta Group is a service mark of Meta Group, Inc. Yankee Group is a service mark of The Yankee Group, Inc. ERPWORLD.COM is a trademark of Advanced Logic Solutions, Inc. Comdex is a trademark of Comdex Inc. Sprint is a service mark of Sprint Communications Company L.P. All other products and company names mentioned herein are the trademarks or registered trademarks of their respective owners.

Printed in the United States of America

10 9 8 7 6 5 4 3 2 1

ISBN 0-13-085731-9

Prentice-Hall International (UK) Limited, *London*
Prentice-Hall of Australia Pty. Limited, *Sydney*
Prentice-Hall Canada Inc., *Toronto*
Prentice-Hall Hispanoamericana, S.A., *Mexico*
Prentice-Hall of India Private Limited, *New Delhi*
Prentice-Hall of Japan, Inc., *Tokyo*
Pearson Education Asia Pte. Ltd.
Editora Prentice-Hall do Brasil, Ltda., *Rio de Janeiro*

For the fullness of love and joy, expressed and reciprocated,
we dedicate this book to our most precious little pumpkin, Geneviève.

Contents

Chapter 2
"Do or Die" The Case of International Air   19

Chapter 3
Detailed Analysis of The Case of International Air   29

Chapter 4
Starting Point: Planning   59

Chapter 5
Request for Proposal   83

Chapter 6
"Even the Small Can Triumph"
The Case of Keller Manufacturing   103

Chapter 7
Detailed Analysis of The Case of Keller Manufacturing   109

Chapter 8
Information Search

Chapter 9
"Investigate, Investigate, Investigate"
The Case of Energy Systems Corporation (ESC)

Chapter 10
Detailed Analysis of The Case of
Energy Systems Corporation (ESC)

Foreword

T his book arises from an area with a clear business requirement. The market for enterprise software has arisen in response to the pragmatic need by corporations for software that handles everything from finance to human resources. Because most of the requirements for this type of software are similar across business areas, it has become cost-effective to consider packaged solutions from enterprise software vendors. The need to revise software for Y2K created a trigger for many enterprise software purchases in the late 90s, but the underlying value from enterprise software makes it a sustaining market. Generally, the message given for corporations in this book is that it is more cost-effective to rely on vendors of these solutions. However, this is an objectively presented book, not one with an axe to grind, and one of the case studies actually decides not to buy, but to build, in-house because of source code control and pricing issues.

One key message from the book is that enterprise software decisions are a business decision, not just an IT decision. Enterprise software affects not just the technical aspects of the IT infrastructure, but also the business processes used by employees as they conduct their business. Hence, the decision processes on enterprise software are months long and involve employees from all parts of a business. Indeed, the early involvement and buy-in of non-IT end users into the choice of enterprise software is given as a key critical success factor.

There are many other such gems to be found in the book. It covers the process from the initial decision to consider the company's enterprise software strategy through planning, evaluation, decision, negotiation, and implementation. Various critical success factors are identified throughout the discussions. All are very pragmatic, and some are not so obvious. For example, the involvement of a non-IT procurement manager early in the process can not only ease the internal acquisition process, but also bring negotiating leverage against the vendors right from the beginning. The combination of key principles such as these with practical examples of checklists for RFPs, legal due diligence, vendor questions, and other areas make this book well worth reading cover to cover.

What I found attractive about this book is the original topic covered using information from real world case studies. It takes the veil off the previously hidden happenings that surround a major corporate software purchase. This unique coverage makes this a valuable book to read for those involved in the IT evaluation, purchase, and implementation of corporate software. Although the book focuses on Enterprise Resource Planning software, many of the lessons are general and apply to any type of major IT procurement.

I am pleased to have been involved in the review of Dr. Verville's and Ms. Halingten's book. I found it very interesting to see all the contortions that corporations go through in evaluating enterprise software. It was very educational and well-written with authentic employee quotes. I am sure you will enjoy reading it too.

Dr. David Spuler
February 5, 2000

Preface

This book represents a compilation of the knowledge we have gained both from our professional experiences and from the study of *how* organizations acquire complex technological solutions. The insights we have acquired from our vantage points as both vendors and buyers of information technology have been incorporated into this book. As for the study, it involved two Fortune 500 companies, one Fortune 1000 company and one medium-size company that had just recently purchased Enterprise Software solutions. The decision process they went through to choose the enterprise solution most suited to their organizational needs was examined.

We have written this book with several intentions.

First, our hope is that it will provide small- to medium-sized companies who are contemplating the purchase of Enterprise Software packages (also known as Enterprise Resource Planning [ERP] software) or other software such as Customer Relationship Management (CRMs), Manufacturing Execution Software (MES), and so forth, but who may not have the resources (whether expertise, financial, or other) necessary to help them in their decision process, with the appropriate guidance and direction that they need in this type of buying situation.

Second, we hope this book will provide large organizations, which may or may not have already been through the experience of trying to implement an enterprise solution, with insights that will make their next foray into Enterprise Software territory less problematic and less costly.

Another objective of the book is to raise the level of awareness of those involved, whether directly or indirectly, in this type of endeavor, to the point of recognizing the significance and importance of certain factors to the successful outcome of this buying task.

To this end, we present a process—end-to-end help, from planning to negotiations—that can be used for proceeding with the acquisition of Enterprise Software (ES) solutions or any other type of complex software. This process, based primarily on our own belief of how these types of purchases should be carried out, has been substantiated by four real world cases, each of which were in the market for different types of ES. These cases are included in this book.

The ES Acquisition Process and each of its constituent parts are described in this book in great detail. Numerous quotes have been included from participants in the Acquisition process which infuse additional insights into the whys and wherefores of the decisions that were made. With the help of this book and the points of reference that are provided, any organization, whether small, medium, or large, should be able to navigate through the process and arrive at a point of choosing the solution that is best suited for its needs.

Among the points of reference, we have included information on:

- forming the Acquisition Team, acquisition strategies and issues, defining requirements and criteria for the selection and evaluation of both the vendors and the software
- tips on what to watch out for during the search for information on vendors/software, the need for both positive and negative information, and the significance of a source's credibility and reliability on the overall acquisition process
- different types and levels of evaluations for the vendors and the ES, the criteria that are involved, and the questions that should be asked to determine the organization's requirements
- the not-so-easy resolution of a final ES choice
- a subtle yet effective "new" approach to negotiations, and software-related issues that are important in the negotiation process
- influences and critical success factors (CSFs) for software acquisitions

We have also included information that we believe will be of value in the construction of a Request for Proposal (RFP) for Enterprise Software. Numerous lists and examples have also been provided and are peppered throughout the book.

Sprinkled among the process chapters are the four cases. The format we have used for them is somewhat similar and this will be noted, especially when it comes to their accompanying analysis chapters. These chapters serve to highlight some very important elements of the ES Acquisition Process that we wanted to reinforce. Without getting into them now, it is sufficient to say that you will know them well by the end of this book.

Our book would not be complete without a discussion on the implementation of the software. Although not the focus of the book, we do touch on the critical issues that are pertinent to both the acquisition of Enterprise Software and its implementation. You will note that most of the issues that are critical to a successful implementation are issues that are addressed during the Acquisition process. And this, as we say, is as it should be.

The ES Acquisition Process is not an isolated process that is limited solely to buying-task-related activities (e.g., issue RFP, review responses, choose the least expensive system, sign contract, issue P.O., take delivery). Rather, its scope is quite broad and complex. In addition to the actual buying task, the Acquisition process involves many people, addresses numerous and varied enterprise-wide issues, depends on several key factors, and lays the foundation upon which the ES's subsequent implementation rests. While some evidence of the success of the process is apparent by the end of the Acquisition process (satisfaction with and user buy-in of the final choice of ES, for example), final judgement on the success or failure of the process will only be rendered when the ES is in the midst of implementation and subsequent to that, rolled out into production. With the weight, then, of these consequences and their far-reaching effects, it is easy to see that a great deal depends on the quality and rigor with which the ES Acquisition Process is carried out.

Whether this book is looked upon as a "how to guide" or as a "starting point" for the buying process, it should help to reduce some of the uncertainty that is associated with these types of buying decisions. Unfortunately, for some who would have wished otherwise and were hoping to find it in this book, we do not advocate any particular packaged ES solution. That is not the intent of this book. While some would have wanted us to render our endorsement of certain tier-1 or tier-2 solutions as the best ones out there, we have purposefully refrained from doing so. We firmly believe that no one is in a position to advocate one solution over another, regardless of the claims in the marketplace. It would also be a highly evident about-face from the stance that we have taken in our book. Throughout the text, we return again and again to the position that an organization needs to choose a packaged ES solution based on its needs. Put another way, the organization will need to appropriately match its needs with the capabilities of the software. Finding the right fit is critical. So while the claims and marketing hype might spout "We're #1," it might in fact be #2 or #3 or #4, and so forth, that would be best suited to your organization's needs. But, who are we to say? We don't know your organization. Hence, if we were to endorse any one or only a few vendors, it would not only be contradictory to what we are advocating, but it would also be a disservice to the organizations that would have purchased a specific ES based on our recommendation. That is just the opposite of the service that we are trying to provide here.

This book has been written for a wide range of business professionals who are or will in some way be involved with ES:

1. For the business executives and senior decision makers who are or will be in the market for ES, whether for small, medium, or large-size companies, including:

   - CIOs
   - VPs of IT
   - IS/IT Directors and Managers
   - Department Managers
   - Project Managers

2. For the consultants, industry analysts, software vendors and their staff who are in some way connected with the sales of ES, as it provides an inside look into the buying cycle and the "contortions" that organizations go through when buying this type of technology.
3. For curricula either at the College or University level in Marketing, Information Systems/Technology, and Project Management.

We have been told that this book is a veritable treasure trove of information that will enable readers to grasp the complexities associated with buying these types of systems. We have enjoyed putting it together and we offer it to you in the hope that it will serve you well.

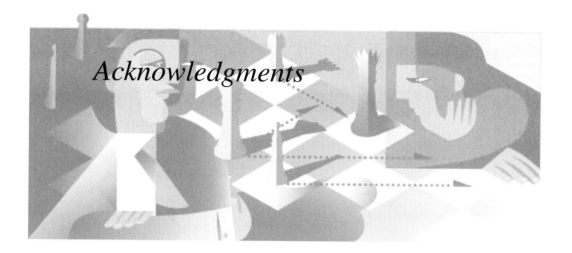

Acknowledgments

Having begun this book at the tail end of Jacques' dissertation, we were coasting on fumes of exhaustion. Our gratitude, therefore, goes to our editor at Prentice Hall, Tim Moore, for his encouragement to "just have fun" with the book and let our personalities show through. His advice became our much-needed second wind that enabled us to complete our book in a timely manner.

We would like to express our thanks to Dr. David A. Spuler for his review of our initial manuscript. His comments and suggestions were greatly appreciated and helped to spur us on to digging out more "gems" for the book.

Our thanks also go to the organizations that agreed to participate in the research project. The knowledge that was gained as a result of the cases helped to substantiate our own beliefs about the Enterprise Software (ES) Acquisition Process.

Thanks are also extended to the many people behind the scenes at Prentice Hall who were involved in bringing our book to market.

Our thanks and appreciation also go to Becky Norlin, Renee Johnson, and the child care providers at MTU Little Huskies in Houghton, MI. They provided such good daycare for our infant daughter, Geneviève, that we were able to work worry-free on our manuscript.

Our thanks and kisses go to our baby daughter, Geneviève, for being such an adorable distraction to the stress and constraints inherent with trying to bring a book to press.

We would also like to acknowledge each other's strengths and contributions. This book represents a veritable team effort between us, truly a coming together of minds, to the point where it is hard to distinguish where the input of one of us ends and the other begins. The spirit of oneness from which this book was conceived is a testament to our unity as a couple, our belief in and our commitment to each other, and our partnership in life and in love.

Last but not least, our deepest gratitude must be extended to that greatest of all Sources that fed us and inspired us when we had no more left to give. Thank you, Father.

Introduction

So, you've got a large task in front of you and you're wondering how we might be able to make it easier for you. You might also be wondering what the big deal is and what makes the acquisition of Enterprise Software (ES) so special that a book has been written about it.

Well, first of all, let us make no bones about it—this is no easy task that you are about to undertake. What's more, this may well be one of the toughest projects your organization has ever gone through. So, if you think buying ES is going to be a "walk in the park," think again. It's very serious business. As you will see, there is so much that goes into it, so many details that need to be considered and attended to—perhaps even more than you might have imagined—that you will be surprised at how such a seemingly simple and straightforward task is, in actual fact, rather complex and arduous.

Second, there is a lot riding on the outcome of this buying task. Don't think for a minute that you will be able to go out and buy an ES package and have it work wonders for your organization—PRESTO!—just like that. Or that, if there are glitches, they can all be fixed during the implementation. Just one look at the headlines of any of the major newspapers or magazines in recent years should tell you that such an approach doesn't work. The headlines recount the horror stories that have been told by several large companies of their troubled attempts, delays, and the millions of dollars in cost overruns that they have spent trying to implement Enterprise Resource Planning (ERP) software. If anything, these stories should be warnings of how high the stakes really are for these types of projects. In some instances, the very existence of those companies has been jeopardized. But, that's not the end of it. More organizations will also suffer the same fate if a better way is not found. What we propose is that better way.

1.1   *WHY ENTERPRISE SOFTWARE?*

In today's intensely competitive international marketplace, information delivery is critical to successful business operations and management. For this, organizations require numerous applications to satisfy their information needs. They are also seeking, more and more, to integrate these numerous applications into one comprehensive, enterprise-wide information system. However, the platform incompatibility between many or all of their systems and the inability of many software applications to integrate or exchange information greatly impede this effort. Organizations are, therefore, turning to packaged enterprise-wide applications such as Enterprise Resource Planning (ERP) software in response to their needs.

Coined in the early to mid-1990s, the term "ERP" originally referred to a suite of integrated software applications that connected back-office operations such as manufacturing, financials, and human resources into one system. Today, however, ERP software consists of applications that link not only back-office operations, but also front-office operations and internal and external supply chains. As such, ERP software has evolved to a much broader scope of applicability in the organization and has literally become the center of the organization's application architecture, or what some have referred to as "the enterprise backbone," linking its functional areas and its business processes.

It is probably for this reason that ERPs, now more commonly referred to as Enterprise Software (ES), have become a viable alternative to in-house development. This may also explain why it has become one of the fastest growing segments of the information technology (IT) industry, with growth rates averaging 30 to 40% per year. While 1999 was the exception (owing to Y2K issues), it is estimated that by the year 2001, worldwide sales of ES will exceed 22 billion dollars (PricewaterhouseCoopers, 1998; Yankee Group, 1998). It is further estimated that by the year 2002, packaged applications will represent a significant portion of most IT portfolios. As it is, overall IT expenditures already represent a significant portion of ongoing capital expenditures for many organizations and will continue to increase. Since the mid to late 1990s, many organizations have concluded that it is more efficient and less costly to replace their aging systems with new packaged software applications. With the goal of imparting new functionality to the organization and solving other issues (one issue being Europe's conversion to a single currency), the acquisition of new packaged ES applications is being looked to as a way to decrease internal development costs.

For organizations both inside and outside of Europe that must deal with the European Monetary Union (EMU), the EMU issue may prove to be more lengthy and hence more costly than Y2K retrofitting was (Pricewaterhouse-Coopers, 1998). With the conversion by countries in the European Union to a common currency called the "Euro" beginning in 1999 with a mandatory December 31, 2001 deadline, European organizations currently have to calculate in two different currencies (the Euro and the currency of the country in which they are located; PricewaterhouseCoopers, 1998). Meanwhile, for organizations with subsidiaries in Europe, their situations are further complicated with having to calculate in at least three different currencies (the Euro, the currency of the country in which the subsidiary is located, and the currency of the country in which the home office resides).

Other factors that will stimulate the growth of the ES market include the expansion of ES into the front-office area (e.g., sales force automation, customer relationship management) as well as into the areas of supply-chain management and electronic commerce (e-commerce), electronic business (e-business), and the diminishing ES life-cycle from 15 to 8 or fewer years (Yankee Group, 1998). Deeper penetration within existing ERP (ES) accounts and continued penetration and servicing of the high-end market will also impact the continued growth of the ES market, not to mention the entire IT industry.

Further growth of the ES market will be stimulated by the expansion by ES vendors into the middle market. Only now are these vendors beginning to target the middle market with full-featured ES solutions that they are tailoring to specific industry business processes. Besides the tailoring that will be done to suit the industry-specific process needs of these mid-sized organizations, the strategy for this market will encompass several other approaches, one of which will be "componentizing" the application implementations so as to reduce complexity, costs, time, and effort (PricewaterhouseCoopers, 1998; Yankee Group, 1998).

The expansion of the ES market, while providing unprecedented opportunities for organizations, also opens them to some potentially significant problems. Among the problems, how to acquire this type of software? Although more and more organizations are turning to ES packages to meet their needs, most have little knowledge about what is involved in acquiring this type of software, let alone the best way of doing so. Since ES packages can cost several thousands, hundreds of thousands, and even millions of dollars, a lack of knowledge about the best or optimum way of acquiring these packages only adds to the already sizable risk involved with choosing ES. It just makes sense then to find out what the best way is for acquiring ES applications.

For organizations, the purchase of ES packages is a high-expenditure activity that consumes a significant portion of their capital budgets. It is also an activity that is fraught with a high level of risk and uncertainty. Why? First of all, if a wrong purchase is made, it can adversely affect the organization as a whole, in several different areas and on several different levels, even to the point of jeopardizing the very existence of the organization. This highlights the obvious need for making the right choice of software. It also brings to light the need for finding the best possible way for acquiring this type of software so that the right choice can be made. The second reason that this activity has a high level of risk and uncertainty is because of the implementation and the risk of it going awry. This risk can be reduced, however, and the chances of a successful implementation increased if the proper foundation is laid beforehand. The Acquisition process set forth in this book will guide organizations in doing just that.

1.2 *THE IMPLEMENTATION OF ENTERPRISE SOFTWARE SOLUTIONS*

ES implementations are said to be the single business initiative most likely to go wrong. Since a successful implementation is dependent on several factors, exclusion of any one or more of them could increase the risk of a less-than-optimal outcome. Several factors, many of which are typically regarded as standard project management guidelines, are critical for the successful implementation of ES, including:

- upper management commitment
- incumbent need for process reengineering or redesign
- appropriately and highly skilled project team
- availability of full-time staffing resources
- in-house project manager
- clearly defined method for tracking and resolving issues
- well-defined project management structure
- application of limits to the project's scope
- recognition of the ES system's limitations
- ability to find experienced implementation partners
- adequate investment in change management (i.e., training programs, process design work, issue resolution, communication to end-users, and post-implementation support)
- a "fit-gap" analysis
- recognition of the two-fold nature of an ES project—that it is as much about people as it is about the technology
- communication
- user buy-in

Necessarily, then, the implementation of ES requires much careful and well-thought-out planning.

1.2.1   ES Implementation Horror Stories

However, waiting until the implementation to consider these issues is, in effect, waiting until it is too late. Consider the following example. An organization approves the purchase of an ES system for financial management, budgeting, human resources, and payroll systems. The technology is purchased. Then, when the organization is in its implementation preparation phase, it proceeds to define its business requirements, determine its business strategy, perform some business process redesign, and define the project scope. Within the same time frame, the project team conducts an analysis of the organization's "as is" and "to be" states by extrapolating from the results of data identified during the preparation phase. Other major activities during the analysis phase include defining current and future functions and processes. Then later, the project team begins its design phase during which the future business functions and processes (defined in the analysis phase) are mapped to the ES's functions. This results in a fit-gap analysis that shows the discrepancies between the organization's needs and the software's capabilities. The average fit-gap, as it turns out, is 40%, meaning that an average of only 60% of the organization's business functions match the ES's functions. Unfortunately, this organization invested a considerable amount of money in an ES product that only marginally fits its needs.

Clearly, there is something wrong with the logic and sequence of how this project was carried out. Wouldn't it have been more logical for the organization to have conducted its "implementation preparation phase" and its "analysis phase" prior to purchasing the software rather than afterwards? In so keeping, shouldn't the fit-gap issue also have been addressed before the ES was purchased?

As the above example and other similar horror stories in the media demonstrate, many implementations are doomed from the start because organizations simply choose the wrong ES solution for their business needs. In some instances, these buying choices were based solely on the "bandwagon effect" or "because so and so bought it" or the answers to "Which ES vendor is #1?" or "What is the best ES solution out there?" Then, in trying to implement the ES, these organizations experienced significant cost overruns and major delays—delays to the point where the systems were still not up and running after 2 years. It seems apparent, then, that while these implementations may not have been "doomed" to fail, they were undoubtedly doomed to experience delays and cost overruns from the modifications that were needed to retrofit the software to their needs.

Certainly, there are many potential benefits to having these systems. The drawbacks, however, are that there can also be numerous costs and risks associated with their implementation. In a study conducted by the Harvard Business

School, 65% of executives believe that ES systems have at least a moderate chance of hurting their business because of potential implementation problems. While it would seem that there are already enough things that can go wrong during an implementation, why would anyone want to further encumber it with the added burden of trying to make right an ill-suited choice?

As previously stated, if the organization waits until the implementation to consider its needs, the fit of the software, etc., it is quite simply waiting until it is too late and inviting trouble. The cause and effect relationship between the acquisition and the implementation is such that if you pick the wrong system, you can expect problems during the implementation. There is no way around it. While the system may be the best in its class, it may not be the best for your organization's needs.

The way to avoid such a situation, though, is as follows. Conduct a careful study prior to the implementation, as we advocate, during which many of the issues that give rise to the risks and additional costs can be addressed. This is one way of reducing and potentially avoiding the delays that could arise, for example, from the need to retrofit technology to the organization during the implementation process. Since many of the issues that should be addressed for the acquisition are also critical to the implementation of the software, attention to these issues at the time of the acquisition could subsequently help to minimize or, perhaps even, avoid delays and cost overruns during the software's implementation, or worse still, noncompletion of the implementation.

1.2.2   Corporate Case Studies

Examples of the type of careful study that should be undertaken for the acquisition of an ES solution are included in this book. These are in the form of four corporate case studies of organizations that went through an extensive Acquisition process to buy packaged ES solutions. The organizations (pseudonymously named, with the exception of Keller) were:

- International Air: a large, international airline corporation that purchased PeopleSoft's ES solution for the sum of US$86 million. The ES Acquisition Process that International Air went through took approximately 9 months and was completed by the summer of 1996. Its subsequent implementation was completed in the scheduled time frame and was regarded a success.
- ESC: a holding company (gas and utilities) that completed the purchase of Oracle's ES solution at a cost of US$6.5 million in March of 1997. Its ES Acquisition Process took approximately 6 months from

start to finish. This case is especially significant because it highlights the need to verify sources of information.

- Telecom International: an international telecommunications organization that began but did not complete the purchase of a proposed US$10 million packaged ES solution. As a result of the strategic nature of the intended purchase, an impasse on the issues of code ownership and cost brought the business negotiations to a halt. The ES Acquisition Process that the organization went through was, nevertheless, quite rigorous and presents some interesting insights and lessons that would be of value to other organizations, including the influence of new management on the overall process.
- Keller Manufacturing Company Inc.: a mid-sized furniture manufacturer that purchased an ES solution from Effective Management Systems (EMS) Inc. for approximately US$1 million. Keller's ES Acquisition Process took approximately 11 months and was completed in August of 1996. Regarded as a great success, the implementation of EMS' software was completed within the scheduled time frame with only a few minor problems.

Many, if not all, of the issues and factors that have already been presented here should be considered during the Acquisition process. These factors, which are deemed as "critical" to the implementation, are equally important and pertinent to the acquisition. There are, however, several other factors that are also critical to the successful acquisition of ES solutions, including:

- Planning—an absolute must if the acquisition is to be a success
- Cross-over of Acquisition Team members to the Implementation project, which provides:
  - continuity,
  - rationale and background,
  - and makes use of the information that was gathered during the Acquisition process and eliminates trying to "re-invent the wheel"
- Careful selection of the Acquisition Team members,
  - including a representative from the Purchasing department
- Interdisciplinary/cross-functional skills of the Acquisition Team's members
- Formality in the structure of the Acquisition process
- Rigor
- Leadership
- Clear and unambiguous authority

- Strong management commitment
- Definition of the requirements—an absolute must prior to even beginning to look at vendors/solutions
- Establishing selection and evaluation criteria—another absolute must prior to looking at vendors/solutions
- Thorough vendor, functional, and technical evaluations
- Scripted vendor demonstrations
- User involvement in the ES Acquisition Process itself
- User involvement in the vendor demonstrations
- User buy-in of the final choice

As will be seen throughout this book, these and numerous other factors need to be addressed and incorporated into the Acquisition process, and for each of the four organizations, these factors played important roles.

One of the objectives, then, for organizations to go through an extensive ES Acquisition Process is to avoid being the casualty of an enterprise project that spins out of control, grows considerably beyond its originally intended scope, and consumes vast amounts of money, time, and effort. Unfortunately, for many companies that have already been down that path and that have fallen victim to such out of control ES projects, if they had known of a better way to approach such projects, one that would have helped them to minimize the risks during implementation, they would most likely have followed it. Instead, though, they had to walk away from their ES projects poorer by tens or even hundreds of millions of dollars with nothing to show for them.

1.2.3   A New Way to Look at Implementation Projects

It is understandable then, with the multitude of organizations that have experienced major delays and significant cost overruns, that organizations embarking on this type of project should be concerned about the ramifications of implementing an integrated ES solution. We believe, however, that these problems arise in part from how these projects are looked at.

Typically, organizations refer to this type of project as an "implementation project" and lump all activities of the project under this general label. In so doing, the major part of the focus and attention is given to the actual implementation of the software and the other activities of the project are considered of secondary or lesser importance. This limited focus, in effect, isolates the implementation into a sort of "vacuum" and has those involved (whether directly or indirectly) in the implementation believing that it is the "end all and be all." Is it any wonder then, with the standard approach being to focus on the implementation, that organizations are experiencing significant cost overruns and delays?

We believe that this singular focus on the end result may be responsible, at least in part, for some of the problems being faced by organizations during ES implementations. This standard approach, it would seem, no longer works. Why?

While many find the actual implementation to be the only interesting and important part of the ES project, we contend:

- First, there is more to an ES project than just the implementation of the software
- Second, the acquisition constitutes the first principal piece of the ES project puzzle
- Third, the process for acquiring the right ES is equally as important and interesting, not to mention challenging, as the implementation

Hence, we believe that by segregating the acquisition for the packaged software from the implementation and looking at these as two separate yet related phases or processes, the attention that has been sorely needed for choosing and buying the software solution could at last be given to the Acquisition process. These two processes, together, provide a more comprehensive view of the whole ES project. Also, instead of thinking of projects solely as "implementation projects," we argue that it would be more accurate and appropriate, at least for Enterprise Software, to refer to them as "ES projects," with the understanding that they consist of two principal and distinct yet related phases: the acquisition phase and the implementation phase.

1.3 THE ENTERPRISE SOFTWARE ACQUISITION PROCESS

The ES Acquisition Process is quite broad and complex. Its scope is not limited to regular buying-task-related activities (e.g., issue RFP, review responses, choose the least expensive system, sign contract, issue P.O.); it also involves:

- numerous people
- addressing a broad and varied range of enterprise-wide issues
- depending on several key factors
- the process itself laying the foundation upon which the ES's subsequent implementation rests

While some evidence of the success of the process is apparent by the end of the acquisition, final judgement on the success or failure of the process cannot truly be rendered until the ES is in the midst of implementation and subsequent to that, rolled out into production. With the weight, then, of these consequences and their far-reaching effects, it is easy to see that a great deal depends on the quality and rigor with which the ES Acquisition Process is carried out.

We present our ES Acquisition Process as a guide or at least a starting point for those organizations that do not know where to begin their journey into ES territory. Unfortunately, we cannot guarantee 100% that your organization will decide to buy the right ES solution for its needs. However, we do know that if the guidelines and recommendations set forth here are closely followed, the organization will stand a much greater chance of arriving at the right choice of ES and of having fewer problems with both the acquisition and the implementation.

For each organization that goes through the Acquisition process, a unique combination of factors (such as the type of technology being sought), participants (individuals and departments involved), CSFs, and influences will conspire to form the overall character of the process. As such, no two acquisition processes will ever be exactly the same. The difference stems more from the dynamics involved in the overall Acquisition process rather than the mechanics of the process itself. What do we mean by this? Well, since each acquisition is different, the Acquisition process (and hence the evaluation processes) will necessarily take on slightly different twists depending on the technological solution that is desired, the internal customers, the culture of the organization, and sometimes even the approval process that needs to be followed to get funding. What does this mean to your organization? It means two things:

1. The structure of the ES Acquisition Process will remain the same for most, if not all, of your ES acquisitions.
2. The constituent details or "nuts 'n bolts" that go into each major component of each process will vary, as will some of the "intangible" elements that influence the process.

The acquisition of ES software involves several major processes. Figure 1–1 shows the inter-related and iterative nature of each of the individual processes.

The ES Acquisition Process (see Figure 1–1) has the following characteristics:

1. Begins with planning
2. Ends with negotiations
3. Some of the processes are done concurrently
4. Each process results in deliverables that are used by another process

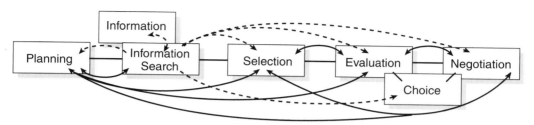

▶ **Figure 1–1**   The Enterprise Software Acquisition Process

1.3.1   The Planning Process

The majority of the time spent during the ES Acquisition Process is in the Planning process with planning and preparations being done for the other parts of the process. This is as it should be.

Planning begins very shortly after the decision is made to purchase an ES. Then, a short time after that (once some initial meetings have occurred to get things underway and the Acquisition Team has been formed and met to do some planning, etc.), the search for information begins. As described in Chapter 8, the search for information would include the gathering of information on the organization's requirements and following that, the establishment of selection and evaluation criteria. At the same time, the Acquisition Team would be developing its acquisition strategies, setting its acquisition project time frame, and looking at issues that are pertinent to the acquisition. Then, a little further into the process, with the organizational and systems requirements defined and various criteria established, the Marketplace Analysis would occur. Information on vendors and their solutions would be screened using high-level vendor, functional, and technical criteria, with the end result being a long-list of vendors/solutions. Beyond this, the Team would be putting together the RFP and sending it to the vendors on its long-list.

The Planning Process contains seven categories that reflect the principal activities that should occur during this phase of the Acquisition process (see Figure 1–2).

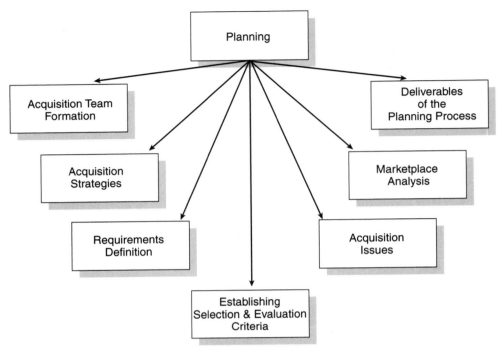

▶ **Figure 1–2**   Planning

Acquisition Team Formation

This first element plays an important role in the success of the acquisition project. In the formation of the Acquisition Team, it will be necessary to:

- Select a project leader. The project leader may or may not be from IT department.
- Identify the skills that will be required for the Acquisition Team. Each individual team member needs to have skills that enable him or her to assume a specific set of tasks or responsibilities within the project.
- Build a cross-functional/multidisciplinary team.
- Define each of the roles of the individuals that would be on the Team. Each individual team member will need to perform a functional and/or advisory role based on his or her abilities or past experiences. Each team member also needs to understand each role as it belongs to each team member, as well as those roles shared among members.

- Assess whether outside experts or consultants are needed to complement the Acquisition Team members' skills.
- Include both users and IT staff. Members of the Acquisition Team can be drawn from the various departments that would be impacted by the ES. User participation is crucial to establishing the buy-in that will improve the chances of a successful implementation later on.
- Include a representative from the Purchasing Department on the Acquisition Team and have him or her involved right from the earliest stages of the acquisition process. This can help the deal and save the company both a lot of time and money.
- Consider the long-term availability of individuals when recruiting them for the Acquisition Team.
- Consider the "cross-over" participation of many of the Acquisition Team's members from the acquisition project to the implementation project.

Acquisition Strategies

The strategies that the Team develops for the ES acquisition should help reduce some of the uncertainty associated with this decision process. Strategies might be developed regarding such things as the scope of the acquisition, and the types of vendors to consider. For example, as a strategy for conducting the Marketplace Analysis (Chapter 4), will the Acquisition Team use the services of a professional research group such as Gartner Group or will the Team conduct its own search? Either way, what criteria do you have for identifying the vendors/products that you will deal with? Where will you look for information? The strategy that your Team decides upon will have an impact on how you conduct the Marketplace Analysis as well as the Information Search process (Chapter 8). It will also start you thinking about the different types and levels of criteria that you will need to establish for your search, more of which is discussed in Chapter 12. Other strategies for the acquisition that will be discussed include:

- Vendor awareness session
- Scripted vendor demonstrations
- Videotaped presentations

Requirements Definition

The Acquisition Team will need to define the organization's requirements for the ES solution. To do so, the Team will have to analyze and/or define:

- Organization's current technological environment
- Functional requirements

- Technical requirements
- Organizational (business, procedural, policy) requirements
- Different user areas and functions
- Existing processes in the areas that will be affected by the new software
- As many problems and opportunities as possible

This information will be used to construct the RFP and will also provide the basis from which selection and evaluation criteria can be established.

Establish Selection and Evaluation Criteria

The Team will also need to establish its selection and evaluation criteria prior to contacting any vendor or looking at ES solutions. These criteria should be based on information that has been gathered from the users and other sources. Once established, these will be used in the RFP that will be sent to potential ES vendors. In addition, these will also be used, in part, for the Marketplace Analysis, the Selection process, and for the three different areas/types of evaluation that will need to be performed during the Acquisition process. These may also be used to create questionnaires and grids/matrices that could be useful during the Evaluation process.

Acquisition Issues

The Acquisition Team will benefit by considering as many issues, factors, and concerns as possible that might affect the acquisition at hand. In doing so, the Team could plan for how to handle potential problems that might arise later in the Acquisition process. Since these issues might also affect the implementation of the ES, the Acquisition Team should approach these issues with an eye toward the implementation. One such acquisition issue is Business Process Reengineering (BPR) and its ramifications. A major implication of buying an ES solution is that it will require the redesign of existing processes in the areas in which the software will be applied. Some common acquisition issues are BPR and management commitment.

Marketplace Analysis

During this analysis, the Acquisition Team is able to determine who the major players are in the marketplace for the ES that they are seeking. This analysis is conducted using high-level criteria to evaluate both the vendors and the functional and technical features of the software and results in a short long-list of potential vendors and solutions.

Deliverables

Various deliverables result from the execution of each of the foregoing elements. A few examples of the deliverables from the Planning process include the construction of the RFP (the primary deliverable), the formation of the Acquisition Team, and the creation of a short long-list of vendors.

1.3.2   The Information Search Process

One of the stages that occurs concurrently to the Planning process is the Information Search process. As one can discern, information feeds the Acquisition process. As information is obtained, certain issues, activities, and even entire stages are developed by the Acquisition Teams for all parts of the Acquisition process. One might also deduce, therefore, that the quality of the information that is obtained would have a significant impact on the results of the Acquisition process. Hence, both the sources and types of information that are gathered require due consideration during the Information Search process of the Acquisition process, and both will be discussed later in Chapter 8.

Since information is always feeding the Acquisition process, the Information Search process is an iterative one. It consists of two principal elements: information screening and information sources.

Information sources, both internal and external, provide the Acquisition process with differing types of information. This information is screened in accordance with the level of scrutiny warranted by the stage at which the Acquisition Team is in the Acquisition process. Put another way, initial searches only require high-level screenings of information based on fairly general (high-level) criteria; subsequent searches and reviews require increasingly intensive levels of scrutiny against more detailed criteria. Several key factors regarding information come into play during this process and among them are:

- Type or nature of the information gathered
- Credibility and reliability of the sources, whether internal or external
- Credibility and reliability of the information obtained
- Outside references including client referrals from the vendors
- Possibility of information overload and confusion

1.3.3   The Selection Process

The Selection process is the intermediate stage between the Planning process and the Evaluation process. It consists of only two principal elements: evaluate RFP/RFQs and create a short-list of vendors and technologies.

The Selection process begins following the return of the RFPs from the vendors. A review of the RFP responses (using lower level criteria to evaluate the vendors and the ES's functionalities and technical dimensions) would occur and the vendors deemed most likely to meet the organization's needs would be retained. A more intense evaluation of the vendors might also occur at this point using Dunn & Bradstreet (D&B) reports, among others.

1.3.4 The Evaluation Process

The Evaluation process consists of three distinct areas of evaluation: Vendor, Functional, and Technical. The criteria and strategies that are established during the Planning process are used to implement all three types of evaluations.

The Vendor Evaluation process is carried out in part during the Planning process and the Marketplace Analysis. Vendor Evaluation is also ongoing throughout the rest of the process during the Selection process's review of the RFPs, the Evaluation process (with client referrals and input from other sources), and the Business Negotiations process (on-going dealings with the vendors). Functional and Technical Evaluations are carried out partially during the Selection process and then more intensively during the Functional and Technical Evaluation processes. Since the evaluation of the software (using scripted demonstrations) takes center stage at this point in the Acquisition process, somewhat lesser attention is given to the Vendor Evaluation process.

1.3.5 The Choice Process

Choice follows as a natural result of the preceding processes. For the most part, the Choice process stands on its own and typically involves the conveyance of a final recommendation to an outside group (Steering Committee or Board of Directors) for authorization of the final choice.

1.3.6 The Negotiations Process

The Negotiation process is divided into two types of negotiations: Business and Legal. The Business Negotiation process is an informal but continuous subtone throughout most of the ES Acquisition Process. As many issues as possible should be addressed during the Business Negotiation phase. Then, once tentative agreements are reached and the choice is made, Legal Negotiations can proceed leading to the completion and sign-off of the final contract. Although the majority of the issues that need to be included in the final negotiations should have been covered during the Business Negotiations, the Legal Negotiations process will undoubtedly require new information as the final details are worked out for the contract.

1.4   *INFLUENCES AND CRITICAL SUCCESS FACTORS*

Several different influences will affect the ES Acquisition Process. While some of these have an impact on the Acquisition process, others have more of an impact on the Acquisition Team or the final choice of ES solution. While the subtlety of their impacts may seem negligible, a disregard of these may lead to potentially undesirable consequences. Such influences that are discussed here include:

- Organizational culture
- User buy-in
- Strong management commitment
- Leadership
- Acquisition Team composition
- Past experience

As with the influences, there are numerous factors (as previously noted) that are critical to the successful outcome of this process, including:

- Planning
- Cross-over of Acquisition Team members to the Implementation project
- Interdisciplinary nature of the Acquisition Team
- Clear and unambiguous authority
- Definition of the requirements
- Evaluations—Vendor, Functional, and Technical
- Structured process
- Rigorous
- User participation

1.5   *REFERENCES*

PricewaterhouseCoopers. (1998). *Technology forecast: 1999*. (10th anniversary ed.). Menlo Park, CA: PricewaterhouseCoopers Technology Centre.

Yankee Group. (1998). "ERP software market: Is the replacement cycle over?" *Enterprise Applications*, *3*(8).

2

"Do or Die"
The Case of
International Air

This chapter presents the case of International Air, a large international airline corporation that completed the purchase of a well-known ES solution in the summer of 1996. The chapter begins with a presentation of International Air's corporate profile and is followed by a background description of the circumstances that led to the decision to buy a packaged ES solution. Following that, an overview of the ES Acquisition Process that International Air went through to arrive at its final choice is presented.

2.1 ORGANIZATIONAL PROFILE

International Air, a large international carrier, provides air transportation services for passengers and cargo both to domestic and international arenas. Together with its regional partners, International Air's route network provides transportation services to 125 cities worldwide, including 97 cities in North America and 22 cities in Europe, Asia, the Middle East, and the Caribbean. It also provides charter services to six international destinations as well as cargo services to 65 destinations worldwide.

International Air's operations include a large aircraft and engine maintenance business that provides maintenance services to airlines and other customers. Other services that are also offered include computer and ground-handling services to airlines and other customers. Among its holdings, International Air retains 100% interest in five regional airlines, one of the largest computer reservation systems, and a major tour operator. It also holds minority interests in other travel- and transportation-related businesses.

2.2   BACKGROUND

By 1995, International Air's Honeywell-Bull mainframe system was running
with hardware and software that was more than 10 years old. The system contained information that was extremely important to International Air's daily
operations. With the system due for changes (whether through upgrade, conversion, or replacement), action needed to be taken soon, but how long could International Air postpone the inevitable without impeding or hindering its
operations?

2.2.1   Getting Underway

In August of 1990, International Air's Strategic and Technological Planning
Group presented the Board of Directors with a request for a "global" authority
for commitment (AFC) for a strategy to replace the Honeywell-Bull system. (An
AFC is a proof of commitment or sign-off that must be obtained from International Air's Board of Directors and Steering Committee before work can proceed on a project.) The strategy would involve the replacement of the
Honeywell-Bull with an IBM mainframe and the conversion or replacement of
more than 5,000 applications that were then executing on the Bull system. The
funds requested with this AFC (each AFC represents an allotment of funds that
is committed whether to a specific phase of a project or to an entire project), in
the amount of US$36 million, would be used to convert 1,500 Bull programs to
the IBM mainframe platform, while the remaining applications would be
replaced with new applications under separate projects. (Since the "Bull Migration Project" actually comprised many projects spanning several years, several
AFCs needed to be obtained, in some cases, for each major phase of each
project.) The request was approved.

Since then, a number of initiatives were undertaken to execute this strategy.
The Board subsequently approved the replacement of the revenue accounting
system for the Finance Branch and the procurement, inventory management,
and aircraft maintenance systems for the Technical Operations Branch. These
initiatives represented somewhat less than 40% of all the applications that were
on the Honeywell-Bull system.

Five years later (1995), more than 60% of the 5,000+ applications still
remained (in whole or in part) on the Bull, awaiting conversion or replacement.
While various projects involving the initial 1,500 programs were progressing,
these had yet to be all delivered, and numerous others still needed to be started.
Major upgrades of both hardware and software were needed to support critical
applications, such as payroll and the airline schedule. Other major areas
included Finance, Human Resources, and Sales Reporting. In the interim, continued maintenance was being provided for the Bull, though without any new
enhancements.

2.2.2 Y2K Systems Failures

Up to this point, International Air had, for the most part, adopted a status quo approach. However, status quo was no longer feasible. In January 1995, the urgency of this situation was escalated when one of the applications on the Bull failed. An investigation into the problem revealed that the application had tried to perform a forward-looking date function (looking 5 years ahead) that the Bull's operating system did not support. It became evident that other applications would experience the same problems and serious system failures on the Bull were imminent. Thus, the Y2K issue became a major problem for International Air, the impact of which would be felt starting in 1999.

So it was that in the fall of 1995, the IT Group presented a revised "global" AFC to the Steering Committee covering the planning phase, for eventual presentation and approval by the Board in May 1996 (date later changed to August 1996). This AFC, for more than US$2 million (which was approved), would authorize the IT Group to proceed, in the first part, with an in-depth evaluation of the different alternatives available to International Air and to recommend either re-investment in the Bull technology or completion of the Bull de-hosting program.

Several key issues influenced the evaluation by the IT Group, the most significant of which were the reliability (or rather, the unreliability) of the Bull platform and the inability of the applications and processing environment to support the Y2K problem. Given the uncertain condition of the Bull and the critical nature of systems such as finance and human resources, some applications had been partially migrated, some had been duplicated, and still others had been developed on an IBM host system; both systems (the Bull and the IBM host) were then integrated through a series of interfaces. Because of the gradual and partial migration, and to provide better integration, functionality, data integrity, and overall architecture to facilitate their maintenance, the IT Group's evaluation also included the reassessment of some of the applications that were already transferred (in whole or in part) to the IBM host.

2.2.3 Investigating Options

In light of these issues, the IT Group examined four possible scenarios with which to meet this situation involving the Bull environment (hardware, software, and peripherally affected systems):

1. Upgrade the current Bull environment and stay with the current applications
2. Upgrade the current Bull environment and renew the applications

3. Convert the remaining Bull applications to an IBM compatible environment and invest the minimum required on the Bull system
4. Eliminate the Bull system completely and
   (a) purchase new software packages or
   (b) convert or
   (c) rewrite the applications for their IBM systems or
   (d) outsource the functions

The first two scenarios were considered unfeasible given the probability that the vendor, Honeywell-Bull, would be moving toward open systems over the next few years and that they would be providing decreasing support to their mainframe product line. From International Air's perspective and relative to their goals, Honeywell-Bull would not be the strategic mainframe "vendor-of-choice" for the long term and, hence, the decision was made to move away from this platform.

The third scenario of converting applications to the IBM platform would allow International Air to continue to operate. However, it would not address the issue of inadequate functionality or the gap between what was provided by these systems and what is required to run the business in an increasingly competitive and complex environment.

Lastly, the fourth option would eliminate the Bull host completely and would position International Air for the future with either new software packages, modified and enhanced applications, or with the functions being outsourced. All of the applications that remained on the Bull system were reviewed against these four scenarios.

The IT Group also evaluated these scenarios on the basis of financial considerations (cost and benefits) which they included in their Business Case and which are summarized here:

COST:

- With the third scenario, straight conversion (without enhancement), over the next 10 years, of all remaining applications (Finance, Human Resources, Payroll, etc.) from the Bull to an IBM-compatible environment with minimal investment on the Bull system, was estimated at US$65 million.
- With the fourth scenario, the same applications could be replaced and enhanced for an additional US$15 million, hence US$80 million, over the same 10-year period. However, in this case, there would be significant benefits.

BENEFITS:

- With the third scenario, there were no foreseeable benefits.
- With the fourth scenario, headcount could be reduced by 37, representing a savings of US$9 million. An additional US$12 million could be saved as a result of improved cash management and expense control. Additional benefits estimated at US$110 million could be derived through access to valuable management information, mainly in the areas of profitability and sales. (The economic justification was based on the realization of the headcount savings, the cost reductions and 25% of the management information benefits. The IT Group also estimated that this implementation could yield a return of 20.5% and would better position International Air for the future.)

While the IT Group concluded that the third and fourth scenarios were the only two viable options available to International Air, they recommended the fourth, which would lead to the elimination of the Bull system.

2.2.4   Buy, Convert, Rewrite, or Outsource?

The IT Group then proceeded, in the second part, to evaluate the options available to them in the fourth scenario, namely, the options of buying a software package(s), converting, rewriting, or outsourcing the applications. For this, they performed functional requirement analyses, developed the request for supplier proposals, and developed the business case and schedule required to complete the project. This second part (with some overlap from the first part) of the AFC was referred to as the "preliminary analysis and planning phase of the Bull replacement project."

In their evaluation of the fourth scenario, the IT Group determined that for some of the applications, conversion would be the most feasible option available to them due to the specificity and uniqueness of the software functions for International Air. For other applications, rewriting was the best solution. For others still, the purchase of a software package offered the most cost effective and timely solution.

2.2.5   Final Recommendation and "Go-Ahead"

A summary of the IT Group's final recommendations and project plan were presented to the Board and included:

1. Remove International Air completely from the Bull
2. Renew or replace the applications and thereby provide enhanced functionality for International Air users
3. Reduce application maintenance costs
4. Improve system and functionality integration by renewing or replacing systems
5. Assist in improving International Air's business processes

The Board granted their AFC providing the go-ahead for the IT Group to commence the Bull replacement project.

2.2.6   One Issue Still Outstanding—Buy or Build?

The only decision that remained was whether to build or to buy. While the option of rewriting the Finance, Human Resources, and Payroll applications was initially reviewed, it was discarded early on (February 1996) in favor of buying a packaged solution. It was readily agreed that "in the 1990s, you do not build, you buy, especially if it is software that is a generic application or in generic use by the industry." With the decision being made to purchase a packaged ES, International Air's Project Leaders proceeded to plan a set of activities which they would use to select the appropriate technological solution.

"In the 1990s, you don't build—you buy!"

A Request for Proposal (RFP) was subsequently issued in March 1996 to several software vendors, four of which responded and three of which were thoroughly evaluated. In July 1996, the packaged software solution by PeopleSoft Inc., a recognized industry leader, was chosen to provide International Air with its integrated Finance, Human Resources, and Payroll applications. Not only would this packaged software allow them to implement within a short time frame (especially given the imposing deadline of 1999 less than 3 years in the future), but International Air surmised that the use of a standard software package would allow them to rapidly implement new functions developed by the software provider and would also reduce their internal development cycle for modifying the software to meet their own unique requirements. Again, the argument presented by the team was that when software is already available on the market for a generic function or is in generic use by the industry, "you don't build, you buy." International Air's management reasoned that since every company has financial and human resource systems, it makes little sense to invest time, money, and effort to build when state-of-the-art software is readily available. Other factors that affected the decision to buy an integrated solution included the 1999/Y2K deadline, then just 2½ years away, and the restrictions that it imposed.

2.3 *INTERNATIONAL AIR'S ES ACQUISITION PROCESS*

The ES solution that International Air decided to purchase needed to meet all of the finance, payroll, and human resource software requirements of the following business sectors:

- Payroll
- Pension
- Administration
- Time and Labor
- Collection
- Finance
- General Ledger
- Budgeting
- Forecasting
- Corporate Reporting
- Accounts Payable
- Accounts Receivable

Hence, the solution would need to be consistent with the vision of each of the business areas covered by the scope of this acquisition as well as that of the Technology Strategy Group. The solution would also need to support International Air's operations on an international scale. Given the strategic nature of the software, it would have to integrate well into International Air's global environment. Other objectives included the capability of the packaged ES to correctly handle the processing associated with Y2K and beyond, and the ability to implement it no later than December 1998.

> **International Air's ES Objectives**
> - Meet software requirements of 12 business sectors
> - Consistency with the vision of each business sector
> - Support operations on an international scale
> - Integrate into International Air's global environment
> - Handle Y2K and beyond processing needs
> - To be up and running by December 1998

2.3.1   First Things First—Planning

With these objectives clearly defined, International Air began the Acquisition process by planning a set of activities to select and purchase the packaged ES. This set of activities (plan) consisted of a series of processes that were based in part on formally defined standard purchasing procedures and routine project management protocols. The plan was also sufficiently flexible to accommodate unknown variables that would arise during the Acquisition process as a result of the special nature and complexity of the software package being purchased. Also, because this was International Air's first time purchase of a complex software package, they did not know what to expect or how exactly to proceed.

The software acquisition planning process that was part of International Air's initial planning phase began in 1996, and signaled the start of the acquisition. Given the broad scope of the proposed acquisition, International Air required additional staff to gather information on the requirements of each of the areas. They also had to build a team of individuals that would not only be part of this initial phase (the acquisition), but that would, for the most part, continue on to the next phase (the implementation of the software). In addition, they had to establish the requirements that would eventually go into an RFP and subsequently be forwarded to the vendors.

Within this planning process, International Air's team outlined strategies and tactics that would be used in the search for the software. They established criteria by which each of the vendors and their products would be evaluated, criteria that included, among others, architecture, functionality, market share of the vendor, and financial viability of the vendor.

Also in this planning process, International Air sought out information (internal and external) on who the major players in the market place were for fully integrated software packages. Then they held an information session where they invited the potential vendors to attend. As part of International Air's strategy, this information session let each vendor know who they would be competing against and also informed them of precisely what International Air was looking for. After this session, one of the major vendors, ORACLE, bowed out. Following this information session, an RFP was issued (on March 1, 1996) and the vendors were given 1 month to respond.

2.3.2 Eliminating Prospects

After the initial review of the RFP responses, International Air realized that they had to go back to the vendors for more information due to some modifications they had made to the initial RFP. They realized just how much each vendor's pricing of the product differed and the extreme difficulty they would have in making one-to-one or side-by-side comparisons of the software package offerings. Consequently, International Air issued an addendum to each of the potential vendors that stipulated the method according to which the product was to be cost out. A 1-week deadline was given, following which International Air did an evaluation of the responses (early May 1996). From an initial group of approximately seven vendors, the list was narrowed down to three vendors—SAP, PeopleSoft, and D&B.

International Air subsequently began (in June 1996) a more intensified evaluation of the products from each of these three vendors. Each vendor was invited to put together a 3-day session where International Air brought in approximately 50 of their users to evaluate the functionality aspects of the software. As part of their strategy, they supplied each vendor with scripted scenarios in which specific functions needed to be demonstrated. These were the most complex and demanding requirements that International Air had. The performance of the software in each of the specified areas would allow International Air to differentiate each of the vendors' products from each other. Also, as part of these 3-day sessions, International Air wanted to gain a better understanding of the vendors technologies and to see how their software would perform. These sessions also enabled International Air to evaluate and validate the information that was provided in the vendors' RFP responses by comparing it with what was shown in the scripted demonstrations.

2.3.3 And the Winner Is . . .

Based on the results of these evaluations, International Air was able to reduce their list to two vendors—PeopleSoft (the primary choice) and SAP. At this point, International Air began to negotiate with their primary vendor.

In July 1996, International Air entered into general business negotiations (as opposed to contractual negotiations with the final terms and conditions) with PeopleSoft. The business negotiations process allowed International Air to agree informally on all of the terms and conditions that were critical to their business, ranging from product support to cost. (All that remained was to translate the business terms into legal terms and conditions.) The objective of this process was to produce a revised proposal, which International Air called a "business understanding document," whose purpose was to clarify all that International Air had negotiated with their primary vendor. Another objective of this document was to serve as a "letter of intent" to the preferred vendor, PeopleSoft, declaring International Air's intention (commitment) to buy their (PeopleSoft's) ES solution.

Later in July 1996, with the "business understanding document" in hand, International Air went to their Board for final approval. Once approval from the Board was given, the final contract was put together. One of the critical items that led to the successful closure of the whole negotiation process was a performance clause that International Air steadfastly insisted upon and was finally agreed to by the vendor. The final contract was then signed.

From the point shortly after the decision to buy an ES was made to the signing of the final contract, the ES Acquisition Process that International Air went through took approximately 9 months to complete. The final choice was People-Soft's packaged ES at a cost of US$86 million. Its subsequent implementation was completed in the scheduled time frame and was regarded a success. According to all involved in both the ES Acquisition Process and the implementation process, the PeopleSoft solution was the right choice for International Air.

In the next chapter, the ES Acquisition Process that International Air used will be looked at more closely. Beginning with Planning, each of the processes that make up the Acquisition process will be broken down and the activities that International Air undertook will be discussed.

3

Detailed Analysis of The Case of International Air

This chapter presents a detailed account of the processes and activities that International Air completed for the acquisition of PeopleSoft's ES solution. The case of International Air is an excellent example of the level of focus and care that needs to be given to the ES Acquisition Process. It is particularly noteworthy for the thoroughness and painstaking attention to detail that was given to the Planning process. This attention resulted in an Acquisition Team that was very well prepared for the challenge of the ES Acquisition Process and the choice of an ES solution that was right for the International Air organization.

3.1   PLANNING PROCESS

> The more work you do before selecting the package, the better. It decreases the surprises and allows you to prepare ahead of time all things that have to be considered in order to put the package into place—and there are certainly quite a number of them. (Project Manager–Technical)

For International Air, planning marked the beginning of the Acquisition process. Planning encompassed all of the activities that International Air deemed necessary to pursue this endeavor. In global terms, planning included meetings to determine schedules, priorities, participants, and resources that would be required; activities and tasks that would need to be completed; types and sources of information to be sought; and so forth. Although the Manager of Capital Equipment Purchasing at International Air did not use the word "planning," he spoke of meetings in which issues were discussed and goals, milestones, and so forth, were set forth:

> . . . meeting that included . . . Project Director, myself (Purchasing) and . . . Project Manager (technical). We wanted to establish our "P" (proposal) process, exactly what our goals would be, what the timeline was, and what the transit conditions of the RFP would be, etc.

As for the Project Director, he spoke of planning in the context of project management:

> . . . project management approach in terms of defining a detailed plan, assigning responsibilities, startup dates, milestones, planning, tracking, and steering committee reporting.

It is clear that there was a great deal of planning done by International Air for this acquisition. Much thought and attention was given to every stage of the ES Acquisition Process during this phase (Planning) so as to lay the foundation for undertaking the acquisition. The planning that was done by International Air addressed the following issues:

- Participants: Who would participate in the different phases of the acquisition?
- Acquisition Strategies: How would the organization approach and deal with the vendors?
- Establishing Requirements: What are our organizational needs in each of the areas that would be affected by the software?
- Establishing Evaluation Criteria: How would we evaluate the software and against what criteria?
- Contingencies: What contingencies do we have to fall back on should there be a delay or if the final negotiations fail or we are unable to find a suitable packaged solution?

3.1.1   Participants

The Director of Enterprise Systems/IT was responsible for the acquisition project and he selected the main person (Project Director) who would lead the Acquisition process for this project. Responsibility of the overall process/project was given to the Project Director who, in turn, had to select the various managers, leaders, and individuals who would participate in the process. Individuals were recruited from within the organization. These individuals were from the various departments that would be immediately affected by the new technology. In all, International Air's Acquisition Team consisted of a core team and several smaller teams, one for each of the 12 business sectors that would be directly impacted by the new technology. Each of the teams also included an IT (technical) representative. External consultants (IT specialists) were also hired for this project.

One of the Project Director's objectives in recruiting people for this acquisition project was his concern for the long-term buy-in and support of the users for the chosen software. One of the keys to ensuring that buy-in and support would occur was to make certain that many of the individuals from International Air's core team would participate not only on the project team for the acquisition of the packaged solution, but that they would also be part of the implementation project. As per the Project Director:

> . . . on the project team, I tried to bring in people that would to be part of the selection and also would be part of the implementation. So that they could not say, "Why did you pick this product? That would never work!" So you wanted to avoid that, so I brought in users and project people that were going to carry this thing through right to the end. So they had a vested interest in picking one they could make work.

For International Air, this approach worked very well. Participant continuity (team members and end-users) for the acquisition through to full implementation helped to ensure user buy-in of the chosen solution.

As one can see from the aforementioned quote, users played an important role in International Air's decision process. It was important to International Air's management that users buy in to (actively endorse and support) the new technology. Without this buy-in, International Air's management felt that the project would be in jeopardy. According to the Director of Enterprise Systems/IT, what International Air wanted was "a consensus from the users for the decision." By having heavy user involvement in the project, management believed that the Acquisition Team would have the support or buy-in from International Air's user community that they (both management and the Project Team) needed. Hence, management wanted each "sector of activity to be represented" by users "so that we would have the buy-in." User participation in the project gave International Air a sense of partnership "with the various users communities and let them come up with a recommendation that they felt comfortable with" (Project Director).

International Air's Steering Committee also had a role in this Acquisition process—they oversaw the project. The Steering Committee was able to allow the Acquisition process to flow relatively unencumbered by alleviating obstacles. As per the Director of Enterprise Systems/IT:

> We had a couple of key decisions made by our Steering Committee during our planning phase, which was earlier on—let's stop considering the Bull scenarios, such as upgrading the Bull; let's stop wasting time elaborating the Bull upgrade scenarios. That freed up our time to work on the other scenarios.

> Another key decision was, if it is out there in the market, we are not going to consider coding. That was another key decision that freed us up. You could have elaborated hundreds of scenarios in this type of acquisition. We would have been all over the place and working on poor scenarios. Fortunately, our Steering Committee helped us eliminate scenarios.

The Purchasing Department also had a role that began early in the Acquisition process and that was facilitated by a partnership approach initiated by the Project Director. During the Planning phase, the Project Director met with both the Manager of Capital Equipment Purchasing and the Project Manager–Technical to establish their RFP process—exactly what their goals would be for the RFP, what their timeline was, and what the transit conditions of the RFP would be. Although the Manager of Capital Equipment Purchasing described his role in this process and that of his department as primarily being to "negotiate and get the terms and conditions under a contract that involved our insurance people, taxation people, our law branch, myself, the user group, and the user group firming up the specifications," this example illustrates how Purchasing can play a role in the Acquisition process for more than just the final contract and issuing of a P.O.

3.1.2   Acquisition Strategies

Acquisition Strategies are strategies International Air employed that impacted their Selection process. International Air's strategy for approaching the various vendors was to bring them all together in a central location and present them with an overview of the type of technology they were looking for. International Air felt that this would enable them to reduce the list of potential vendors and thus eliminate incompatible technologies or solutions early in the process. It also provided another means for International Air to gather more information on each of the vendors. As stated by the Manager of Capital Equipment Purchasing:

> . . . a meeting in Toronto of all potential investors [vendors]. This is unusual because normally we would keep the vendors in the dark about whom they would be competing against. In this particular case, we wanted to get a feel for who could do the work for us and also allow some of them the opportunity to team up or partner together in order to give us the full scope or full sweep of applications which was, ultimately, what we wanted.

This is further supported by the Project Director:

> The first formal step is that we invited all of the potential bidders to an information session. We had all the competitors come in the same room and listen as we gave them, in advance, an understanding of our requirements . . . So we wanted to get a head start, an early advance so that they could prepare, wind up (motivate) their staff, determine the resources required to respond to our requirements. We also wanted to qualify them.

> The good thing it did is that they all knew who their competitors were. So it set an early expectation. As a result of this, one actually dropped out . . . So they saved us a lot of time and they saved themselves a lot of time.

This approach is an example of an unconventional and unusual Acquisition (Buying) Strategy that International Air employed to deal with the vendors. While some companies have lists of qualified vendors that are accessible by the public, this apparently was not the practice at International Air. Hence, for International Air, it was unusual that the competitors were made aware of each other. Also, what made it unconventional was that they gathered the competing vendors together at a neutral site; that is, a conference room in a hotel. This, apparently, gave the "knowingness" an edge that had an effect on the vendors in attendance (with one dropping out of the competition).

Another strategy that International Air planned was to have the short-listed vendors present, over a 2- or 3-day period, their proposed technological solutions. For their presentations, each vendor would be required to use pre-determined scenarios supplied by International Air. According to the Project Director, this would give International Air the opportunity to better understand each vendor's technology:

> . . . gave them (the vendors) some scripts with specific functions that they had to demonstrate to us which were probably some of the most complex and demanding requirements that we had. These we thought

would differentiate one [vendor/technology] from another. As part of this, we also wanted to understand their technology and be able to really see their system, their demo system, in operation.

3.1.3 Establishing Requirements

Given the wide-sweeping range of areas that the software solution was expected to cover, International Air had to determine exactly what requirements would need to be met by the technology as well as what their own business requirements would be, both current and future. They looked at their current resources—what they had, what they were lacking. They determined what they wanted that was not being met by their current systems. In addition to looking at the requirements that would need to be met by the new technology, they also ascertained the resources that would be required to acquire and implement this technology. Hence, they assessed their staffing resources, considered the time requirements, looked at the financial requirements (how much it would cost to add more staff), examined their own systems architecture (would it be sufficient to support the new technology), and so on. They covered all areas of the organization. As per the Director of Enterprise Systems/IT:

> . . . since a lot of areas were to be covered, we needed people to gather requirements in each of these areas and so we had to staff up and start defining the requirements to put into an RFP. We looked at our business requirements, both current and future, and from this, we evaluated the software against those requirements and we said, "This is covered, this is not covered, here there is a gap, etc." We took the list of gaps and said, "How would we bridge those gaps? Do we need to bridge those gaps, and if so, how do we bridge those gaps?"

We then estimated the work needed to bridge the gaps. It was mostly based on current requirements; future requirements were mostly through the acquisition (the software does something that we did not do before) which does bring some benefits. The gaps were mostly to do with features that we already have in our current system that are not found in a packaged solution.

3.1.4 Establishing Evaluation Criteria

International Air's Acquisition Team established criteria for three distinct types of evaluation:

- Vendor
- Functionality
- Technical

Vendor evaluation criteria included size, financial stability, reputation of the vendor, and so forth. Functionality criteria dealt with the features of the software and included functionalities specific to front-end interfaces, user-friendliness, and so on. Technical criteria dealt with the specifics of systems architecture, performance, security, and other related issues.

International Air established all of the evaluation criteria (with very few exceptions) for all three areas early in the Acquisition process (during the Planning process) because the majority of these were needed for incorporation into the RFP that would be sent to the vendors. This document would inform the vendors, in great detail, of the criteria against which their companies and their software solutions would be evaluated. As per the Director of Enterprise Systems/IT:

> We had evaluation criteria and we put them in the RFP. Implicitly, the evaluation criteria were all in the RFP as we were asking vendors to describe each process for each business sector, how they were doing this, if they had software to handle this.

3.1.5 Contingencies

Given the possibility of not being able to find a packaged ES solution that would meet the needs of the organization—what would they do? With International Air, there was no contingency plan per se. Although they did allocate a budgetary buffer of US$3.5 million in case of delays in the implementation of the chosen solution, this was not a full contingency plan. So, while they had contingency money, they did not have a contingency plan.

For International Air, this project offered no alternatives. There was no room for, "what will we do if we cannot find an ES solution?" They had to succeed. They had to find an ES solution that would work for the organization. This was a "do or die" project.

3.1.6 Recap of the Planning Process

Everything that was determined during the Planning process was implemented in the other stages of the Acquisition process.

- The acquisition strategies that were discussed earlier had an impact on or were directly involved in the Information Search and the Selection processes.
- With the requirements and the evaluation and selection criteria established, the Acquisition Team was able to proceed by using this information, in part, for:
  - Narrowing their list of vendors (a deliverable of the Planning process)
  - Constructing the RFP (another deliverable of the Planning process)
  - Doing preliminary evaluations of the vendors' RFP responses (during the Selection process)
  - Completing more thorough evaluations of the software (during the Evaluation process)

Some of these elements or tasks worked hand-in-hand, such as for selecting and narrowing the list of vendors. International Air used information that was gathered from all sources, both internal and external, including the vendor awareness session, for example, with information determined through the course of Establishing Evaluation Criteria and Establishing Requirements. This was also the case for evaluating the functionality and technical aspects of the software.

The bottom line is that everything that was set forth during the Planning process was applied in the Information Search process, the Selection process, the Evaluation Process, and so forth. Several deliverables were noted as a result of the Planning process, including:

- The RFP
- The long-list of vendors
- Determination of the selection and evaluation criteria
- The formation of the Acquisition Team
- The determination of acquisition strategies

3.2   INFORMATION SEARCH PROCESS

What is most significant about the Information Search process in this case are the sources of information. Two types of sources were used by the Acquisition Team: internal and external.

As to the internal information sources, International Air availed themselves of information from various sources within the organization that included individual users, team members, and internal consultants. These internal sources provided information primarily on the organization's requirements (existing and forecast) at all of the levels and in all of the areas that the technology would impact (discussed in Section 3.1.3).

External sources were sought to provide information about software solutions that might best meet their needs. International Air conducted a marketplace search, gathering information from such varied sources as external consultants, publications, trade shows, conferences, references, professional networks, the Internet and research services (such as the Gartner Group). Many of these sources are referred to by International Air's Project Director:

> We are a member of the Meta Group, which is a research organization. We also have access to Gartner information through our business partners. These were probably the two major research firms. Then we searched through the Internet and we did a pretty extensive search there. We also did some financial research through D&B in terms of viability of the company. I also talked to my stockbroker . . . and they have a research organization and I gave them the names of the companies to get an assessment of how solid they are and what their long-term viability is. The financial department also took a look at the financial statements and did some assessment there.

> Essentially, those were our sources of information. The rest of them was by talking to clients, asking them who they considered in their selection process. References were either supplied by the vendors or through our research. Those clients that went through an evaluation stage helped us foresee what we could expect which allowed us to either drill down a little deeper into some of the areas that were areas of concern or anticipate some of the surprises that might not present themselves to us, so that we poked at those things much better. So, I would say that the other companies that we talked to also helped us.

Other means that International Air used for obtaining information from the vendors were a Request for Information (RFI) and an information session. International Air used the RFI to gather information from the vendors in order to "size the cost of the software" (Director of Enterprise Systems/IT), among other things. This, coupled with the information session that was discussed in "Acquisition Strategies" in Section 3.1.2, enabled International Air to determine, among other things, its long-list of vendors.

It should also be noted that the credibility of the source of information was important, considering the amount of readily available and oftentimes unreliable information out there. As per International Air's Project Control Officer, they found Gartner Group to be a credible source of information—"You can rely on them."

3.3   SELECTION PROCESS

Concurrent to the Planning process, several iterations of screenings (which could be considered as part of the Selection process) were done during the Information Search process prior to arriving at a short long-list of vendors. Selection and evaluation criteria pertaining to both vendors and technologies were used to screen for vendors that could supply the type of software solution International Air was seeking. According to the Project Director, some of the vendors "we knew were well-known, worldwide corporations that supplied systems. I think that the list included PeopleSoft, SAP, Oracle, . . . Computron, D&B, etc." Then, working from their short long-list (a deliverable from the Planning process), International Air submitted the RFPs to the vendors.

For the most part, the Selection process began at the point when International Air received the RFP responses back from the vendors. With the RFP responses in hand, International Air then proceeded with the paper evaluation of the vendors' packages, that is, they evaluated the responses as they were presented, at face value, on paper. During their evaluation of the responses, International Air became aware of discrepancies in how the costing was done from vendor to vendor, a problem they attributed to their own lack of clarification. Nevertheless, they proceeded to narrow their selection to arrive at their short-list of three vendors. At this point, though, International Air asked the three short-listed vendors to resubmit certain parts of their responses, requesting that costing be done along specific lines and that clarification be made on some items. As indicated by the Project Control Officer:

> There was a lot of clarification that had to happen. Obviously, your proposal is never quite what you want it to be. We had to have the three short-listed vendors do things like re-quote because we were not as precise as we should have been, in terms of how we wanted to quote pricing . . . this was done to provide a consistent view so that we could really, truly compare to make sure that we had the same numbers, viewers, same size of user communities. And, of course, every vendor is different—some by users, some by size of mainframe, and whatever.

Once the requoted responses were received from the vendors and International Air had reviewed them, International Air proceeded to invite the three short-listed vendors to do on-site presentations of their software solutions. Although the Screening of Information could be considered as part of the Selection process, it occurred during and is commonly understood to be a necessary part of any search for information. During their search, International Air performed high-level screenings of information to narrow the field of possible vendors/solutions. As per International Air's Project Manager:

> We had set general criteria, some of which were that we wanted an integrated package, for example, we wanted one that supports our operations not only in Canada, but elsewhere also; and, we wanted one that fits into the [International Air] technology environment, so over and above some of the business requirements, we had some other considerations that we looked for.

So, while it is commonly understood that information screening is done iteratively throughout any process, we are not considering it as part of the Selection process proper, but rather as an integral part of the Information Search process.

Hence, we have chosen to demarcate the Selection process as beginning with the activities following the return of the RFP responses from the vendors. In the case of International Air, their course of action for the Selection process involved two primary objectives/tasks, those being the evaluation of the RFPs and the formation of the short-list of vendors.

3.4 *EVALUATION PROCESS*

There were three distinct types of evaluation that were conducted by International Air: vendor, functionality, and technical. Evaluation criteria for all three types were developed in the Planning phase of the Acquisition process.

3.4.1 Vendor Evaluation

The Vendor Evaluation was conducted based on criteria that were established during the Planning process. Each of the vendors was evaluated in terms of its financial stability, reputation, and so forth, based on D&B reports and other information. According to the Manager of Capital Equipment Purchasing, the vendors were asked to supply "references . . . annual reports . . . and a list of customers that they are dealing with." While evaluation of each vendor's financial stability rested with Purchasing, other aspects of the vendor evaluation rested with a team(s) that was dedicated to "going through each of the vendors references and scoring them" in order to evaluate their long-term viability, among other things.

3.4.2   Functional Evaluation

Responsibility for the evaluation of each technology's functionality rested with the Project Control Officer while responsibility for the evaluation of its technical aspects rested with the Project Manager–Technical. The Functional Evaluation proved to be in and of itself an important process for International Air. It was during the Functional Evaluation that users participated in the decision process. As per the Director of Enterprise Systems/IT, "In a company like ours . . . the users have a lot of say (weight) in those decisions." Functional criteria that were established and questionnaires and scenarios that were developed during the Planning phase of the Acquisition process were implemented. Short-listed vendors were invited to participate in a 2- or 3-day demonstration of their technological solution. According to International Air's Director of Enterprise Systems/IT:

> We then proceeded with demos, three-day long demos with our users. In each case, we had about 50 people (business analysts, project managers, but mostly regular users) who attended these demos.

3.4.3   Technical Evaluation

In parallel with the Functional Evaluation, International Air "also had a team of technical architects looking at the technical aspect of it" (Director of Enterprise Systems/IT). Most of the technical criteria that had been established during the Planning stage and included in the RFP were now tested with the technology. In addition to this, the Project Manager–Technical utilized a methodology developed by IBM called "World-Wide Application Development and System Design Method." This methodology forced the team to identify:

> . . . the key defining characteristics of this system from the point of view of the users, the functions that users wanted to execute, the data that was to be used, the relationship between those three; the locations, the existing equipment into which you were putting this system and the requirements from the point of view of systems management; how available that it would have to be, how fast it would have to be; what . . . the security requirements were; what . . . all the systems management requirements were; and the costs, risks, and implementability.

This allowed the Team to "work with the vendor to define what the major building blocks" were as well as to identify:

• "the major components that were part of their solution;

- the servers, workstations, network components, database management systems, etc.; and
- the processing of data on each of those."

What International Air's Technical Evaluation team learned provided them with an understanding of the "interplay between the various components, workstations, server, traffic going over the network and what the impact of that would be—'Is there a lot of traffic?' and 'What would the response time characteristics be on a local network versus a WAN?'" The Technical Evaluation team also had to determine:

- the "volume of data,
- the volume of processing, and
- the sizing of the various components that were necessary to support all the processing and data that resides on them."

In addition to this, the team "looked at the ability of the whole infrastructure, end-to-end, to support the availability characteristics. In other words, if I lose a terminal, I lose a line, I lose a router, I lose a server, what would happen and what would I have to do to be able to maintain the availability?" The Technical Evaluation team also looked at the software's security from the standpoint of how it was defined and managed. Moreover, they had to:

> . . . take a look at what type of performance we would expect to get; what systems management tools had to be procured; and what systems management processes would have to be executed if they had to have software data distribution across the network, etc.; and from that, they could assess the ability of the overall network to support the business functionality and to integrate into the current environment, and . . . drive out cost for both hardware and software as well as network and manpower.

Again, many of the above requirements were established during the Planning process and added to the RFP.

3.4.4   Evaluation Tools

As part of their Evaluation process, International Air used pair-wise comparisons and assigned weights and scores to the various areas of evaluation. The Project Director describes what they did:

> We had a very "scientific" approach to it, we broke it down into major categories and within each one of those categories, we had multiple

questions. Then we used an evaluation tool to do pair-wise comparisons for each functionality or each characteristic and give it some weighting so that we had a quantifiable assessment on how they met our requirements in the different categories that we had defined, whether for a functionality, technology, support and so on.

What we did was, we established a weighting for each one of those categories. In each category, we had a breakdown in detail, and we had over 400 elements to evaluate, function by function, or characteristic by characteristic, and they were grouped into 7 or 8 major categories, and each of those categories carried a different weight so that we had a quantifying bottom line.

3.5 CHOICE PROCESS

The Acquisition process culminates in the Choice process and consists of the "final choice" or "recommendation." The final choice or recommendation that resulted for International Air, according to the Project Control Officer, "matched the evaluations all the way through."

In addition to the pair-wise comparison that was done in the Evaluation process, a meeting was convened of all of the representatives of the various business groups to see if there was a consensus on which technological solution was the most appropriate for International Air. A "round robin" format was adopted and each business sector representative was able to review the cumulative scores and present a brief summary of the reasons for their scores. It was during this meeting (which lasted 10 hours) that International Air's Acquisition Teams reached a consensus, though not unanimous—one group, Time and Attendance, felt that SAP met their needs much better than PeopleSoft. Nevertheless, once all of the arguments were presented and the Time and Attendance team members became aware of all of the factors relating to the choice of PeopleSoft, they accepted (perhaps reluctantly, perhaps not) the arguments presented by the majority of the teams. It was also made clear during that meeting that International Air's management was committed to "bridging the gap in Time & Attendance with PeopleSoft somehow" (Project Director). Hence, they voted for PeopleSoft.

> . . . when that person listened to all the arguments from everybody, they rallied behind the decision because it was obvious that there were more reasons to choose PeopleSoft than to choose SAP. (Director of Enterprise Systems/IT)

As seen in the following quotation, the final choice (the Choice process) is clearly described by International Air's Director of Enterprise Systems/IT:

> At the end, in one big meeting of 10 hours, we reviewed each area for each business sector. The meeting consisted of 25 people, each representing their sector of activity. Each, as we reviewed the evaluations, presented a summary of the reasons for their scores. What we wanted was a consensus from the users . . . for the decision. With heavy user representation, we would have their buy-in. We wanted each sector of activity to be represented there so that we would have buy-in.

> We did not have unanimity. We chose PeopleSoft, but for Time and Attendance, SAP was better. . . . We did not take a formal vote, we just did a final round-table, and I think based on that, we chose PeopleSoft. The person representing payroll said, "Time and Attendance is much better on SAP, so I vote SAP." But, when that person listened to all the arguments from everybody, they rallied behind the decision because it was obvious that there were more reasons to choose PeopleSoft than to choose SAP. We said that we will bridge the gap in Time and Attendance with PeopleSoft somehow . . .

> My decision . . . and my recommendation to the team was for PeopleSoft because it gives us the flexibility to change while with SAP, you have to implement SAP as is otherwise you get into big trouble—this is when a 2-year project turns into a 5-year project if you try to change too much.

It can be noted that the user community had enthusiastically embraced the PeopleSoft product. If the teams had chosen SAP, they would have had much greater difficulty selling it to their user community than the PeopleSoft product. The Director of Enterprise Systems/IT was very aware of this and believed that it would have been difficult to achieve success without user buy-in and acceptance of the new technology:

> . . . the users outside the room who had participated in the demos were convinced that we were choosing PeopleSoft. They were convinced that PeopleSoft was the best. Choosing SAP would have required one hell of a selling job. We would have had quite a sales job to do [for SAP] as they were very much impressed by the demos they saw [for PeopleSoft].

It should be noted that while PeopleSoft was the Acquisition Team's choice, it was in fact their "recommendation" because it had to be presented to the Board of Directors for their final approval.

The Choice process that was noted in the International Air case consisted of one element, a final recommendation or choice. This recommendation was subsequently conveyed to a body outside the Acquisition Team, the Steering Committee (Board of Directors), for final approval.

As a note about this case regarding the final recommendation, International Air could have been influenced by the fact that they had previously acquired financial or accounting software from Dunn & Bradstreet (D&B). While International Air had considered D&B's solution (D&B was on International Air's short-list of three vendors), the issue of D&B being a former supplier to International Air did not appear to have had much (if any) impact on their final choice of software solution. As per the Director of Enterprise Systems/IT:

> We also thought that we should still look at D&B, though, and there was still a life scenario where we would use D&B for finance and perhaps one of the two other vendors (PeopleSoft or SAP) for HR since we were on D&B for our GL (General Ledger) and we figured that there might be some advantage to converting from the old GL to the new GL and so we wanted to explore that a little bit more. As it turned out, there was really no advantage.

Again, if it had been an issue, in all probability, it would have been dealt with during the Selection process. Moreover, if, as a former supplier, D&B had been more favorably considered, then we speculate that International Air would have ranked them first on their short-list.

3.6   NEGOTIATION PROCESS

Negotiations were pervasive throughout most of the Acquisition process. However, there were, in effect, two distinct types of negotiation processes that took place and this is supported by the Project Director:

> There were two types of negotiations, the business negotiations and then the legal negotiations.

The Business Negotiations were characterized as being informal, while the Legal Negotiations were characterized as formal. According to the Director of Enterprise Systems/IT, they entered serious business negotiations with both their primary and secondary vendors of choice, PeopleSoft and SAP.

> We kept the two vendors in the loop until we had a final contract with PeopleSoft. We did play one against the other for a while. One of the

things that we wanted to negotiate with them both had to do with their pricing structures. We managed to get PeopleSoft to be more flexible on their pricing structure, but SAP stayed quite rigid as we expected. SAP has a reputation for being rigid either in contract negotiations or in technical negotiations, technical issues resolution. Then we proceeded to sign a contract when we figured the negotiations were the way we wanted them to be (Director of Enterprise Systems/IT).

For International Air, it was the Project Director and the Manager of Capital Equipment Purchasing who conducted the Business Negotiations. As per the Project Director:

> We were in a partnership mode with them (Purchasing) and every time there were any negotiations, both of us would be sitting with the vendor.

The Manager of Capital Equipment Purchasing was also involved for the signing of the final contract. According to the Director of Enterprise Systems/IT:

> Then we proceeded to sign a contract when we figured the negotiations were the way we wanted them to be. For this, we involved the Purchasing Group [the Manager of Capital Equipment Purchasing] who helped us through this.

According to the Project Director, the objective of the Business Negotiations was to iron out the "major issues, come to an agreement, and agree on the words to put in the final letter" which they referred to as a "business understanding document." The issues that were negotiated included terms and conditions, implementation, scheduling, performance, and training, among others.

> . . . we entered a business negotiation phase as opposed to a contractual negotiation phase. That phase was to agree on all of the terms and conditions that were critical to the business, anywhere from product support to key terms and conditions. The only thing that we did not do there was to translate that into legal terms.

> The objective was to produce a final revised proposal which was what we called a "business understanding document," a letter of a few pages that clarified everything that we had been negotiating. . . . The objective at the end of this was to give them a letter of intent and advise the other vendor that they had lost.

In the process, we visited the vendor on their site and then renegotiated every term that we thought was critical. That gave us a final price and allowed us to complete our business case. (Project Director)

Once an agreement was made with the vendor of choice (PeopleSoft), "the legal people were ready and available to start the legal negotiations process." The Project Director relates the following:

As soon as we got the funding approved, then we went into legal negotiations. That is so much more detailed—looking at terms and conditions and what happens if [International Air] buys a company or sells a company or if, the supplier, went bankrupt or all those other possibilities of ownership, escrow agreements; and all of those types of terms and conditions. That allowed us to put together a final contract and then sign it, and we just made it in time to take delivery as agreed to during the business agreement negotiations phase.

According to the Director of Enterprise Systems/IT, the Legal Negotiations involved "some intense discussions with our lawyers, their lawyers, and there were some points that we could not agree on." One of the critical issues that concerned International Air related to the performance of the software on a wide-area network (WAN).

The last issue was performance. We wanted a performance clause guaranteeing us that the system would work better in the future releases. We even went to see for ourselves, since we had heard rumors, and the industry was unanimous in saying that over a WAN, for remote users, the system is slow. This is due to the high traffic. . . . It does generate a lot of traffic over the network, and on the WAN, with lower line speeds, the response time is slow.

So we went to San Francisco to their office with some of our performance people. We put devices called "sniffers" on the line and simulated a WAN. We brought our own network equipment, our own sniffers, and really analyzed the behavior of the application over the WAN.

Since this was the number one issue with PeopleSoft, we went and dug very deep to understand how it worked. We talked to their VPs—the VP for PeopleTools, the VP for Performance, the VP for Applications, and we discussed their future plans. We did all of this before we signed the final contract.

At the end, we did discuss and argue about performance clauses and penalties, and we were able to get that in. So once that was settled, we signed the contract.

As to how this process could be characterized, it appeared to us that the Business Negotiations were fluid throughout most of the process. When asked to characterize the Negotiation process, the Manager of Capital Equipment Purchasing replied that "the negotiations were ongoing—it is an evolutionary process," that they start "the minute we begin contact with the vendor," and that they are "fluid" throughout the Acquisition process.

3.7   *INFLUENCES*

Several influences were noted in the case of International Air. They are presented as to the principal targets of their effects. Hence, the influences are categorized according to their effects on the Acquisition process, the final choice of ES solution or the Acquisition Team.

3.7.1   Influences on the Acquisition Process

The following items had varying influences on International Air's ES Acquisition Process:

- Obsolete systems
- Y2K
- Project management techniques
- Technical aspects of the ES system
- User community

Obsolete Systems

This factor was a definite influence for International Air. In fact, since the Bull systems were no longer being supported by either the vendor or third party providers, and personnel trained on these systems are extremely difficult to find, it was the primary reason for deciding to undertake the Bull replacement project, and following that, the ES acquisition project.

Y2K

Another factor that influenced International Air's process was Y2K. The Project Manager–Technical commented that:

[International Air] came to a realization they had to do something with certain systems in human resources and finance and others that existed on legacy systems, specifically the Bull and some on the IBM mainframe systems, from the point of view of functionality as well as obsolescence of the technology, both hardware and logically software, because it wasn't year 2000 compliant.

Project Management Techniques

The project management techniques that were used to structure the Acquisition process were a procedural type of influence.

> We used the traditional project management approach in terms of defining a detailed plan, assigning responsibilities, startup dates, milestones, planning, tracking, and steering committee reporting. So, we handled this as a significant project actually and we spent a couple of million dollars going through that process. (Project Director)

Since project management techniques are normally used by the MIS/IT department (and probably less so by user departments) in an organization to structure IT projects, they are familiar tools that were relied upon for this process. As such, these techniques influenced the structure of the Acquisition process that resulted at International Air.

Technical Aspects of the ES System

Other influences arising from the technical aspects of the software, including such issues as performance, influenced both the Business and Legal Negotiations. This specific issue gave rise to a clause guaranteeing performance that became a part of the final contract between International Air and PeopleSoft. This influence also affected the final choice of ES.

User Community

One influence that played a significant part in this case came from the user community within International Air. According to the Director of Enterprise Systems/IT, "users have a lot of power in determining their functionality." The reason for the heavy user involvement within the Acquisition process was that their buy-in would weigh heavily in determining the final recommendation. As iterated by the Director of Enterprise Systems/IT, to "get the buy-in from the users—make sure that their input was considered and make sure that they were involved in the decision."

3.7.2 Influences on the Final Choice of ES

The following items had varying influences on International Air's final choice of ES:

- Economic factors
- Support for geographically dispersed global operations
- Single vendor solution
- Business process reengineering
- Vendor demonstrations

Economic Factors

Economic factors, in terms of the various costs that are associated with this type acquisition, influenced the process and consequently, the final choice of ES solution. According to the Project Director, "the recommendation had to take into account all the costs associated with not only the software, but the implementation of the software."

Support for Geographically Dispersed Global Operations

First, it was of major importance to International Air that the vendor be capable of supporting the software in International Air's geographically dispersed global operations. As one of International Air's criteria for the evaluation of the vendors, this factor influenced their selection process.

Single Vendor Solution

Another influence arose from the desire, by International Air, for a single vendor solution. According to the Director of Enterprise Systems/IT: "We did prefer a single vendor."

Business Process Reengineering

Another factor that influenced the final choice of ES was Business Process Reengineering (BPR). As part of the functionality of the software solution, International Air wanted to be able to incorporate some aspects of BPR into their existing processes. However, the amount of reengineering that would or rather could be successfully incorporated into their existing processes would be influenced not only by the user community, but by the overall organizational culture at International Air. As stated by the Director or Enterprise Systems/IT:

Business Process Reengineering is difficult in a company like ours because the users have a lot of say (weight) in those decisions. That's the culture of the company.

According to the Director of Enterprise Systems/IT, to implement BPR at International Air would be a major task, not only because of the reengineering process itself, but because implementing such changes to existing processes within International Air would require a substantial effort to obtain user buy-in. As per the Director of Enterprise Systems/IT, this was one of the reasons why International Air chose PeopleSoft over SAP:

> . . . decision factor and my recommendation to the team was for People-Soft because it gives us the flexibility to change while with SAP, you have to implement SAP as is otherwise you get into big trouble. (Director of Enterprise Systems/IT)

Vendor Demonstrations

Vendor demonstrations were yet another influence. Vendor demonstrations, specifically with their flashy "bells and whistles," can influence users (particularly casual or less experienced users) to lose their objectivity regarding the effectiveness of a software tool for the jobs/tasks that they perform. Since the Director of Enterprise Systems/IT and other project team members were aware of this possibility, they endeavored to maintain their own objectivity during all of the vendor demonstration.

> We had to be very careful that we were not influenced too much by the enthusiasm of the users as we have to look not only at the "color of the car and at the nice flashy paint job," but also at "what's under the hood" as well. We had to make some kind of abstraction of the enthusiasm. While we had to take it into account, we had to also make sure that we were analyzing the product itself very objectively. (Director of Enterprise Systems/IT)

3.7.3   Influences on the Acquisition Team

The following items had varying influences on International Air's Acquisition Team:

- Leadership
- Competency
- Interdisciplinary nature of the Acquisition Team

- User participation
- Past experience

Leadership

Leadership was a driving factor in the Acquisition process. The leadership exhibited by the Director of Enterprise Systems/IT and the Project Director drove the process. Though not stated directly, the impact of the Project Director's leadership skills were apparent on all of the processes within the Acquisition process. Moreover, the data reflect the confidence that the Steering Committeeand the Board of Directors had in the leadership abilities of these individuals and, consequently, in the Acquisition Team:

> So all the way along we proved and gained credibility which is very instrumental to management support which has been very instrumental all the way along. (Project Manager–Technical)

As a group, International Air's Steering Committee also took a leadership role by removing several administrative obstacles that were part of International Air's standard administrative processes. By doing so, they enabled the acquisition project to progress more quickly. As stated by the Director of Enterprise Systems/IT when asked if the Steering Committee had an influence on the direction:

> Fortunately, our Steering Committee helped us eliminate scenarios. Each scenario can become ten different scenarios once you break it down into smaller pieces. We tried to keep focus on the main scenarios which we thought were the right ones and not waste time on some other perhaps plausible scenarios . . . this did help us to stay focused. In other words, typically at International Air, you may be asked to over-analyze something—breakdown scenarios into small pieces, investigate this, that, etc., and that was a concern. This would have made the process much longer if we had to spin-off scenario 1A, 1B, etc. We presented the broad scenarios and eliminated some as we went along.

Competency

The competency of the various Project Managers and the Project Control Officer was another factor that influenced the process. This factor is a testament to the skill of the Director of Enterprise Systems/IT and the Project Director in selecting team members for the acquisition project. As per the Project Manager–Technical:

> . . . we had a project director, . . . who was just loaded with common sense and has the wide ability to understand issues and questions and to boil things down to what is absolutely necessary to understand. I think there were other people in the project that had that ability also.

> The second thing, I guess, is the experience that people had, the variety of backgrounds. We brought in people from [International Air] as well as from outside that were from many different firms, so we really had a diversity of viewpoints and experiences that contributed quite success-fully to things that we did. I think, for example, that . . . brought in a lot of rigor and a lot of insight into the package acquisition process. It was he that came up with the idea of the pair-wise comparison for the evaluation. Good tools, good communications between the project members, lots and lots of meetings that were long but contributed to the communications.

Interdisciplinary Nature of the Acquisition Team

First, the Acquisition Team was interdisciplinary, composed of highly moti-vated professionals, and each team was very cohesive. This factor was important not only to the outcome of the process, but was also a definite influence on the process itself. As stated by the Project Director–Technical:

> . . . we worked very well together as a team: free exchange of ideas, . . . a real professional desire to get the job done. Highly motivated. People excited about the project.

User Participation

Because of the influence of the user community on International Air's Acqui-sition process, user participation played an important part in and had an impact on the process. According to the Director of Enterprise Systems/IT:

> What we wanted was a consensus from the users for the decision. With heavy user representation, we would have their buy-in.

Once again, it comes down to user buy-in. However, without user participa-tion, International Air would not have obtained user buy-in.

Past Experience

Another influence that affected the Acquisition process came from the past experience, either positive or negative, of individuals involved in the Acquisition process. In International Air's case, the effect of a negative past experience (i.e., a previous failure in the attempt to develop this system in-house) was noticeable in the attitudes of various individuals involved in this process.

This negative past experience also served as a motivational influence. For certain of the individuals who were involved in the failed project, that experience was a major motivating factor for completing this project successfully.

> Also another motivating factor was the need to accomplish the task. Interesting to note too that [International Air] had many false starts and I think that was, in my mind, a motivating factor, that we were not going to be another false start. Past experience was not going to reproduce itself. (Project Manager–Technical)

Although not tangible elements of the process, the memories of that past failure produced an underlying tension or need to succeed that was pervasive throughout the ES Acquisition Process and which could be seen in the level of detail that was attended to during the Planning process.

For International Air, past experience was both a positive influence (learning from their past experience) and a benign negative influence which brought with it a fear of the possibility of history repeating itself. The newcomers to the organization who were involved in the process had to deal with this dichotomy throughout the Acquisition process.

> [International Air's] past experience having been part way through this process and having had another vendor, this was around 1990, where at that point they chose to go through a development process as opposed to purchase or do an acquisition. I think that had a very strong influence because we certainly had a number of people in the project team that had been through that experience and they brought the good and bad with them.

> That had a strong influence because people would bring some bad history with them and you always had to work at saying, "That was the last time. We are not going to make that mistake. We are going to try to do something different this time." You had to work on that, and it was hard to understand from all of us being outsiders since you do not have that history. So it was hard to make sure that you are always aware of that. (Project Control Officer)

This fear (of history repeating itself, of another failure) was apparent not only at the level of the individual team members, but also at the management level. For instance, from the Director of Enterprise Systems/IT, there seemed to be a strong need on his/Management's part for successful completion of this acquisition. This need was two-fold. The first and most obvious reason was the fate of the company—this was a "do or die" project. Second, there seemed to be some personal stakes involved relating to the credibility of the IT department. With the image of the past failure still lingering in Management's memories, it was imperative that this project succeed. For one or both of these reasons, the urgent need to successfully complete the task was apparent.

Linked with past experience was the influencing factor of Y2K and the realization that if they did not succeed in replacing their aging systems, International Air would suffer dire consequences. According to the Project Manager–Technical:

> . . . one motivating factor, interestingly enough, was the realization on the part of International Air, especially, and the project team, that we had to absolutely do something since we were facing the year 2000 and if we didn't do something, if we didn't get these systems off the legacy mainframes in time, they would "blow-up," and International Air's existence would be at stake.

3.8   CHARACTERISTICS AND CRITICAL SUCCESS FACTORS (CSFS)

Several factors were noted about the ES Acquisition Process in this case that were critical to its successful outcome. In addition, some of the influences that were discussed in the previous section were also CSFs of the process and these are included here. The following list includes all of the CSFs for International Air:

- Planning
- Evaluation—Vendor, Functional, and Technical
- Formal process
- Structured process
- Rigorous
- User-driven
- Partnership
- Leadership
- Competency/skills of the Acquisition Team members
- Interdisciplinary nature of the Acquisition Team
- User participation

Various elements from the Planning and Evaluation processes were critical to International Air's ES Acquisition Process. Their omission would have resulted in a less-than-optimal outcome for the International Air organization. For International Air, the elements that stand out the most are as follows:

- **Planning:** The most outstanding characteristic and CSF of the ES Acquisition Process for International Air was that it was planned. The successful outcome of the Acquisition process can be attributed in large part to the level and rigor of planning and preparation that International Air's Acquisition Team did.
- **Evaluation:** Another outstanding characteristic and CSF of International Air's ES Acquisition Process was the detailed manner in which the evaluation criteria were established and the care with which the evaluations of the ES vendors and software solutions were carried out. This was critical to the determination of the right fit of ES for International Air.
- **Formal process:** The process that the Team developed for this acquisition was very formal. As attested by the Manager of Capital Equipment Purchasing:

  > The key characteristic that sticks out the most is the structure (the planning) that was put together by the Project Director. It had a high degree of formalization—it was well planned. Also, keeping some flexibility in the process. The process can be described as fluid.

- **Structured process:** Another characteristic of the Acquisition process for International Air is that it was a structured process. This characteristic could also be considered one of this process' CSFs. In addition to the previous quotation from the Manager–Capital Equipment Purchasing, the Director of Enterprise Systems/IT stated the following about the structure of the process:

  > Since we had to cover 12 or so sectors of activities, we had to put a structure around this to be able to get it done. . . . We did plan, at the lower level, the steps that we were going to take as part of the selection process. . . . We invented this process, not as we went along, but we had to plan for it ahead of time and then execute. There was no documentation at the time at [International Air]. Because of the magnitude of all the sectors involved, we had to put a structure around it because of the size, the number of people involved, and the complexity.

- **Rigorous:** According to the Project Control Officer, International Air designed a formal process that was very rigorous.

  > We needed a formal process and so we designed a very formal process, very rigorous, very quantitative, everything can be backed up, you name it, we have it documented. . . . the documentation was very rigorous and the process was very rigorous. (Project Control Officer)

- **User-driven:** It is worth noting that, in this case, a CSF of International Air's Acquisition process is that it was user-driven. This was considered by each of the participants to be very important to the successful outcome of their process. According to the Director of Enterprise Systems/IT and the Project Director, to ensure the success of the acquisition and full user buy-in, they had heavy user involvement in the decision process, with user representation from each sector of activity:

  > Get the buy-in from the users—make sure that their input was considered and make sure that they were involved in the decision.

- **Partnership:** Similarly, another CSF of the process, according to the Director of Enterprise Systems/IT, is the sense of partnership that the Team worked to establish not only with various user communities and Purchasing, but also with the potential vendor:

  > I think in that sense I tried to create more of a partnership approach internally with the various user communities and let them come up with a recommendation that they felt comfortable with. Similarly with Purchasing, right from the beginning, we worked in a partnership approach. We tried to establish the same working relationship with the vendor to avoid a conflictual approach.

Other factors that were noted in the previous section as influences were also CSFs of International Air's ES Acquisition Process: Leadership, Competency/skills of the Acquisition Team members, Interdisciplinary nature of the Acquisition Team, and User buy-in.

3.9 LESSONS LEARNED

Although International Air was a large organization already well versed in the exercise of making very large purchases, the Acquisition process for the People-Soft ES was nevertheless a learning experience for it. Some of the lessons that were learned from this experience were that:

1. **They had to develop new procedures for dealing with ES acquisitions.** As described by the Director of Enterprise Systems/IT:

> We invented this process, not as we went along, but we had to plan for it ahead of time and then execute. There was no documentation at the time at [International Air]. Because of the magnitude of all the sectors involved, we had to put a structure around it because of the size, the number people involved, and the complexity.

   With this having been a first-time purchase of packaged software of this complexity and magnitude, there were no procedures in place that the Acquisition Team could follow for this purchase. One might nevertheless presume that, at the very least, there were some fundamental processes (procedures) or guidelines in place for International Air's Acquisition Team to follow for proceeding with certain aspects of the buying task. In large part, though, various procedures had to be developed ad hoc to deal with this "new" buying situation.

2. **They had to modify existing purchasing procedures.** Among some of the fundamental procedures that were already in place within International Air for the Acquisition Team to follow, were standard procedures for purchasing. However, those standard purchasing procedures needed to be modified to suit the complexity of this acquisition. According to the Project Control Officer:

> We do not typically do this in IT [reference here is to incredibly large purchases of IT such as for this acquisition], so the process wasn't geared to an IT purchase. So we had to make some adjustments . . . We had to make adjustments to terms and conditions that Purchasing provided because they did not quite match the kinds of things you want to have guaranteed when you are buying something like this. . . . So although they were used to this type of process and buying things, [vehicles], of this magnitude, . . . a lot of rigor was added by the outside consultants that were brought in.

3. **They had to take into account past experience.** Though intangible, past experience was a factor that the Acquisition Team members learned to deal with during this experience.

For this experience, International Air's Acquisition Team took extra care to formally document the process. Since a number of individuals involved in this acquisition were not directly employed by International Air, the Team wanted to leave behind some documentation explaining the rationale that was used and the decisions that were made for choosing the PeopleSoft technology over another. As a result, the Team contributed a documented history of what transpired during this acquisition process to the organizational memory.

> We needed a formal process and so we designed a very formal process, very rigorous, very quantitative, everything can be backed up, you name it, we have it documented. We really went formally for a couple of reasons: most of us were not [International Air's] people, so we wanted to make sure that we left behind the appropriate rationale as opposed to a more typical situation where we would all be done with a company and we could always rely on someone's memory—that may or may not have happened here. Since no one really knew who would continue on the project, the documentation was very rigorous and the process was very rigorous. (Project Control Officer)

4 *Starting Point: Planning*

Okay. So it's been decided that the organization needs Enterprise Software and you've been asked or "designated" to go out and buy it. You've heard about this type of software. You may even have had some prior experience from a previous job with using it, but you weren't involved in buying it. So, now what? Where do you begin? What do you look for? Who are the vendors? Who should be involved in buying it—can you do it alone or can you have someone, say from the Purchasing department do it, or do more people have to be involved? How much does this kind of software cost? And what exactly does your organization need? And what other issues should you be considering? There are a million and one questions.

So, where should you begin? This is where planning comes in. If we had to state what the most critical phase of the Acquisition process is, we would have to say "planning." The depth of planning that is done for an ES acquisition is what is going to give you the edge. The more detail and the more angles that are covered, the better your chances are of succeeding and choosing the right ES solution for your organization. It is during the planning phase that you look at the "Total Cost of Ownership" of the technological solution. By total cost of ownership, we mean all of the tangible and intangible elements that are involved in the purchase. This means more than just looking at the cost of the software itself. The total cost of ownership includes the costs associated with support, maintenance, training, potential disruptions, as well as many other elements and issues that will be discussed throughout this book. It is during the Planning phase that the composition of the Acquisition Team(s) is determined. It is during the Planning phase that buying strategies are developed, selection and evaluation criteria are established, and that the initial marketplace analysis is conducted to investigate the overall ES market. It is during the Planning phase when organizational and other acquisition related issues are identified and addressed. It is also during the Planning phase that the requirements are defined and that a detailed RFP is constructed.

Without going any further right now, it should be safe to say that our point has been made. Planning is highly critical to the ES Acquisition Process. Since there is so much that needs to be planned for and prepared, the odds of succeeding with the Acquisition process will be greatly increased with the more care that is taken to do the Planning process well. Our hope is that, with the information provided here, we can help to make this phase of the ES Acquisition Process a little easier for you.

4.1   THE CONCEPT OF STRATEGIC THINKING

Now, before we continue, we feel that it is important to introduce the concept of "Strategic Thinking" and the role that it can play in the Planning process. Because of the opportunity that is afforded, by the Planning process, to take time out from the normal day-to-day operating tasks to think about and plan for the ES acquisition, the added element of strategic thinking can be brought into play—hence, another reason for the importance of planning or the Planning process.

Beyond the tasks that need to be planned for the ES Acquisition Process, the Acquisition Team has the opportunity to think strategically regarding the needs of the organization and about how the software will meet those needs and help the organization to achieve its goals. It should be noted, however, that strategic thinking requires a certain mindset. It necessitates that the Acquisition Team think of the organization as a whole, a single entity, a cross-functional unit, and not as a group of individual or independent departments. In doing so, the Team will look not only at what the needs are for particular departments or divisions, but they will also look at what the needs are, at least at a higher level, for the whole organization. This exercise really helps to point out whether the two are in sync and in line with the corporate vision, or at odds with each other and counterproductive to the progress of the organization as a single unit. A prime example of this can be seen in the case of Keller Manufacturing. Keller received a recommendation from an outside agency to replace their existing systems in Finance and Human Resources. However, when the Acquisition Team began the ES Acquisition Process, in the Planning process, the Team decided to look at the organization as a whole and asked questions in line with the following:

- "What do we need to do to become more competitive?"
- "What are the areas that we need to look at to make us better?"

- "Where do our problems lie?"
- "What is our 'bread and butter' (that is, what is crucial to our business)?"

What the Team discovered was the need to do something tactical in manufacturing. At the same time, though, they realized that they had to keep in mind the long-term plans of the organization. Thus, in order to meet both objectives—their immediate and pressing needs in manufacturing and the long-term plans of the organization—they had to look at a technological solution for manufacturing that could, at some point in the future, be integrated with Financials, Human Resources, and Payroll. This demonstrates the concept of strategic thinking and how Keller's Acquisition Team used it when they looked at the organization's goals in conjunction with their current needs. Consequently, integratibility became a criterion for selection and evaluation and Keller chose a package that would help them now and in the future.

Another example of strategic thinking comes from the International Air case. During the Planning process (as well as other times during the ES Acquisition Process), the Acquisition Team consulted regularly with International Air's Corporate Strategic Planning Group to ensure that they were in line with the long-term corporate objectives. So, although International Air was looking primarily at Human Resources, Payroll, and Financials, they also had to consider an ES solution that would benefit them, in the long term, in other areas of the organization. In so doing, the Acquisition Team was not only concentrating on their immediate needs, but was also keeping in mind the organization's long-term objectives.

Each of these examples illustrates how the concept of strategic thinking was used. They show the importance of going beyond just doing the acquisition or the buying task routinely, and of considering the long-term objectives of the organization.

Now that we've shared with you our concept of strategic thinking and how you might incorporate it into your planning efforts, let's get started.

4.2   THE ES ACQUISITION PLANNING PROCESS

The Planning process is the phase of the Acquisition process during which the Acquisition Team takes the opportunity to address important issues and answer basic questions regarding all aspects of the acquisition. "Planning," as a process, marks the beginning of the ES Acquisition Process and "planning," as an activity or task, is rather broadly defined. Generally speaking, though, all planning is conducted in the form of meetings, which in some cases can be very formal and in other cases very informal. It is during these meetings that as many major issues, concerns, and questions as possible should be addressed. This is where activities need to be planned for each of the subsequent stages (processes) of the acquisition. Planning, at the level that we saw in the case of International Air, can be likened to the blueprint for a home with all of the specifications set forth so that everyone knows exactly what needs to be done.

There are at least six specific sets of activities that should be completed for the acquisition of ES. These sets of activities and issues, each with its own set of deliverables, are:

- Acquisition Team formation
- Acquisition strategies
- Requirements definition
- Establishing selection and evaluation criteria
- Acquisition issues
- Marketplace analysis

Figure 4–1 illustrates the sets of activities involved in the Planning process.

In addition to these activities/deliverables, the Planning process results in the construction of the RFP that is sent to the vendors. Chapter 5 covers what should go into the making of an RFP for ES.

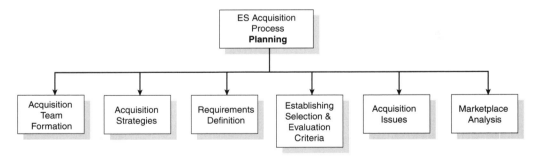

▶ **Figure 4–1**   Planning

4.2.1   Acquisition Team Formation

Once your organization decides that it is going to acquire an ES solution, the selection of who will be responsible for overseeing the Acquisition process and who will participate in it needs to be undertaken. As was seen in the case of International Air and as will be seen in the other three cases, it was a senior executive and/or a Steering Committee comprised of senior executives that designated the individual who would be responsible for overseeing the entire process. For International Air, that person was the Director of Enterprise Systems/IT; for Energy Systems Corporation (ESC), it was the Director of IT; for Keller Manufacturing, it was the CEO/President; and for Telecom International, it was the VP of IT. It was then up to this individual to select a team director or manager (depending on the organization) to head the acquisition project and form an Acquisition Team. As was seen in the case of International Air, the overall responsibility of the Acquisition process for the ES was given to the Director of Information Technology. A Project Director was then appointed to select the Acquisition Team, facilitate the Acquisition process, and coordinate all necessary activities.

For this type of acquisition, the criteria for the selection of the individual who will manage the project will vary. It will depend on the nature, impact, cost, schedule, sensitivity of the requirements, and technological solution that is needed for the organization. While there is no "hard and fast" rule stipulating that only IT personnel should lead a project such as this, typically we have found (through our conversations with other organizations who have completed ES acquisitions and from our own prior experiences) that it is IT/IS professionals with experience in projects that are designated "Project Director" or "Project Manager." Having said that, two of our cases defied that stereotype. In the case of ESC, it was a User Manager from Finance who was designated Project Manager, and in the case of Keller, it was the VP of Engineering/Quality Control who became the VP of IS (but who, in fact, had little experience in IS). These User Managers were identified very early in the process. These individuals either originated the request or were senior members of the user staff. (Formal identification and appointment of these individuals was critical to the success of their organizations' acquisition projects.)

Of equal importance to the selection of a Project Director or Manager is the selection of the members of the Acquisition Team. The organization of the Acquisition Team needs to reflect the activities and tasks that will be undertaken during the ES Acquisition Process. It will also change as the Acquisition process progresses. In so keeping, the composition of the Team will need to be given careful consideration. The Acquisition Team will be responsible for the analysis, documentation, solution design, procurement, and development of criteria and procedures for the selection and evaluation of the technological solution. Its members, therefore, will require specific skills and competencies.

With this in mind, the Project Director and/or Manager will need to develop a detailed list of individuals for the project. This is an important step that should be completed early in the Planning process. It will require identifying and ascertaining the availability of users and management staff from key areas of the organization, as well as obtaining their commitment to participate in the project.

You will also want to consider the following when recruiting individuals for the Acquisition Team—the "cross-over" participation of many of these individuals from the acquisition project to the implementation. Not only would these individuals be involved on the Acquisition Team and be responsible for recommending the appropriate technological solution, but certain individuals among this group would also be involved in its implementation. This is a good strategy to consider. If you think about it, how better to ensure the continuity of a process that was begun with the acquisition and to provide other members of the Implementation Team (who were not involved with the acquisition) with the reasons and background for selecting a certain software, than to have members of the Acquisition Team as part of the implementation.

An example of how one organization approached the formation of an Acquisition Team for this project comes from International Air. At the earliest stages of the Planning process, International Air's management realized that they had to identify the skills that would be required for the Acquisition Team. They concluded that a combination of consultant (internal and external) and client (individuals from the various areas of International Air) expertise would best meet their needs. They also defined the roles of each of the individuals who would be on the Team.

In almost all instances, the role of each individual on the Acquisition Team is determined in part by their skills and in part by the department they represent (these usually correlate). While a few examples are given regarding some of the team members' roles and responsibilities, the focus of roles in this text is on the part (role) that the departments play in the process. Since the team members represented specific departments on the Team, with each department playing a role in the process, the team members assumed those roles on the Team.

One example of a role that was already discussed is that of team leader, which at International Air was referred to as Project Manager. Another example comes from the case of Telecom International. In both International Air and Telecom International's cases, a team member was designated to conduct the Marketplace Analysis that was part of the Information Search process.

The conceptualization of teams as structures of positions and roles is an integral part of a project. While the careful selection of team members is critical for any project, it is especially critical for the acquisition of ES. Since this type of technological solution is so complex and diverse in nature, the Acquisition Team needs to be equally diverse in the skills that are required of its team members. Hence, each individual team member needs to have skills that enable him or her to assume a specific set of tasks or responsibilities within the project. Moreover, each individual team member needs to be selected to perform a functional and/or advisory role based on his or her abilities or past experiences. Examples of this are drawn from the case of International Air. Prior to this acquisition project, several of the team members had participated in an internal development project for HR, Finance, and Accounting applications, which was unsuccessful. This example is two-fold—first, these individuals were selected because of the abilities (technical and other) that they brought to this acquisition project; second, they already had the experience they had gained from having worked on that past project. There is, however, more to the latter part of this example than is apparent at first glance. (Refer to Chapter 16 for more on the influence of past experience on the Acquisition process.)

It is also important that each team member understand each role as it belongs to each team member, as well as those roles which are shared among members. This last factor especially implies the need for a cross-functional/multidisciplinary team. By the careful selection of Acquisition Team members, the Team will benefit from each individual team member's talents, knowledge, and past experiences.

Since ES solutions are often strategic in nature, spanning a wide range of sectors in an organization, the Acquisition Team will necessarily be composed of highly skilled individuals from within the organization and, when needed, outside experts and consultants. As was seen in the case of International Air and as will also be seen in the case of ESC, outside experts were hired to complement the Acquisition Team members' skills. For International Air, consultants from Advantis were hired; for ESC, the consultants were from Arthur Andersen Business Consulting. For this acquisition, the organizations had to deal with a plethora of information technologies (databases, programming languages, platforms, operating systems, etc.) and needed to draw on experts in each of these areas. In addition to the expertise that these consultants had in their respective areas, in the case of International Air they were needed to supplement its existing staff for the project. In the case of ESC, the Acquisition Team's Project Manager–Financial System hired outside consultants for assistance and guidance throughout the Acquisition process.

Figure 4–2 illustrates the areas having key roles on the Acquisition Team.

Interdisciplinary Nature of the Team(s)

As we now can see, the composition of the Acquisition Team is an important factor to be considered. Representation within the teams should be interdisciplinary. The participants on the Acquisition Team can be drawn from the various departments that are associated with the technological solution being acquired. Depending on the technological solution that the organization wants to purchase, membership should include key users[1] and IT staff, as well as people from other application areas that would be impacted by the new solution.

---

1. The users indicated in Figure 4–2 are key users who were part of the Acquisition Team. Besides the key users, user groups were also involved in the Acquisition process, though at a later stage (during the Evaluation process). While they were not part of the Acquisition Team per se, their buy-in weighed heavily in the final choice.

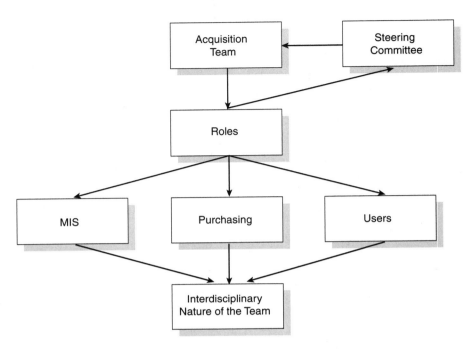

▶ **Figure 4–2**   Acquisition Team Formation

In the cases of International Air, ESC, and Keller, the Acquisition Teams consisted of members from various functional areas—Finance, Accounting, Human Resources (for International Air only), Manufacturing (for Keller only), and MIS. The Acquisition Team was similarly composed at Telecom International, though on a much smaller basis. For Telecom International's Acquisition Team, not only did it have members from similar areas as mentioned earlier, but it also had a member from Marketing who was responsible for establishing contact with key users both in Canada and the United States. In addition to this, Telecom International had a team member whose responsibility it was to gather the necessary information to enable the process. This individual also acted as the sole contact person for the vendors. Keller was an exception to all of the cases. Not having an actual MIS department within the organization, this role was assumed by the VP of Engineering/Quality Control who became the VP of Information Systems.

What is important to remember regarding the interdisciplinary nature of the teams, is that each department and/or functional area plays a role and that role is assumed by the team member(s) from those areas. In the following section, we will discuss the major roles that should be assumed in the project.

The Roles of the Steering Committee, MIS, Purchasing, and Users

Role of the Steering Committee. A Steering Committee provides periodic management direction to the Acquisition Team and one of its roles is to support the team. This committee is usually made up of senior-level individuals from all business areas of the organization that will be affected by, or will share in the development of, the final system solution. Its major role is to validate the emerging solution, with special emphasis on the perspective of the end-user. On a regular or periodic basis, the Committee monitors the Team's progress against the forecasted plan, and its expenditures against its budget. As was observed in all of the cases, the Steering Committees were kept informed on the progress and the status of the acquisition projects with periodic reports that were supplied by the Project Directors/Managers.

When required, the Steering Committee can also make decisions regarding functional and design changes, authorize changes in schedule and budget (as appropriate), and approve changes in resource allocation (when required). The Committee can ensure that financial and human resource issues are adequately addressed in the context of corporate and business unit priorities and policies. An example of this can be seen in International Air's case. The Steering Committee allocated a budget of over US$2 million to examine, among other issues, their human resource needs for this project. As mentioned previously, it was during the earliest stages of the Planning process (what might be considered a "Pre-Planning process" stage) that International Air determined a combination of both consultant (external to the organization) and client (users and IT staff internal to the organization) expertise would be needed to complete this process.

When required, the Steering Committee would also be responsible for conveying the Acquisition Team's final recommendation to a higher authority for final approval, be it the organization's senior executives or the Board of Directors. This was the case for International Air and ESC. In Keller's case, the final authority was left with the head of the Steering Committee, who discussed the decision with the organization's CEO. As for Telecom International, the final recommendation was conveyed to the CIO who then had discussions with Telecom International's top executives.

Role of MIS. In each of the cases the role and responsibility of MIS on the Acquisition Team was five-fold:

1. MIS was considered an internal consultant to the internal clients (the individuals, areas, or departments within the organization for whom the ES was being purchased)
2. MIS was responsible for the technical evaluation of the proposed technological solution

3. MIS was responsible for providing an overall view and description of the organization's existing (and desired) architecture

4. MIS had to match the needs of the users with the most appropriate technological solution and integrate them into their systems. To meet these responsibilities, MIS needed to work closely with end-users associated with the acquisition to determine their needs

5. MIS was responsible for the training and support (in conjunction with the vendor) of internal clients in the proper use of the new technology

With this in mind, the Acquisition Teams planned for and included these criteria as part of their RFPs.

In the cases of International Air, Telecom International, and ESC, the acquisition project was divided into two distinct areas, user and technical. The team members who handled the user-related aspects of the project had the responsibility to coordinate activities that were associated with the various client departments (whether for activities that were department-specific, or for those that required interdepartmental or enterprise-wide coordination). Those team members (MIS and external technical consultants) designated to handle the technical aspects of the acquisition were responsible for reviewing the overall architecture of the organization and of the proposed emerging technology.

Role of Purchasing. As with other types of purchases, and pursuant to normal practice, the Purchasing Department was brought in for its input of terms and conditions into the RFP near the end of the Planning process and then again at the latter part of the Acquisition process. Most often, their mandated role on the Acquisition Team is to supply procurement terms and conditions, and to participate in vendor evaluations and negotiations. In all of the cases, however, it was found that standard terms and conditions were not suitable for acquiring ES. These required special amendments to accommodate the complexities and anomalies of this type of purchase, two of which included ownership of the code and performance clauses.

While their involvement in the overall process can be viewed as limited, it should be noted that the "timely involvement" of the Purchasing Department's representative (as a member of the Acquisition Team) at different stages throughout the Acquisition process could be of benefit to the entire team as well as the organization. Contrary to other types of purchasing activities which involve the Purchasing Department at the end of the buying process, the Purchasing Department could play an important role in the Acquisition process for packaged software if they became involved during the initial stages of the project. An example of this comes from the case involving Telecom International whose Purchasing Manager noted that had his department been brought in sooner, the Acquisition Team would have been aware of Telecom International's requirements for ISO-certified vendors and products and hence could have saved the Team valuable time and effort that was otherwise lost looking at vendors who did not meet this basic criterion. Yet another example comes from International Air's case. International Air's Manager–Capital Equipment Purchasing noted that if he had known how complex the process was, he would have found it beneficial to have a member of his purchasing staff involved from the early stages of the process.

It is our belief, therefore, that a representative from the Purchasing Department should participate in the project right from the earliest stages of the ES Acquisition Process. In addition to providing the Acquisition Team with information that could impact the Acquisition process (as we saw in the earlier example from Telecom International), the benefits that could be gained by the Purchasing Department are as follows:

1. Awareness of the issues that influence the purchase of complex technological solutions, such as ESs, so that the focus of Purchasing takes more into account than simply the cost (as it currently does) when they are brought in only at the end of the process

2. Knowingness of the terminology that is particular to software or IT in general

3. Understanding or at least an awareness of the IT infrastructure of the organization and what it consists of so that they (Purchasing) can be better able to assist in the decision process for other types of IT acquisitions (from small to large technological purchases)

4. First-hand knowledge of the issues that are pertinent to ES or other IT acquisitions so that the Purchasing representative will be better able to modify the standard terms and conditions so as to accommodate the complexities and anomalies of these types of purchase

5. Negotiation advice—since negotiations start almost immediately, though informally, Purchasing may help advise earlier in the process (e.g., how to play off competitors, how to structure the costing/pricing details in the RFP, etc.)

Moreover, we will even go so far as to state the following—we believe that there should be an individual within each organization's procurement department who has a background or training in MIS, or at least more than just casual knowledge or experience with IT. If your organization is among those for whom the acquisition of IT (software and hardware) is becoming a way of life, then it makes good business sense to go this route. For example, in the case of ESC, the representative from Purchasing did not understand the term "client-server" and so did not understand the implications of them going from a "mainframe" environment to a "client-server" environment.

Role of Users. The role of users, whether on the Acquisition Team or as part of the Acquisition process, is an important factor in the acquisition of an ES solution. To match the capabilities of available products with user needs, careful attention needs to be given to analyzing and defining all aspects of the present and future user environment. To do this, user participation within the Acquisition process is crucial. In each of the cases, we found that the successful outcome of the acquisition project, that is, the future success of the selected ES solution within the organization, was greatly dependent upon the immediate "buy-in" of the users.

For International Air, user buy-in was considered a key factor in their decision process. By bringing together users and project people for the acquisition project, International Air hoped to minimize conflict with their user communities by involving them in the process, by addressing their needs, by seriously considering their input, and by obtaining their buy-in. To get the "buy-in" from their users (executives, directors, and users from each business sector including Purchasing), that is, to make certain that their input was considered and that they were involved in the decision, the Acquisition Team involved them in the vendor demonstrations. While there was a danger that the users become overly enthused by the "fluff and flash" of the presentations (similar to when an individual purchases a new vehicle and is caught up in its color and "bells and whistles"), International Air's management chose to take the risk nevertheless. There is a case-in-point here. Fortunately for International Air, the Acquisition Team's primary candidate (PeopleSoft), following the demonstrations and evaluations, was the same as the one selected by the users—had it gone the other way, that is, had International Air's Acquisition Team recommended their second candidate (SAP), the Team would have had a much harder time getting the users' "buy-in." However, with the assured buy-in from the users for the primary candidate, International Air was more confident that everyone concerned with the software would be able to live with the final choice.

User buy-in was also important for another reason. User involvement was sought not only for the Acquisition process itself, but also for the implementation of the chosen ES solution. The reasoning behind this was rather simple—by bringing together users and project people who would not only be part of the Acquisition process, but who would also be involved with the subsequent implementation[2] of the ES, International Air hoped to avoid potential conflict and

---

2. It was noted that only certain key users and MIS individuals remained with the project throughout the entire Acquisition process and on into the implementation. They provided "project memory" (comparable to organizational memory) and continuity during the implementation stage.

assure the success of the entire acquisition and implementation project. Thus, International Air was able to create a sense of partnership with the various user communities in their organization and let them have "a say" in the final recommendation.

Similarly, Keller wanted their acquisition to be user-driven. User representation came from all of their plants and from all different levels of the organization. A few users participated in site visits that were arranged to see how the various technological solutions that Keller's Acquisition Team was considering performed in manufacturing environments similar to their own. Several groups of users were involved in the vendor demonstrations, and each had their chance to present different scenarios, relevant to the tasks they performed, to see whether or not the software could meet their challenges. Since Keller was introducing numerous changes to the organization, management felt very strongly that "buy-in" from the various sectors of the organization was important. To reinforce user involvement, weekly information notices were published and distributed to the employees to keep them abreast of the situation regarding the selection of the software. Thus, each employee was informed as to where the Acquisition Team was in the process. Representatives from the various user groups (manufacturing and operations, high-level production people, supervisors, employees) were also brought together to form an Employee Advisory Committee (EAC). While the EAC did not have a direct say in the decision process, input from the Committee was highly effective in that several of its recommendations were implemented by the Acquisition Team. One of the EAC's recommendations that was implemented and that was contrary to the Acquisition Team's initial decision was for the installation of PCs at each of the workstations on the shop floor, instead of bar code scanners. PCs, the committee members argued, would provide each employee with the means for more accurate data verification, production tracking, and feedback than bar code scanners could allow.

While users played a role in Telecom International and ESC's Acquisition process as well, these examples from International Air and Keller best illustrate the importance of the roles that users and user buy-in played in the Acquisition process.

4.2.2 Acquisition Strategies

It is a daunting task to develop strategies for a new acquisition, especially in an area undergoing revolutionary technological changes. Nevertheless, your Acquisition Team should do so, because you can be guaranteed of one thing—the vendors will have selling and marketing strategies for dealing with you.

The essence of strategy, then, is the deliberate decision to perform, in a manner other than might ordinarily occur, certain activities that may be different from those ordinarily selected to be done. Strategy, relative to the Acquisition process, denotes the approaches and specific activities that the Acquisition Team decides to use to accomplish the task of buying ES.

The following examples illustrate some of the strategies that were developed by the Acquisition Teams during the Planning phase of the Acquisition process:

- Vendor awareness session
- Vendor demonstrations
  - At vendor's site
  - At organization's site
    - Canned presentation—Vendor defines the tasks and features shown
    - Scripted presentation—Customer defines the tasks shown
- Videotaped presentations
- Visit vendor referrals
- Limited access of vendors to the Acquisition Team

These strategies may help to reduce some of the uncertainty associated with the decision process. The Acquisition Teams, in each of the cases here, were faced with a high level of uncertainty, not only with regard to the needs of the organization, the products and services that were available in the marketplace, and the mix of activities and technologies that would be required to deliver the optimal solution, but also with regard to the Acquisition process itself.

One strategy that was developed had to do with approaching the vendors. In International Air's case, the Team decided to hold a vendor awareness session prior to sending out their RFP. All of the vendors that were on their short long-list were invited to attend the information session. Beyond providing the vendors with general information about the type of solution and time frame they were looking at and letting the vendors ask questions, the main purpose of this session was to let each vendor know who they were competing with.

Another strategy that was adopted by three of the cases involved the product demonstrations. Instead of letting each vendor do their own demonstrations (i.e., canned demonstrations), International Air, ESC, and Keller developed scenarios of their own (called "scripted" demonstrations) which they gave to the vendors prior to the demonstration sessions. These scenarios represented various tasks that they wanted the application(s) to perform. In two of the cases (International Air and ESC), one of the vendors' technological solutions failed to meet the demands of the scenarios.

Although not observed in any of the cases presented here, one strategy that could have been useful for each of the Acquisition Teams would have been for them to have videotaped[3] the product demonstrations. International Air's scripted demonstrations lasted 3 days for each vendor, ESC's lasted 2 days, and Keller's lasted 1 full day for each vendor. If they had all videotaped the demonstrations, the tapes could have been used to review the presentations and reduce the risk of choosing a software based on the excellence or weakness of the vendors' presentation skills. These videotaped recordings would also have served as "accurate memory" for the Acquisition Teams to return to and review at their leisure, to confirm what was presented or correct a miss-association (when something is remembered as belonging to one vendor or product, when, in fact, it belongs to another), or to help with "information overload." They could also have been viewed by users or others who could not be present at the demonstrations.

Unlike International Air and ESC, one of Keller's primary strategies was to visit reference sites[4] of the vendors that they were interested in to see how the technology performed for those organizations. The reason for this strategy was three-fold:

1. See first-hand how the technology performed in manufacturing environments similar to their own
2. Identify which platform the technology performed the best on
3. Help them refine their requirements

Another strategy that was used by Telecom International was limiting access of the vendors to the Acquisition Team members. Because of Telecom International's past experience with vendors who had tried to influence different members of the organization with "gifts" (very common are things like fancy restaurant meals, travel to vendor user groups or "training" sessions, etc.), Telecom International deliberately restricted contact between this Acquisition Team and the vendors to a single person. Hence, all communication between the vendors and the Team was via this contact person and the vendors were not permitted to contact other individual team members.

4.2.3 Defining the Requirements

One of the tasks that the Acquisition Team will undertake during the Planning process is the definition of the organization's requirements for the ES solution. This activity is important. It will identify the specific needs of the organization and enable the Acquisition Team to find the right match of ES vendor and soft-

---

3. If vendors object to videotaping the session for whatever reasons (confidentiality, for example), their concerns can be alleviated if it is indicated that the videotapes will be used only as a tool in the decision process and that they can either be returned to them upon completion of the Acquisition process or destroyed. The Acquisition Team could also express its willingness to sign a nondisclosure agreement as it concerns the use of the videotapes.

4. Customer references were also used by the other cases, though they were not a primary strategy.

ware. The Team will need to define the organization's needs at all of its different levels and in all of the functional areas where the ES will have direct or indirect impact. An analysis and definition should be done of:

- The organization's current technological environment
- The different user areas
- The different existing processes/procedures
- The different user functions
- Personnel requirements
- Organizational IT objectives
- Business needs
- Shortcomings of the current systems
- As many existing problems as possible
- As many potential opportunities as possible

This information will, in turn, be used to establish the evaluation and selection criteria that will be used during the different phases of the ES Acquisition Process and will also be part of the RFP that will be sent to the vendors. The following examples provide a limited sampling of the type of information that is needed to define the requirements of an organization's existing and future technological environment:

- What is our current technological environment (infrastructure/architecture)?
- What architecture do we envision for the proposed system?
- What problems are we aware of with the current systems?
- What user areas will be impacted by the proposed system?
- What are our current processes and procedures?
- What functionalities are needed?
- What is our current status regarding IT personnel?
- Do we have adequate staff to handle the proposed system?
- Do we have adequate in-house IT expertise?
- What are the objectives of the proposed environment?
- What are the shortcomings of the existing systems?
- What are the processing objectives or what would we like them to be?
- What additional functionalities would be needed to meet these objectives?
- What additional information would be needed?
- What functionalities would be needed to increase revenues?
- What functionalities would be needed to avoid additional costs?
- What functionalities would increase customer service?

- What are the global requirements (enterprise-wide or international)?
- What impact will the proposed changes have on the current environment?
- What peripheral applications and/or hardware will be affected by the changes?
- What interfaces, if any, will require changes or will specialized interfaces need to be built?
- Will the new applications give access to additional information?
- What opportunities would a new system allow for?
- What benefits are to be gained from the proposed solution?
- What impact (both positive and negative) will the new systems have on our organization?

The Acquisition Teams from all four of the cases went through an extensive exercise to define their technological (functional and technical) and organizational requirements. It is important to note, though, that for three of the four cases (International Air, ESC, and Keller), this activity (requirements definition) as well as the overall Acquisition process appears to have been driven by the needs of the users. Because of the emphasis that was placed on this factor, careful attention was given to analyzing and defining all aspects of the present and future user environment so as to make the best possible match of user needs with available product capabilities (functionalities).

4.2.4   Establishing Selection and Evaluation Criteria

In addition to defining the requirements of the organization, its users, and the functional and technical requirements of the proposed systems, the Acquisition Team will need to address how it is going to select and evaluate the vendors and their solutions. Therefore, it is critical that the Team establish its selection and evaluation criteria prior to contacting any vendor or looking at ES solutions—this cannot be stressed enough. Simply contacting a vendor is not the way to select a complex system because, more often than not, it will lead to a wrong choice. Or, simply having some vague notion about what you are seeking is also not enough. This is why the Planning process, with each of its constituent phases, is so important. It is the part of the Acquisition process during which the Team focuses on identifying the organization's needs and, subsequent to that, on determining what will be required to meet those needs. Once that is done, the Team is then in a position to establish its selection and evaluation criteria for both the vendors and the solutions. Following that, it may conduct its external information search, but then and only then (discussed in Section 4.2.6, "Marketplace Analysis," and in Chapter 8).

As seen in all four of the cases, the Acquisition Teams defined the selection and evaluation criteria during the Planning process. These criteria were established based on information that was gathered from the users and other sources, and were used in part for the Marketplace Analysis, the Selection process, and for the three different areas/types of evaluation that were performed during the ES Acquisition Process. They were also used to create questionnaires and grids/matrices that were used during the Evaluation phase of the ES Acquisition Process. Most of these criteria were presented to the vendors in the RFP so that they knew what would be required of them and of their solutions. The following are examples of the criteria that were important to all of the cases:

- Integratibility of the solution with other applications
- Vendor strength
- Support services
- Cost

See Chapter 12 for a discussion of the three different types of criteria that need to be established for selecting and evaluating vendors and their solutions.

4.2.5   Acquisition Issues

Among the activities that will be completed during the Planning process for the ES acquisition, the Acquisition Team should consider as many issues, factors, and concerns as possible that could help, hinder, or impinge upon the acquisition at hand. In doing so, it could plan for what to do in case potential problems arise later in the Acquisition process or perhaps even in the Implementation process, and also plan how to avert them. It's better to be safe than sorry, especially when you consider the amount of time, effort, and money that will be invested in this type of system, not to mention the impact of this purchase on the organization.

As we know, one of the most pressing issues for organizations during the latter half of the 1990s has been Y2K. For both International Air and ESC, this was the driving force behind their decision to replace their existing legacy systems. This issue imposed time constraints on the process, not only for choosing the most appropriate technology, but also for the implementation of the chosen solution. Milestones had to be established early in the process to make the vendors aware of the tight scheduling constraints. For ESC, this issue affected their initial primary candidate. While ESC's Acquisition Team had expressed an interest in Hyperion's solution, Hyperion declined to reply to their RFP due to the tight time constraints that ESC had imposed and other unknown reasons.

Another issue that should be considered with this type of acquisition is Business Process Reengineering (BPR) and its ramifications. A major implication of buying an ES solution is that it will, in all instances, require the redesign of some, if not all, of the existing processes in the areas in which the software will be applied. Although many organizations have already implemented BPR prior to buying an ES solution, the ES solution will most likely necessitate further redesign of processes. Why is this? Because the basic philosophy behind ES solutions is that they exemplify[5] the "best practices" for a given area (i.e., Accounting, Finance, Human Resources, Materials Management, etc.). Here are a few examples of the types of questions that should be asked:

- Which processes should we change?
- How much of a change can we expect?
- Will the proposed changes improve our existing processes?
- What impact will these changes have on our organization? On the users?
- How much change will our organization's culture accept?

The answers to these questions are very important—they will provide you with one of the keys to determining which ES solution will best meet your organizational needs.

In three of the cases (International Air, ESC, and Keller), the BPR capabilities of the software were a consideration. In the case of Keller, for example, with this acquisition, they would be introducing new technology into their manufacturing process and the technology was going to drastically change many of the ways that their existing processes were being done. (To minimize the uncertainty and the negative impact that these changes could have in their organization, Keller adopted a strategy to keep its employees informed throughout the entire Acquisition process.) International Air, on the other hand, wanted the technology that they chose to have some BPR capabilities built into it should a decision be made to alter some of their existing processes. However, the amount and type of change that the technology was going to require still had to be addressed, as well as its impact on their organizational culture.

Another issue that your Project Manager might want to consider is financing. Of all the cases here, only one organization addressed this issue. As will be seen in the case of ESC, the Project Manager found out, through the "grapevine," that one of the vendors was offering no interest for 2 years. The Project Manager,[6]

---

5. We are not saying that this is necessarily true of all modules within a given ES package. As we advocate in this text, the responsibility remains with the Acquisition Team to do as thorough a job as possible in discerning the marketing "fluff" from the facts and in assessing the overall appropriateness of a solution for their needs.

6. If not the Project Manager, then the representative from Purchasing or Finance. Here is yet another reason to support the involvement of Purchasing (especially if Purchasing is involved in the "cost" and "contractual" aspects of the acquisition) from the early stages of the Acquisition process. This example also illustrates the importance of having an interdisciplinary team where the expertise of its members can be drawn upon.

being from Finance, used this option to negotiate a reduced cost for the technology by factoring in a standard interest rate; that is, he calculated the interest lost to the vendor and subtracted that amount from the overall cost of the technology.

Issues can arise in many forms and the relative importance of an issue varies according to each organization. As we observed in each of the cases, management commitment in the early part of the process and their ongoing commitment to the process was an important factor. For one of the cases, the issue of organizational strategic planning was noted. Only International Air's Acquisition Team conferred with the individual responsible for organizational planning to ascertain that the technology being considered met or helped in the overall achievement of International Air's organizational goals.

As with these and the other issues noted in this section, Acquisition Issues are factors that are important to *your* organization and that should be part of the consideration that goes into the initial stages or Planning process for any major acquisition that is undertaken.

4.2.6   Marketplace Analysis

A Marketplace Analysis (part of the Information Search process that is embedded in Planning) should be performed during the Planning process. This analysis allows the Team to determine who the major players are in the marketplace for the technological solution they are seeking. It plays an important role in the construction of a list of potential vendors and is highly dependent upon the prior completion of the requirements definition and the establishment of selection and evaluation criteria, as noted earlier.

Working closely with key users, the Acquisition Teams from each of the cases carried out an extensive search for existing technological solutions that appeared to meet their defined requirements and their high-level selection and evaluation criteria (see Chapter 8 for a discussion of the different levels of screening). Information concerning specialized technological solutions was obtained from a variety of sources, including technical and trade publications, referrals, and professional research organizations. The names and locations of each possible solution and vendor were identified. Vendors of potential solutions were then contacted and requested to send all available documentation about their products to the Acquisition Team.

Once the information was gathered, each of the Acquisition Teams reviewed (based on the documentation that they had received) each technology's capabilities against their defined requirements (the functional capabilities that the software needed to possess as identified during the Planning process) using the selection and evaluation criteria that they had defined during the Planning process. Any products that were found to lack any of the essential capabilities during this review were eliminated from further consideration. Each of the Acquisition Teams was then able to produce a shorter long-list of potential vendors and solutions that either appeared to meet or were believed capable of meeting their requirements.

Other factors that were also taken into consideration during the review were nonquantifiable or nonspecific impressions that the Teams had formed about any product or vendor. These included any sense of uneasiness arising from difficulty in contacting knowledgeable people from the vendor organization or from inadequate or unclear documentation, as well as positive feelings arising from technology options or overall design of the potential software solutions.

The purpose of the Marketplace Analysis is to produce a short long-list of vendors (and technologies) to whom RFPs will be sent. Following their review of the marketplace (which was based on a list of vendors that appeared in a trade publication they subscribe to), Keller made initial contact with 63 vendors by mail with a letter and a list of critical requirements. These together could be called an informal Request for Information (RFI). Based on the replies that were received, they were able to reduce their list first to 30 vendors and then to 15. To reduce this list even further (i.e., to their final 3 vendors), they relied on customer referrals, site visits, Dunn and Bradstreet (D&B) financial reports, and other vendor and product evaluation criteria to help them narrow their selection. As for International Air, their Marketplace Analysis in conjunction with their vendor information/awareness session enabled them to reduce their short long-listto 7 potential vendors, each of whom was forwarded an RFP. Both ESC and Telecom International, on the other hand, were quickly able to reduce their lists to 3 and 5 vendors, respectively, as a result of their Marketplace Analysis findings.

4.2.7 Deliverables from the Planning Process

The Planning process produces deliverables[7] that will be used to proceed to the next phase of the ES Acquisition Process. In each of the cases, we were able to identify what we term as "deliverables," some examples of which include:

- Formation of the Acquisition Team
- List of requirements
- Map of the current processes/procedures
- Selection and evaluation criteria
- Timetable and milestones

---

7. A "deliverable" is defined here as a product, whether tangible or intangible, that is produced as a result of one or more activities/tasks. Examples of a deliverable can be a decision, a list, a document, a set of modules, and so forth.

- Marketplace report (which was used to create a short long-list of potential vendors and their products)
- Short long-list of potential vendors and their products

Another deliverable of the Planning process for all of the cases except Keller was the RFP. It was during the Planning process that the Acquisition Teams defined and refined their requirements and these were then assembled into an RFP document.

In the next chapter, we discuss in greater detail the type of information that could be included in an RFP for packaged ES.

4.3 SUMMARY

One of the major differences between buying ES and other types of organizational buying is the element of planning. The cost of the packaged ES, the impact of the acquisition on the organization, and the type and sheer volume of issues that require consideration all more than adequately justify in-depth planning for the acquisition. For these reasons, the Planning process is highly critical and necessary to the success of the ES Acquisition Process.

This chapter presented the issues and activities that the Acquisition Teams need to plan for and complete in order to lay the foundation for the other phases of the ES Acquisition Process—plan strategies, identify issues that are relevant to the acquisition, define the requirements, establish selection and evaluation criteria, prepare questionnaires and grids/matrices, and so on. With the exception of the formation of the Acquisition Team, all of the deliverables that result from the Planning process will be used in other stages (processes) of the ES Acquisition Process.

Although the Planning process is one of the least glamorous parts of the ES Acquisition Process, entailing some of the most rigorously painstaking and tedious work for the definition and establishment of requirements and criteria, the payoff from the thoroughness of these efforts is substantial:

1. They are essential for identifying the exact needs of the organization
2. They are essential during the Marketplace Analysis for searching and screening information and for matching potential vendors/ES solutions to the organization's needs
3. They are vital to the construction of a solid RFP
4. They are essential to the Selection process for the review of the RFP responses from the vendors
5. They are essential to the three types of Evaluation processes

6. They constitute the elements and issues that are negotiated during the Business and Legal negotiations

7. They answer to some of the issues and needs of the software's implementation

As one can plainly see from this list, the payoff will make the effort spent extremely worthwhile.

5 *Request for Proposal*

The focus of this chapter is on the RFP. While the RFP is a highly visible deliverable of the Planning process, it is in fact a compilation of almost all of the organization's requirements and criteria for the desired ES. Since this information is vital to the construction of a solid RFP, thoroughness in the completion of these activities is essential.

5.1   CONSTRUCTION OF THE RFP

As we have already seen in the case of International Air, a significant effort was made on the part of the Acquisition Team to be very thorough right from the start of the Acquisition process. The Team planned for and then defined each of the following requirements, which were subsequently included in its RFP:

- All of the business functionalities that they wanted to see in the proposed software package
- The technical pre-requisites and co-requisites; that is, the platforms on which the software should ideally operate
- The database management systems that should be used

The RFP also included other information as well as questions to the vendors that needed to be answered. International Air wanted to know:

- Strategic position of the vendor
- Vendor's plans regarding the long-term strategic position of their (the vendor's) company and product

- Vendor's ability to maintain their vision
- Vendor's ability and expertise to assist them (International Air) in the implementation of the ES
- Availability of third-party partners to provide support

Each of the cases (with the exception of Keller) followed a similar route, more or less, in the development of their RFP. However, none of the organizations presented here developed the quintessential RFP for packaged ES.

What we believe to be the principal elements for the basis of a solid RFP for a packaged ES solution are presented next. With these as a starting point, the reader can begin building an RFP that is appropriately tailored for the specific needs and requirements of their organization.

These elements also provide another example of the types of issues that should be addressed and the level of detail that needs to be (or would be best) defined early in the Acquisition process.

5.1.1   Principal Elements of an RFP for Packaged ES

The purpose of the RFP is two-fold:

1. Provide the vendor with information on the organization
2. Request information from the vendor about their proposed solution

Terms and Conditions

- **Procurement Terms and Conditions**
  This is where you would indicate your organization's standard terms and conditions for vendors who are responding to the RFP.
- **Terms and Conditions for the Software**
  In addition, you may wish to add some of the following Terms and Conditions that are pertinent to software applications:
  - **Virus**
    The Vendor warrants that it has tested the delivered System to the best of its ability, using commercially reasonable scanning procedures, to determine that the System contains no threats known as viruses, time bombs, logic bombs, Trojan horses, trap doors, or other malicious computer instructions, intention devices, or techniques that were designed to infect, attack, assault, vandalize, disrupt, or shut down a computer system or any component of such

computer system ("Virus"). If the organization can document that the System contains a Virus which originated from the Vendor, then the Vendor will provide the Organization with a Virus-free replacement copy of the System.

– **Data Ownership**
The Vendor shall not be granted ownership rights for any data developed with the use of the System. All data which is generated or stored through the use of this System will remain the sole property of the Organization.

– **Time-Dependent Keys**
The Vendor will not include any mechanism in their software that would cause the software to stop functioning or shut down.

– **Duplication and Distribution**
The Vendor acknowledges that the Organization may need to copy or duplicate portions of the System, including documentation, for backup, development, and/or testing purposes. The Organization agrees not to copy or duplicate all or any portion of the System except as may be necessary for its own use and to maintain and control all full or partial copies thereof as if such were originals and to reproduce on all such copies Vendor's proprietary legends and/or copyright notices. The Organization agrees to protect its own confidential and proprietary information.

– **Increases to Maintenance and Support Fees**
The base maintenance rate (annual fee for support) may only be changed by the Vendor one time in any 12-month period to reflect changing costs, circumstances, and equipment usage. Any rate increase to annual Maintenance fees will be limited to a predetermined percentage increase from the previous year of paid Maintenance or limited to the rate of inflation.

– **Response Time**
With the minimal hardware requirements as stated by the Vendor, the Organization here indicates its expectations for "reasonable" response time with online transactions, queries, and batch turnaround. Reasonable is defined as not being a detriment to overall productivity and effectiveness. Also indicated here might be the willingness of the Organization to jointly resolve, with the Vendor, any deviations to these expectations.

– **Escrow Agreements**
This might include such escrow agreements as for source code. For example, the vendor agrees to place in escrow a commented and documented copy of the source code (the "Source Code

Information"). Vendor agrees to update the Source Code Information with replacement Code for all subsequent releases of the System within a specified time frame for general availability of the subsequent release. The Organization shall be entitled to receive a copy of the Source Code Information, or any part thereof, for the maintenance and support of the System if the Vendor ceases to do business, becomes insolvent or party to any bankruptcy or receivership proceedings or makes an assignment for the benefit of creditors, or fails to meet its support obligations pursuant to it maintenance agreement and fails to correct the same within a pre-determined time frame of written notification from the organization. The Organization acknowledges that the Source Code Information is a trade secret of the Vendor and the Organization agrees that the same shall be subject to the confidentiality provisions of this agreement.

Introduction

The introduction of the RFP should contain a breakdown of the following:

- **Objectives of the Acquisition**
  This is where you could present the vendor with a description of your organization's reasons for wanting to acquire an ES solution. The explanation need not be overly long or elaborate. It might also include the time frame in which the ES should be up and running.
- **Organizational Profile**
  This section could contain some information on your organization, its mission, size, and other unique elements.
- **Current Situational Analysis**
  This would be a high-level description of your organization's current IT situation that includes, among others, the platforms being used—mainframe, UNIX, Windows 95/98/NT, Linux, AS 400, OS/2, etc.; the software that is being used—systems management software, existing HR/finance software, Web sites, etc.; and the software that needs to be replaced or converted.
- **Description of the Business and Technical Problems**
  This would be a high-level description of the principal shortcomings of your organization's existing systems (software and hardware).
- **Acquisition Project Schedule**
  This would provide the vendor with a high-level schedule of the principal milestones of the ES Acquisition Process as they relate to the RFP process. The schedule would start from the date of issue of the

RFP, would include among others, the anticipated date of the awarding of the contract, and could end with the anticipated start date of the ES implementation phase.

- **Tentative Implementation Project Schedule**
  Here would be indicated the time constraints, if any, in which your organization would want the software implementation completed.

RFP Process

- **Objective of the RFP**
  Briefly outlines the objectives of the RFP and describes its principal components.
- **Description of the Content of the RFP**
  This section indicates to the vendor what the RFP needs to contain in order for it to be considered and properly evaluated. The RFP response from the vendor should at the very least include:
  - **Cover Letter**
    The cover letter needs to be submitted on the vendor's letterhead and signed by the responsible official in the vendor's organization, certifying the accuracy of all information in the proposal, and certifying that financial details in the proposal will remain valid until a specified date.
  - **Executive Summary**
    This summary, which briefly describes the vendor's proposal, should be no longer than one page.
  - **Vendor Alliances/Partnerships**
    If the solution, in whole or in part, is the result of an alliance between two or more vendors, the principal vendor should provide detailed information on the alliance that has been entered into in order to meet the terms of this RFP. They should also indicate which portions of the software will be supplied by which vendor(s).
  - **Vendor Background**
    Here the vendor is asked to provide information on their organization.
  - **Vendor's Vision Statement**
    This is where you request the vendor's vision statement. This will provide your organization with some insight into the vendor's future plans for the direction of their company, the software, etc. Given that the acquisition of an ES solution necessitates a long-term commitment to a vendor, you could also request here that the vendor inform your organization of its plans to support future environments and technologies.

– Vendor's Key Contact Person
The vendor supplies the name of the key contact person in the event that supplemental information is required, to answer questions, etc.

• **Vendor Response Process**
This section tells the vendor how they should respond as well as the time frame in which they need to respond to the RFP. For example, any questions concerning the RFP must be received within a specified number of days (e.g., 15 days) and will be responded to within a set period (e.g., 25 days). In addition to this, an explanation of how questions should be presented and how they will be responded to would be included in the section titled "RFP Communication Process." The responses to the RFP should follow the format described in the section titled "Format of Vendor Response." You may also wish to include a list of general instructions regarding the preparation of the RFP. For example:
  – All questions must be answered. Any questions that are not answered will be considered a negative response.
  – If the vendor's response is conditional, a detailed explanation of the condition must be provided.

• **RFP Communication Process**
This is where you can indicate to the Vendor that they are not allowed to communicate with any other individuals within the organization. All queries or correspondence should be directed to the Project Director, Leader, or another designated person.

• **Format of Vendor Proposal**
This provides the vendor with general instructions for the preparation and the format of the RFP. For the format of the RFP document, you would indicate this in order to receive uniform responses from all of the vendors. These instructions might include:
  – The exact sections that the RFP should contain
  – How the RFP should be presented (e.g., bound, loose-leaf binders, etc.)
  – Whether brochures are desired
  – Whether reproduced copies of standard manuals may or may not be substituted for the specific recommendation narratives and responses that are required for particular sections, if any, in the RFP
  – The media in which you will accept the RFP (i.e., paper and/or electronic, etc.)

• **Format of Vendor Responses**
This section indicates to the vendor the format of the answers they need to use in their responses to the RFP. For example:

- "Complies" where the proposed solution fully complies with the requirements
- "Partially Complies" where the proposed solution only partially complies with the requirements
- "Complies with Customization" where the solution can be customized or configured by the IT staff themselves or by the vendor, pre-sales or consulting staff to address the requirements
- "Does Not Comply" where the proposed solution does not comply with the requirements. Effort (in person-days) of any modification for the full compliance should be provided, together with complete details of how compliance will be achieved
- "Complies with Alternatives" where the proposed solution does not comply as inferred in the requirements, but the vendor proposes an alternative which is believed to produce the same result; the alternative should be described in detail. If additional effort is required to make the alternative solution fully comply with requirements, the effort (in person-days) should be provided as part of the response

- **Pricing Format**
  This section indicates to the vendor how you want the pricing broken down (e.g., by the number of users, number of licenses, by module, by hardware types, etc., or combinations thereof). In addition, you could request price breakdowns on maintenance, services/consulting, customization work that might need to be done, and so forth. You might also include a request for a summary of the vendor's discounting models for pricing.

- **Evaluation Process**
  This section would provide a high-level indication of the individuals in the organization who will be involved in the evaluation of the software and the primary criteria/requirements against which the vendor's RFP response will be evaluated. For example:
  - Quality of the vendor's proposal
  - Demonstrated understanding by the vendor of the organization's requirements, constraints, and concerns
  - Demonstrated understanding by the vendor of the need to solve specific problems
  - Provision of a comprehensive implementation plan and schedule
  - Degree of compliance with the specified functional requirements
  - Degree of compliance with the organization's technology standards and architecture

- Vendor's qualifications, experience, and demonstrated success in delivering solutions to organizations of a similar size and complexity
- Ability of the vendor to interface their proposed solution into those parts of the organization's environment that will not change as a result of this project
- Experience, business, and technical expertise of the vendor's staff
- Ability of the vendor to offer implementation support to assist in the transition from the current environment to the proposed environment
- Financial strength of the vendor
- Quality of the pricing proposal
- **Glossary of Terms**
  Included in this section or in an appendix, the Glossary of Terms should describe and explain the terms, as understood by your organization, that are used in your RFP. Since there are certain terms and acronyms that may be specific to your organization or industry, it is important to communicate this to the vendor so that you both have the same understanding of what is being asked and answered.

Current Organizational IT Infrastructure

- **IT Systems Overview**
  This is where you describe your organization's current IT systems to the vendor. Since the ES applications may reside on those systems and interface with other applications, this will make the vendor aware of the systems with which the proposed solution will have to effectively integrate.
- **Architecture Guidelines and Initiatives**
  This is where you include your established organizational IT architecture guidelines and initiatives that are pertinent to the RFP. For example:
  - Hardware/software platforms
  - Networks
  - Software initiatives such as help-desk, moves to "follow-the-sun" support
  - Standardization initiatives
  - High availability initiatives
  - Web initiatives such as those for an intranet or enterprise portal
  - Personnel-related initiatives (increase/reduction/changes)
  - Other support initiatives
  Compliance with these architecture guidelines and initiatives will have an influence on the evaluation of the proposed solution.

Global Requirements

- **Global Business Requirements**
  Describe your organization's requirements that are global in nature and that are not unique to the solution being sought (e.g., multiple currencies, multi-lingual support, security and access, reporting, government compliance, etc.).
- **Global Technical Requirements**
  The focus of this area should be on the overall solution as opposed to just the functional applications (e.g., online help facilities, external interfaces, foreign language support, application customization and development, operations management, high availability support, web browser interface support, etc.).

Types of Software Required

- **Users and Locations**
  For each of the areas where a solution (an application within the ES) is being sought, include information on the user communities and their locations (e.g., HR, Finance, Accounting, Materials Management, etc.). For example:
  - User Group name
  - Brief description of what they do
  - Branch of the organization in which they are (if applicable)
  - Location of the User Group
  - Number of employees in the User Group
  - Current hardware in use by them
- **Data Requirements**
  As with "Users and Locations," high-level information on the data requirements for each area where a solution (an application within the ES) is being sought should be supplied here. Here is an example of the type of information that you will need to provide the vendor for the Finance function:
  - High-level data entities
  - Brief description of each entity
  - Average population size/volume
  - Growth/change frequency
  - Process owner
  - Any special requirements

Process and Data Models

The vendor needs to provide process and data models for the proposed solution. The process model is the hierarchical definition of all application processes and the relationships between these processes. The data model is a definition of all data entities and attributes used by the application. In addition, the relationship of which data entity is used by which process is required. Also, the vendor should provide a description of how well the proposed solution and its data and process model can be integrated with your organization's data and process architecture.

Interfaces

Your organization might have certain requirements for the user interfaces of the vendor's solution. In such instances, you would want to ask the vendor to indicate the ability of their solution to comply with your requirements. Additionally, they should describe the process to be used to modify the screens and whether this can be done by your organization, by specially trained contractors, or only by the vendor.

Future Systems Requirements

In this area, you would want to inform the vendor about your organization's future requirements. This would allow the vendor to understand your long-term objectives as they pertain to the ES within your organization. For example, when Keller was looking for an ES solution, they informed the potential vendors of their desire to expand (in subsequent phases) the ES to other areas of the organization such as Accounting, Finance, and Human Resources. If so desired, you might also indicate that this disclosure does not commit your organization to that vendor if they are chosen as the primary provider and that your intent is to purchase the right solution for your needs.

ES Solution Architecture

Here the vendor needs to provide an overall architectural view and description of the proposed solution, which should include:

* All application modules
* Relationships between these modules
* Important relationships to existing organizational applications
* Description of the processing styles of the proposed solutions (e.g., distributed logic, etc.) and why that style was chosen

- Description of important application design characteristics including:
  - Application modularity
  - Application portability
  - Scalability of the solution to increased numbers of users
  - Scalability of the solution to larger processing or data volumes
  - Independence of the application solution from the underlying technology structure
  - Ease of implementation and maintenance
  - Maturity of the solution's components
- **Solution Integration**
  This is where the vendor would indicate the method by which the proposed solution will integrate with existing or other systems.

Technology Infrastructure

Here the vendor would provide a description of a typical technology infrastructure configuration required to support the proposed solution that would be appropriate for the organization. This description might include:

- The hardware, systems software, database management systems, systems management tools, and networking components
- Any additional products or tools which are required to meet the organizational requirements
- Placement of the major application modules and data elements of the proposed solution on the technology infrastructure components
- Important relationships with existing organizational technology infrastructure, including network connectivity
- The capacity planning approach that is used to arrive at the technology infrastructure sizing
- How the organization will be able to validate the final technology infrastructure sizing (i.e., reference, load simulation, benchmarks, etc.)

Technology Requirements

This is where the information gathered about your organization's technological requirements would be used. This information, which provides you with a very clear understanding of your organization's technology requirements, will enable you to make your requests to the vendor as specific as possible. These needs might be indicated as follows:

- Which hardware platforms are supported: Mainframe, UNIX, Windows 95/98/NT, OS/2, AS400, Novell NetWare, etc.?

- Which network protocols, if any, are supported: TCP/IP, IPX/SPX, SNA, WAN, LAN, Dialup, ISDN, etc.?
- Describe your installed customer base that is utilizing a network architecture similar to our organization.
- What is the recommended configuration (not the minimum) for your system in terms of desktop hardware and software, file and print servers, database servers, DBMS?
- Describe your Client/Server development strategy and provide percentages detailing workloads on both the client and the server processors for typical system usage.
- Outline the system's batch versus online processing. Identify those processes which can be run in either mode and provide a breakdown by system.
- Detail the process by which reports and screens can be customized by the user groups.
- Detail your mechanisms, terms, and availability for technical support.
- Detail your training approach, including a list of recommended classes for the technical groups and the user groups along with their cost, location, and availability.
- Detail the origin and development of your software product including the development language and the database structure.
- Which interfaces does the system support: Windows 95/98/NT, X/Motif, Web browser, command-line, text, 3270, cell phones (WML), PDAs, Windows CE, etc.?
- Which interface standards are supported by the system: CORBA, COM/DCOM, etc.?
- Detail the current system interfaces along with all integration capabilities.
- Which integration points does the system support: API, CLI, SDK, etc.?
- Provide an estimate of the current number of users (installed base) of the system.
- Detail the system's ability to support customized applications for each of the business units and lines of business.
- Detail the steps required for a typical client-side installation of your software.
- Detail your organization's and the implementer's experience with data conversions in a multi-platform environment.
- Detail the processes utilized by users to retrieve data in query and report formats.

- Detail the impact on performance and response times during low, moderate, and high ad hoc query periods.
- Detail the system's data retention, archival, and retrieval processes by system.
- What security standards and technologies are supported by the system: Kerberos, SSL, DES, PKI, etc.?
- Detail the system's security measures in terms of local and remote access; ability to create user groups and assign rights by groups; security and the menu, module, and user level.
- Detail your maintenance policy as it pertains to new releases of the development software and DBMS.
- Does the system provide flexibility in restricting use or access?

Here you might remind the vendor of the need for their answers to conform to the format (see "Format of Vendor Responses" on page 88).

Functional Requirements

With regard to the information that has been gathered about functional requirements, this is where you would list all of the existing and desired requirements for each of the functional areas covered by the proposed ES solution, asking for each functionality whether the vendor's proposed solution complies, etc. This section of the RFP, alone, could include several hundred line items. See Chapter 12 for examples of the functional requirements that could be included in this section.

Implementation

- **Issues**
  This is where you would indicate to the vendor your requirements for the implementation of the ES. The vendor would be required in this section to address issues such as, but not limited to, the following:
  - Ease of implementation of the proposed solution
  - Available services to ensure the successful implementation of the proposed solution
  - Provide a conversion/migration plan (application, data, and interfaces) from the existing systems and environment to the proposed solution
  - Provide a schedule with major deliverables and milestones
  - Estimate the effort (IT, user, organization, and third party) required to implement the proposed solution

– Identify any tools, conversion programs, etc. that are available and/or are required
– Provide information on the capacity planning tools and guidelines (metrics) that are available to help size the technological environment that is required to operate the proposed solution
– Indicate if any additional effort is required to tailor the proposed software to meet the organization's requirements and provide a summary of all such effort, by software component

• **Strategy**
This is where you would indicate your implementation strategy preference (e.g., a phased implementation or a parallel conversion or a single, large, "big bang" implementation).

Assumptions

Any assumptions being made by the vendor in their response to this RFP should be clearly defined.

Risks

This is where you explain your organization's understanding that the timing, size, and complexity of the proposed project present considerable risks. However, since there may be risks that are uniquely posed by specific solutions, such as with the use of newly released software, or the use of third party software, this is where you need to ask the vendor to give you an indication of such risks.

Conversely, if the vendor believes that the proposed solution does not present any additional or unique risks, the reason for this belief should be clearly stated.

• **Implementation Risk Reduction Strategy**
The vendor should describe any risk reduction strategies that they use when dealing with an implementation of the proposed solution.

Warranties and/or Guarantees

Here the vendor is requested to supply information on its warranties and/or guarantees for the software.

Intellectual and Industrial Property

This section would contain information explaining your organization's position on patents, trademarks, trade secrets, infringement of copyright, etc.

Also in this section the vendor might be asked about your organization's rights to any new technological developments. For example, if, in the installation of the vendor's software program, the vendor customizes a solution to the organization's specifications that the vendor can subsequently add to software program as an enhancement, what are the rights of your organization to this technological development? In addition, the vendor might be asked as to whether they would provide a royalty arrangement for any systems enhancements that are sold in the future.

This section would also include a request for the vendor to supply information on its rights.

Nondisclosure/Confidentiality Agreement

The organization would here acknowledge that the programs, design, and ideas contained in the system, including any vendor provided modifications or updates thereto, are confidential and proprietary to the vendor.

The organization would also request here that the vendor not disclose to any third party, without the organization's prior written approval, any of the organization's information (obtained in connection with this agreement) that is known by the vendor to be confidential.

Acceptance Procedures

The organization indicates here its procedure for acceptance of the system. Such procedures might include that the vendor notify the organization, in writing, when installation of each module licensed hereunder is complete. Commencing with the date of such notification, the Organization shall have a predetermined period to evaluate the module (the "Acceptance Period"). Such evaluation shall be a determination, agreed to by both parties, as to whether the Module performs in substantial compliance with the User Documentation and passes Vendor's standard acceptance test(s). During the Acceptance Period, the Organization shall notify the Vendor in writing within 24 hours of any material deficiencies that the Organization encounters in the testing process. The Vendor shall make personnel available to assist in diagnosing such material deficiencies and to address them. To the extent that the Vendor determines, or the Organization determines and Vendor concurs, that the deficiencies arise out of the use or operation of the Module, such support will be provided at no added cost to the Organization. If the Vendor determines and the Organization concurs, that the deficiencies do not arise out of the use or operation of the Module, the Organization agrees to reimburse Vendor's standard hourly rate plus reasonable travel and living expenses incurred for time so spent.

If at the expiration of the Acceptance Period, material deficiencies remain, the Organization shall notify the Vendor of such deficiencies in detail, in writing, and the Vendor shall have 90 days from receipt of such notification to cure the remaining material deficiencies at no cost to the Organization. If the Vendor fails to cure the material deficiencies after this 90-day period, the Organization shall have the right to terminate this Agreement and receive a full refund of all license fees paid.

Miscellaneous

For this section, the vendor could be invited to include any brochures or other materials regarding their software and/or the hardware platform that they recommend for this solution.

Table 5–1 summarizes the items that have just been presented.

Table 5–1   RFP—Table of Contents

Terms and Conditions

  Procurement

  Software

    Virus

    Data Ownership

    Time-Dependent Keys

    Duplication and Distribution

    Increases to Maintenance and Support Fees

    Response Time

    Escrow Agreements

Introduction

  Objectives of the Acquisition

  Organizational Profile

  Current Situational Analysis

  Description of Business and Technical Problems

  Acquisition Project Schedule

  Tentative Implementation Project Schedule

RFP Process

  Objective of the RFP

  Description of the Content of the RFP

Table 5–1   RFP—Table of Contents (Continued)

Cover Letter

Executive Summary

Vendor Alliances/Partnerships

Vendor Background

Vendor's Vision Statement

Vendor's Key Contact Person

Vendor Response Process

RFP Communication Process

Format of Vendor Proposal

Format of Vendor Response

Pricing Format

Evaluation Process

Glossary of Terms

Current Organizational IT Infrastructure

IT Systems Overview

Architecture Guidelines and Initiatives

Global Requirements

Global Business Requirements

Global Technical Requirements

Types of Software Required

Users and Locations

Data Requirements

Process and Data Models

Interfaces

Future Systems Requirements

ES Solution Architecture

Solution Integration

Technology Infrastructure

Technology Requirements

Functional Requirements

Implementation

Issues

Strategy

Table 5–1   RFP—Table of Contents (Continued)

Assumptions

Risks

   Implementation Risk Reduction Strategy

Warranties and/or Guarantees

Intellectual and Industrial Property

   Patents, Trademarks, Trade Secrets, Infringement of Copyright

Nondisclosure/Confidentiality Agreement

Acceptance Procedures

Miscellaneous

While this should not be construed as a complete listing of all of the items that could be included in an RFP for packaged ES, it does provide the basis from which to start.

5.2   *THE RFP RESPONSES*

For International Air, Telecom International, and ESC, the quality of the vendor's response was an indication of how seriously the vendor wanted their solution to be considered. It was also an indication of whether the vendor understood the requirements, constraints, and concerns as expressed by the organization. In each of the cases, how the vendor responded to the organization's needs was important in the process.

The approaches used by the different organizations in their RFPs resulted in varying degrees of quality among the responses. The more general the questions were, the more often the vendor responses were simply "yes" or "no" with no further explanations. An example of one such type of question is: "Does the system provide flexibility in restricting use or access?" However, the more specific the questions were in requesting details from the vendors, the more beneficial and useful were the responses. (See "Technology Requirements" on page 93 and "Functional Requirements" on page 95.)

Nothing is for certain, however, because even with specific questions, some vendors will still respond with a simple "yes" or "no" reply. As was noted by Telecom International's Project Manager:

> The most disappointing thing was the responses from the vendors, such as when they replied, "Yes. Yes. No. Yes. Maybe." etc. This was very disappointing. . . . Even if we thought that the vendor was better than

how they looked on paper, it was difficult to give a good assessment to someone who only answered, "Yes. Yes. No. Yes. Maybe."

By comparison, though, International Air took some extra measures in order to avoid this type of situation as much as possible. International Air spelled out both the way that the vendor was to respond and the type of information that the vendor was to supply in its responses. (See "Format of Vendor Responses" on page 88.)

Among the cases, International Air was the only one to include very specific and detailed instructions with their RFP. We noted that, as a result of these extra measures, International Air had fewer problems than Telecom International and ESC with the responses they received. In addition, International Air included a Glossary of Terms to alleviate any misunderstanding or confusion that might arise with the vendor regarding their use of terminology.

6

"Even the Small Can Triumph"
The Case of Keller
Manufacturing

This chapter covers the case of Keller Manufacturing Company Inc., a mid-sized furniture manufacturer. Keller completed the purchase of an ES solution in August of 1996. The chapter begins with a presentation of Keller's corporate profile and is followed by a background description of the circumstances that led to the decision to buy a packaged ES solution. Subsequent to that, an overview of the ES Acquisition Process that Keller Manufacturing went through to arrive at its final choice is presented.

6.1   *ORGANIZATIONAL PROFILE*

Keller Manufacturing Company Inc. was established in 1895 as a manufacturer of farm wagons and remained so until 1943 when it began manufacturing household furniture. Today, this mid-sized organization has over 700 employees in three manufacturing plants in the United States. Two of the plants are located in Indiana (Corydon and New Salisbury) and one is located in Culpepper, Virginia. Keller now manufactures over 2,000 different oak and maple legs, seats, and other components (with over 100 separate procedures) that are required for its solid wood furniture products. In 1995, the company earned profits of $3.1 million on sales of US$46 million. This represented a 76% increase in profits with only a 30% increase in sales from the previous year. In 3 short years, Keller Manufacturing grew from US$35 million in sales to US$54 million in 1996, representing a 54% increase.

6.2   BACKGROUND

During the past few years, Keller changed from a production-oriented company to a very effective market-driven business. It also expanded its product line to include bedroom furniture, a change that proved to be a very successful marketing strategy. Consequently, the reorientation of Keller's marketing strategy with the resulting increase in sales and new product introductions created some production challenges for their manufacturing operation. Manufacturing was having difficulty supporting production demands brought on by the substantial increase in sales. The problem was mainly attributed to the lack of timely and accurate information that was necessary to effectively and efficiently plan for and control production.

6.2.1   Assessing the Situation

At the time, Keller's information systems consisted of a combination of manual procedures and automated systems, with computers only being used by the engineers and in manufacturing. The main computer (an AS400) handled batch-oriented processing and was supported by a number of stand-alone PCs. These stand-alone systems were originally installed in an effort to provide information that was desperately needed to support manufacturing operations. However, with the recent and sizable increase in sales and sales mix (expanded product line), this type of information system (manual and computerized) could no longer effectively support Keller's manufacturing operations.

Unfortunately, the weakness of this information system was not limited to Keller's manufacturing operations. Personnel in other areas of the organization were having difficulty performing their duties effectively because of the inefficiencies of the manual systems involved.

As sales increased, the organization's ability to control costs and provide customers with products on a timely basis became more and more difficult. Competition continued to shorten lead times. Keller was faced with an escalating problem that needed to be urgently addressed—the organization could no longer continue status quo and still remain competitive and profitable. They were forced to seriously consider more "modern" systems that could help them to better utilize their personnel, equipment, and facilities, and provide better service to their customers.

Hence, in 1995, Keller Manufacturing requested the assistance of an outside state-run agency, the Indiana Business Modernization and Technology Commission (IBMTC), to conduct an assessment of its organization. The objective of this study was to identify areas in which modern manufacturing techniques and new technology could benefit the organization in terms of performance and competitiveness.

The study showed that Keller was deficient in several areas, but especially so in manufacturing. The report outlined that Keller's manufacturing operations were controlled by a combination of manual and automated procedures and stand-alone PCs. However, with the growth that they were experiencing, their existing systems and procedures could no longer support operations and provide management with the information that it needed. If no action was taken, the organization's continued growth and ability to support its customer base would be compromised.

6.2.2   Balking the Trend

One of the recommendations that was made by the IBMTC was that Keller eventually invest in a fully integrated manufacturing system, more specifically, a multi-user, multi-tasking, fully integrated, real-time manufacturing resource planning system. The study showed that implementation of a resource planning system could improve scheduling, efficiency in the assembly area (by keeping the lines running), tracking, security, controls over shipping areas, manufacturing processes, and individual performance. This system would reduce setup times and thereby improve efficiency, reduce unreported parts losses, and reduce database and key-entry errors. Also, new employees could be trained more efficiently and effectively with the new system. The IBMTC estimated that it would save the organization approximately US$1.2 million annually.

However, the IBMTC's primary recommendation was that Keller begin its modernization efforts with the implementation of a general ledger system, proceed to order-entry, and then expand a little further. Once these systems were in place and functioning, Keller would then be in a better position to implement a manufacturing system.

Keller took this recommendation under advisement. Again, senior management reviewed their situation, with consideration to the IBMTC's recommendation, and a decision was made. This decision was based on the realization that their existing system could no longer sustain Keller's current rate of growth nor would it allow for them to take full advantage of future market trends. With the life of their organization being directly tied to manufacturing, senior management determined that their most urgent and critical area of need was the shop floor. Hence, in October 1995, Keller's senior management decided—contrary to the IBMTC's recommendation—that the company would acquire a manufacturing execution system (MES), or in effect, an extensive information system for the shop floor.

6.3   KELLER'S ES ACQUISITION PROCESS

Once the decision was made to proceed with the acquisition of a new manufacturing system, meetings were held and a team of 12 individuals was selected to be part of the Acquisition process. The various areas represented on this team were finance, personnel, marketing, engineering, production (manufacturing and operations), and information systems. At the outset, it was decided that the team's task would be to find the very best integrated solution not only to meet Keller's immediate needs in manufacturing (on the shop floor), but also its long-term organizational needs. It was also decided that selection of the system would be user-driven.

6.3.1   Getting the Users Involved

With this in mind, meetings with the line managers at all three plants were arranged during which the Team compiled a "wish list" of requirements for the new system. An employee advisory committee (EAC) was also formed at about this time to bring representatives from various user groups together. Since Keller was going to be introducing numerous changes to the organization, they realized that user buy-in from the various sectors would be very important to the successful outcome of the project. In addition to the EAC, Keller wanted to make certain that all employees were kept abreast of how things were progressing with the acquisition. Hence, weekly notices were published and distributed to all employees to keep them informed throughout the entire process.

6.3.2   So Many Vendors . . .

In the initial phase of the Acquisition process, certain members of the team began looking for companies that had developed this type of manufacturing system. Their principal reference was *Manufacturing Systems Magazine*, which published a list of the top 50 manufacturing software developers/vendors. From this list, they selected the vendors that had MES and ES software. Then, they contacted the Manufacturing Execution Systems Association (MESA) Group, which is an association of 11 member organizations. From this, they created their long-list of 63 vendors and subsequently compiled information on each of them.

At this point, a "Selection Team" of 5 individuals was formed from the initial 12-member team. These 5 individuals took on the task of selecting and evaluating potential vendors and their products. To assist them with this task, they refined the line managers' "wish list" and then expanded it to what became their list of critical requirements. This list was then used as one of their tools of evaluation for the various vendors' products.

6.3.3 Paring Down the List

The Selection Team proceeded to review the information that had been gathered on the 63 vendors. They eliminated 32 of them, then further reduced the list to 15 vendors. These 15 vendors were each sent a letter along with the list of critical requirements that Keller wanted the system to be able to do. After the Selection Team had received and evaluated the vendors' replies, each of the 15 vendors was invited to Keller's head office to meet with the 12-member team and present their software. Of the 15 vendors, 3 submitted reports on their products and 5 came and met with Keller's Acquisition Team for a preliminary meeting and sales presentation. Each of the vendors was evaluated based on their demonstrations and the supplemental information that the Selection Team had gathered on them. At this point, the Selection Team also ran D&B financial reports on each of these 8 vendors. The Team used these reports to rank each vendor based on their number of employees, financial stability, product, and other criteria.

Further to this, 6 site visits were conducted to various vendor locations and customer installations. Additional references were also requested which they subsequently contacted. Some of the information that was received from these referrals provided the Selection Team with more insight into what they should be looking for, and they used this information to further refine their list of critical requirements.

After reviewing the D&B reports, their impressions from the demonstrations, and the input that was received during the site visits and from the referrals, along with their critical requirements list, the Selection Team reduced their list of 8 vendors to a short-list of 3 vendors: Camstar Systems, Symix Computer Systems, and EMS.

6.3.4 Final Choice! Are You Certain?

Next, Keller developed a comprehensive listing of specific performance criteria from their list of critical requirements. The Selection Team then used these requirements to evaluate vendor and software capability in detail. For this, a more in-depth evaluation of the 3 short-listed vendors' proposals was performed. Further, some members of the Selection Team visited 5 companies who were using the systems from their short-listed vendors. Based on these evaluations (using their comprehensive listing of performance criteria and what was found during the 5 site visits), the Selection Team found EMS to be the most capable of fulfilling their information systems needs. Three of the Selection Team members then spent 2 days with EMS during which they learned more about their company, their strategic direction, and their philosophies. All-in-all, the Selection Team determined that EMS would be a good long-term partner for them.

6.3.5   Re-Confirming Their Final Choice

Keller then invited EMS back for an intensive 2-day demonstration for the Selection Team, mill managers, and the EAC, a total of approximately 50 to 60 individuals. These individuals were then polled regarding their impressions of the demonstrations and the responses were overwhelmingly positive. The decision was then made to select EMS' packaged software solution.

The ES Acquisition Process that Keller went through took approximately 11 months to complete, from the point shortly after the decision to buy an ES was made, to the signing of the final contract. The final choice that resulted from the Acquisition process was for the packaged ES from EMS at a cost of approximately US$1 million. Implementation of EMS' software in all three of the Keller manufacturing facilities was completed within the scheduled time frame with only a few minor problems. According to all of the individuals that were involved in both the ES Acquisition Process and the Implementation Process, the EMS solution was the best "fit" and the right choice for the Keller organization. Overall, this project was considered a great success.

In the next chapter, the ES Acquisition Process that Keller went through will be examined more closely. Each of the processes that make up the Acquisition process will be broken down and the activities that Keller undertook will be discussed.

7

Detailed Analysis of The Case of Keller Manufacturing

This chapter presents a more detailed account of the processes and activities that Keller Manufacturing completed for the acquisition of EMS' ES solution. The case of Keller Manufacturing provides a very good example of what can be done by a mid-sized organization with little to no internal IT resources or expertise and no assistance from outside consultants or professional research groups. The Keller case demonstrates how strong leadership, a clearly defined plan, user involvement, an openness to learn from ground zero, and the "pull together" spirit of an organization to get the job done, can work together to find the right solution.

What is also of particular noteworthiness about this case is that it illustrates how one organization, with little knowledge of manufacturing ES going into the Acquisition process, conducted its own marketplace search for information and narrowed its prospects from a large pool of vendors/solutions to a final choice. While all of the cases in this book present good examples of the Information Search process, we think that the Keller case best illustrates the use of the wide variety of information sources that a small to mid-sized organization might have to rely on in this type of situation.

7.1 PLANNING PROCESS

The initial stage of the Acquisition process that was completed by Keller correlates with the Planning process. For Keller, planning marked the beginning of the Acquisition process. The Planning phase encompassed all of the activities that Keller deemed necessary to pursue this endeavor. Keller's Planning process included meetings to determine schedules, priorities, and participants; activities and tasks that would need to be completed; types and sources of information to be sought; and so forth. According to Keller's VP of Information Systems, "a planning scenario as far as timing and dating, defining milestones" was developed and laid out in a Gantt Chart using Microsoft Project Management.

Although the level of planning may not have been as extensive as it could have been (based on the type and magnitude of this acquisition—a first for Keller), planning itself was continuous throughout Keller's Acquisition process. Planning was done iteratively as the Acquisition process progressed, with the plan adjusting as warranted by "new" information as it was received. According to the VP of Information Systems:

> The planning stage, initially, was dating—how long is it going to take us to do this, and do this; and when do we really want this thing done— so, what are the milestones to make sure that we're not slipping. The planning actually continued throughout the project.

This case shows that Keller's Planning phase addressed the following issues:

- Participants
- Acquisition Strategies
- Establishing Evaluation Criteria
- Establishing Requirements
- Present Status Assessment

7.1.1 Participants

The VP of Information Systems was given responsibility for the acquisition project and he had to identify who would participate in the Acquisition process. In addition to this mandate, he had to make sure that the process was user-driven:

> [The President] asked me—I was the VP of Engineering at the time—if I wanted to head that up—I was re-appointed as VP of Information Systems when I accepted to "head up" the new project—because it was obvious at that point that we had decided to do it, that we were going to go for a very extensive information system on the shop floor. He [the President] said that he wanted it driven by the users. (VP of Information Systems)

As leader of the project, he recruited individuals from within the organization to participate in the Acquisition process. These individuals were from the various departments that would be immediately affected by the new technology. Initially, 12 individuals were selected to form the team for this acquisition project. In addition to himself (VP of Information Systems), the other members of the team were:

- VP of Personnel
- VP of Finance
- VP of Marketing
- Two VPs of Production (one Manufacturing, one Operations)
- Current IS person
- Corporate Materials Manager
- Plant Manager
- Assistant Plant Manager
- Representative from Production
- Quality Manager

These members were subsequently divided into two teams: the Steering Committee and the Selection Team (hereafter referred to as the Acquisition Team). The main body, the Steering Committee, consisted of all 12 members and the Acquisition Team consisted of 5 of the Steering Committee members (one of which was the VP of Information Systems) who were most concerned (or involved) with the area of manufacturing. It was the Acquisition Team's responsibility to recommend the appropriate technological solution:

> . . . so 5 of us were picked as what we call the "Selection Team," in other words, 5 of the 12. . . . We had five people who were very concerned [in the Manufacturing side] and also very familiar with what was needed. So, they were appointed as the Selection Team. (VP of Information Systems)

Users also played an important role in the Acquisition process. It was important to Keller's management that users buy in (actively endorse and support) to the new technology. According to the VP of Information Systems, Keller's President/CEO wanted the process to be user-driven:

> He [Keller's President] said that he wanted it driven by the users, so to speak, and I was definitely a user—I knew nothing about MIS, though I had used computers quite a bit and done quite a bit of programming actually, but I was not "trained" MIS. . . . It was not MIS driven—it was not the computer people telling the users what they need.

User participation in the Acquisition process would give Keller employees a sense of ownership and for this reason, Keller decided to involve the users early in the process.

> . . . the user, once again, all the way out to the machine operator. We think we actually got to them—well, we know we did—and tapped their knowledge and opened them up and they told us some things. The supervisors, the prime users of this system, the people who were really going to use it, we got good inputs from them.
>
> The big thing, though, was getting them involved early on and having them a part of the process, trying to make the process theirs. Definitely, the supervisors, our production managers feel that this is their system, it's not something that MIS has pushed down on them. I also think that our employees, even though they would not feel ownership to that extent, I think that they feel that they had a good input and that they were listened to. (VP of Information Systems)

Since Keller was introducing numerous changes to the organization, management felt very strongly that buy-in from the various sectors of the organization was important. User representation came from all of their plants and from all different levels of the organization. A few users participated in site visits to manufacturing environments that were similar to Keller's to see how certain software solutions, that the Acquisition Team was considering, performed. Several groups of users were involved in the vendor demonstrations, and each had their chance to present different scenarios relevant to the tasks they performed to see whether or not the software could meet their challenges.

To further reinforce user involvement, representatives from the various user groups (Manufacturing and Operations, high-level Production people, supervisors, employees) were also brought together, on a voluntary basis, to form an EAC. According to the VP of Information Systems, although the EAC did not have a direct say in the decision process, their input was highly effective in that several of their recommendations were implemented by the Acquisition Team:

> During the latter part of the process, we brought in the hourly people. These were two teams—we called them "Employee Advisory Teams," which is exactly what they were—they were not making decisions, though they ended up making one, but they were advising—and this worked extremely well. In fact, we had them in pretty early in the process as far as requirements and we just wanted them to know what was going on and to be a part of the project. They were not selected . . . we just wanted volunteers. . . . They had major contributions to make.

One of the EAC's recommendations that was implemented and yet was contrary to the Acquisition Team's initial decision was for the installation of PCs at each of the workstations on the shop floor, instead of bar code scanners. PCs, they argued, would provide each employee with the means for more accurate data verification, production tracking, and feedback than bar code scanners could allow. As we can see in the following quotation, the VP of Information Systems credits the users for the significant contribution they made in Keller's decision process:

> During the final demonstrations, they were the ones that actually made one of the major decisions . . . I remember one fella who said, "I don't know a thing about computers, but I can do this," and that statement stuck very deep with us, and that's what led us to the decision, "Okay, this is what we'll do." Now, after being into it for six months, we clearly see that was the right decision, in fact, we would be sick right now had we gone the other way. So, those teams had a major input.

Keller's "hybrid" Steering Committee also had a role in this Acquisition process. In the beginning of the process, it was the Steering Committee that "met and made a lot of the initial decisions" (VP of Information Systems). This Committee (which also included the members of the Acquisition Team) oversaw the project, providing "guidance, management, promotion, and final decisions" (VP of Information Systems). While it is unusual that members of the Acquisition Team are also members of the Steering Committee, from the case, there does not appear to have been an issue of "conflict of interest." In Keller's case, this appeared to have been a "win-win" situation.

In Keller's case, the final choice for the acquisition rested inevitably with the VP of Information Systems. While he wanted to obtain consensus on the decision, the final authority for closing the deal was his, "I looked at all of us as having to agree on it, but the buck stopped with me."

7.1.2 Acquisition Strategies

"Acquisition Strategies" are intended to denote how the organization deals with the vendors. One strategy that Keller chose to employ was to visit the vendors' sites. According to the VP of Information Systems, visiting the various vendors would enable them to further reduce the list of potential vendors and thus eliminate incompatible vendors and/or technologies/solutions early in the process. The site visits also provided another means for Keller to gather more information:

We then had site visits. . . . We visited sites—and I say we, it was not the entire group, it would be various ones of us—I think [the Corporate Materials Manager] and I went to Memphis to look at a SYMIX operation; I think 4 of us went to Jasper to look at a SYMIX operation, for instance. We called a lot of people, a lot of references, before the site visits. In fact, that was one of things that we asked the rep for, "Tell us who is doing, with your software, what you understand that we want to do." That was quite revealing, right there, because many times, they could not come up with someone that they wanted us to talk to. (VP of Information Systems)

Another strategy that Keller planned was to invite a few of the vendors in to do demonstrations of their software products. The short-listed vendors presented, over a 2- or 3-day period, their proposed technological solutions. For their presentations, each vendor would be required to use predetermined scenarios supplied by Keller. According to the VP of Information Systems, this permitted Keller to understand each vendor's technology.

7.1.3   Establishing Evaluation Criteria

We noted in the case that Keller established high-level evaluation and selection criteria early in the Planning process. It is noteworthy that Keller's Acquisition Team refined these criteria/requirements as they proceeded through the various phases of the Acquisition process. As new information was gleaned either from trade publications and/or site visits, Keller refined their requirements.

The case shows that the Keller's Acquisition Team established two distinct types of evaluation criteria early in the Acquisition process: vendor and functional. Vendor Evaluation criteria that the Acquisition Team defined included size, financial stability, reputation of the vendor, etc. Criteria that were established relating to the functionality of the desired software solution dealt with the features of the software and included functionalities specific to front-end interfaces, user-friendliness, and so on. Keller established the Functional Evaluation criteria early in the process. According to the VP of Information Systems:

Our concern was, "What do we want this to do?" So we went to literally every line manager in the company, all three mills, and we asked them, "What would you like to see this system do for you?" They came back with 13 pages of single-spaced, typewritten, "I'd like to have . . ." wish list, so-to-speak. We then condensed that into what we called our "13 requirements"—I think there were 13 or 14 critical requirements, and that's exactly what those words meant. They were the "critical" things and they were required and we approached the project from that standpoint.

> We then condensed the critical requirements—well, let's not say "condensed" them, "expanded" is a better word—into "how will we measure this?" So, if we say, "This is required" then how will we actually measure whether this company or this software can produce that or not? I forget right now what we call that document, but we then expanded those 14—still kept it under the original 14 headings—into a list of what we wanted the system to do, not in generalities, but in specifics.

No technical criteria were established by Keller because, as stated by the VP of Information Systems, the Acquisition Team was "not concerned" with the technical aspects of the technology:

> When we went in, we were open-minded as far as whether to go with UNIX, the AS400, or Windows NT.

Since Keller had no existing infrastructure in place to speak of, they were not required to conform to any particular platform or restricted to any specific architecture. Consequently, they were able to focus primarily on finding the best solution for their needs. Fortunately for them, the software solution that they eventually chose was available for a variety of different platforms so they were free to choose whatever platform they deemed would be best for their organization. As far as determining which platform would best suit their needs, the VP of Information Systems stated:

> A number of MIS professionals that we saw on the site visits and had talked to told us, unequivocally, that if they were in our shoes, what they call "the green field" that we're not tied to any operating system, that there's no question that what they would go with Windows NT, with our size company, under $100 million, and what we wanted it to do, you know, provide a lot of information to a lot of different people. We still were very skeptical, but the more we watched what other people were doing and the more we talked with some users who had gone to it and were very successful with it, then we started leaning towards that platform. Now, we could have brought EMS in on UNIX. A number of users that we looked at were on UNIX, well in fact, they practically all were. Very few were on Windows at the time, but we still chose to come in on this platform.

As evidenced in the aforementioned quotation, it was while they were gathering information on the various software solutions that were available (from talking to various references and during site visits) that they were able to come to a decision on the platform that they would use.

7.1.4   Establishing Requirements

Given the context in which the software was to be used, Keller had to determine exactly what requirements would need to be met by the technology as well as what their own business requirements would be, both current and future. They looked at their current resources—what they had, what was lacking. They examined what was being done on the shop floor. As per the Corporate Materials Manager:

> There were a lot of things that we hadn't thought of that existed out there on the shop floor, and I mean, we thought of a lot of stuff. . . . There's . . . a lot of other stuff that takes place that is particular to the piece-rate system, that's unique to the pay system. . . . [The VP of Information Systems] knew quite a bit about that, but at the same time, there was one or two things that he hadn't thought of. So we slowly uncovered most of these and as we got the software rolled out to the floor, the things that were surprises, were not huge surprises—we were able to work around them and we did not get totally stopped on it.

They also determined what they wanted that was not being met by their current systems. As per the VP of Information Systems:

> The group decided primarily to get input on what we needed. We were interested in results, not databases, platforms, what boxes we were going to run on, networks. These were not our concern. Our concern was, "What do we want this to do?" So we went to literally every line manager in the company, all three mills, and we asked them, "What would you like to see this system do for you?" They came back with 13 pages of single-spaced, typewritten, "I'd like to have . . ." wish list, so-to-speak. We then condensed that into what we called our "13 requirements"—I think there were 13 or 14 critical requirements, and that's exactly what those words meant. They were the "critical" things and they were required and we approached the project from that standpoint.

7.1.5   Present Status Assessment

As has already been presented, Keller closely examined their existing status prior to the commencement of this acquisition project. Keller's existing information technology infrastructure, from both a software and hardware perspective, was inadequate and obsolete and their intention was to "start fresh." As per the Corporate Materials Manager, Keller's existing technology consisted of "a very antiquated AS400 system . . . written in RPG language," several stand-alone PCs, and a modem(s).

7.1.6   Recap of the Planning Process

Everything that Keller's Acquisition Team set forth during the Planning process was applied in the other stages of the Acquisition process—the Information Search process, the Selection process, and so forth. Several deliverables resulted from Keller's Planning process:

- RFI
- Long-list of vendors
- Current status assessment
- Definition of their organizational needs
- Determination of the selection and evaluation criteria
- Formation of the Acquisition Team
- Determination of acquisition strategies

7.2   *INFORMATION SEARCH PROCESS*

Within this case, what is significant about the Information Search process are the sources of information that were used by the Acquisition Team. Two sources were used: internal and external.

As to the internal information sources, Keller availed itself of information from various sources within the organization that included individual users and team members. These internal sources provided information primarily on the organization's requirements (existing) at all of the levels and in all of the areas that the technology would impact (as discussed in Section 7.1.4).

As to external sources, these were sought to provide information about software solutions that might best meet their needs. Keller conducted a market place search, gathering information from:

- Competitors (other furniture manufacturers)
- Trade publications
- Journals
- Seminars (addressing re-engineering in the furniture industry with emphasis on information and technology)
- Professional associations:
    - AFMA (American Furniture Manufacturers Association)
    - SME (Society of Manufacturing Engineers)
    - MESA (Manufacturing Execution Systems Association)
    - APICS (American Production and Inventory Control Society)

According to the VP of Information Systems, Keller approached MESA to obtain information on the various members that provided manufacturing execution systems.

> We then went to the MESA Group which is the Manufacturing Execution Systems Association. They have 11 members—or they did have at the time—and of course, that was their business, manufacturing execution, and so we included all of those people. We ended up with 63 companies from those lists and a few others that we had picked up, on the side, out of the periodicals, that appeared like they had a manufacturing execution system that we could work with, and we got information in on all of those.

Information gathered from the external sources was used by Keller in the construct of their long-list of vendors.

In addition to the external sources listed above, Keller also gathered information from the visits that they conducted to some of the vendors' sites and from vendor references.

To Keller, the credibility of the source of information was important considering the amount of readily available and, often, unreliable information that one has access to. According to Keller's VP of Information Systems, the most credible source of information was the product demonstrations because these showed whether or not the software could do what the vendors were claiming it did:

> Of all of the information, the demonstrations (if you call that "information") were the most credible . . . because they were driven by us, and they were driven specifically by, "How do you do this one little thing?" "Show me this thing," and then we went on to another thing. There were some 60 or 80, as I remember, different items that we asked them to show us.

7.3   SELECTION PROCESS

Concurrent to the Planning process, several iterations of screenings were done during the Information Search process prior to arriving at a short long-list of vendors. Selection and evaluation criteria pertaining to both the vendors and their technologies were used to screen for vendors who could supply the type of software solution that Keller was seeking.

For the most part, the Selection process effectively began at the point when Keller received the RFI responses from the vendors. According to the Corporate

Materials Manager, Keller's Selection process was conducted in two phases. The first phase was conducted upon receipt of the RFI responses from the vendors. With the RFI responses in hand, Keller proceeded with the "paper" evaluation of the vendors' packages; that is, they evaluated the responses as they were presented, at face value, on paper. More precisely, this entailed an initial cursory evaluation that was done by the VP of Information Systems that quickly eliminated more than half of the vendors on the long-list. A second, more detailed evaluation of the remaining vendors was then conducted by the Acquisition Team after which the short long-list was again reduced by half, thereby leaving 15 vendors/software products for consideration. At this point, the second phase of the Selection process began and it involved a second contact with the remaining vendors (via letter with a listing of Keller's critical requirements), more in-depth vendor evaluations using D&B reports, in-house or telephone interviews with vendor representatives, basic product demonstrations, and visits to reference sites.

> There were a couple of different levels in this whole process. The first one would be that we'd bring in a salesman who would give us their best sales pitch, and we weeded some out that way, just by talking. . . . We'd have an initial interview—we'd bring them in, we'd talk to them, and some of them passed that and then we'd bring them to the next level. The next level would be where they would, in more detail rather than maybe just an hour or two, maybe spend all day trying to show us what's going on in more depth, and a lot of them got weeded out there. (Corporate Materials Manager)

Among the factors that Keller considered important in the evaluation of the vendors were financial stability and size:

> We ran D&Bs on every one of them. We looked at the number of people they had employed, some were down around 20, in that area, and we quickly threw them out. These 15 we eventually ranked—in fact, we had a very structured method of ranking—but we had a ranking right at the top, "financial stability," and we had some facts there—their profitability, their annual sales, which we got off of the D&B. . . . Some we threw out instantly just because we said we don't care how capable they are, they're not going to be around in a couple of years or there's a chance they won't, so we did not go any further with them.

One critical factor that the Acquisition Team was looking for was the ability of the vendor to meet Keller's requirements. Keller wanted a single vendor solution. Strategically, this was an important factor for Keller. Although this project was focused on manufacturing, Keller was also thinking of their future requirements in other areas of the organization such as finance.

> Another criteria that was very important to us was that we wanted a company that could do a "turn-key" job. We did not want to buy software [MES] from one person (company), . . . and then later on buy a general ledger package from someone else. We wanted a company that could do the whole thing—an enterprise system. That was not a criterion to the standpoint that we removed people because of it. We wanted the "best of breed" in manufacturing, clearly. If that company could also do these other things and give us the "turn-key" system, . . . then that put them a step ahead of everyone else. But, what we did not want, we did not want to worry about integrating different systems together and we wanted someone who could stand up and say, we will do the whole package for you. (VP of Information Systems)

As noted here, the case shows that information was also gathered on some of the vendors and their software solutions (functional aspects) by means of visits to reference sites. Three reference sites (Best Chair, Aristokraft, and Childcraft) were visited by some of the members of the Acquisition Team and all were found to be valuable sources of information.

According to the VP of Personnel, the objective of the Selection process was to create a short-list of vendors who would later be invited to do scripted in-house demonstrations.

Hence, for our part, we have chosen to demarcate the Selection process as beginning with the activities following the return of the RFI responses from the vendors. Keller's course of action for the Selection process involved two primary objectives/tasks, those being the evaluation of the RFI responses and the formation of the short-list of vendors.

7.4 EVALUATION PROCESS

From the case, we observed two distinct types of evaluation that were conducted by Keller: vendor and functionality. Evaluation criteria for both types were developed in the Planning phase of the Acquisition process.

7.4.1 Vendor Evaluation

As part of the Vendor Evaluation, each of the vendors was evaluated in terms of their financial stability, size, etc., based on reports from D&B as well as other information. The Vendor Evaluation was conducted by Keller's Acquisition Team. In addition to the quantifiable factors (sales volume, the size of the company, etc.), according to the VP of Personnel, consideration was also given to qualitative factors such as the quality of the response, the appropriateness of the response to Keller's particular needs, as well as the impressions made during "face-to-face" meetings with the vendors:

> There were several things, not only financial stability, but the types of programs that they had implemented that could possibly be similar to our situation. Communication—how well did we get along with that group. Information that we requested—how soon did it come, did they present it in writing, was it what we asked for. That was another key in dealing with that individual or organization.

> All that had a lot of say, but we also looked for very financially sound companies. Size, the type of support that we would get. If we brought a company on, if this came about and these were some of the issues, how would you address those, what kind of tactical support could we count on—was it in-house or would they have to go outside and bring in an outside group? We ran across that several times—"Oh, we don't handle that, but we have a partner that would come in and do this part." And, then we started to see who could give us the most overall program and support it after the sale, and these were some of the questions that we would try to find out and cover.

7.4.2 Functional Evaluation

The second type of evaluation that the Acquisition Team conducted focused on the functionality of the software. A high-level Functional Evaluation was conducted on the responses to the first RFI that Keller sent out. (After the evaluation of the responses to the RFIs, they were able to reduce their long-list of vendors from 63 to approximately 30 vendors.) Following a second contact with the vendors for which they had sent out letters (a second RFI) with a detailed breakdown of the functionalities and capabilities they were seeking, Keller then conducted a more in-depth evaluation of the responses that they received. (After the evaluation of the responses to the second RFIs, they were able to reduce their short long-list of vendors from 30 to 15 vendors.) They subsequently evaluated the software's functionalities during standard or "canned" software demonstrations. According to the VP of Information Systems, Keller invited the short-listed vendors to their facilities to conduct in-house demonstrations (sales presentations) of their proposed solutions. Of the 15 vendors from the long short-list of vendors that were invited, only 8 of the vendors responded to Keller's invitation—5 of the vendors went to Keller's facilities and did in-house presentations, while 3 submitted reports on their products:

> . . . we made secondary contacts, we had people in, not doing total demonstrations yet at this point, but talking with some of them here in the office—I would say probably 8 or 9 of the 15) actually came in from all over the country. (VP of Information Systems)

According to the VP of Personnel, these in-house meetings/presentations were a means for the Acquisition Team to narrow the lengthy short-list to a manageable few. It was also a method of educating the Team about the various technologies that were available in the market place.

> At that point, we again went through a narrowing process—starting to lower the group down to a select few—and went through a process then of inviting that group in for an interview—more or less an occasion to get to know each other real well and start to look at the programs being provided. In the interview process, they presented some of the information about what is going on in manufacturing in the area of information development and primarily for manufacturing. We were able to start educating ourselves on the different technologies that were available, some of the trends of that area, and start to see where we would fit into that development. (VP of Personnel)

Lastly, Keller had the primary vendor conduct a scripted in-house product demonstration that was based on the criteria that they had developed to measure the software's capabilities in each of the 14 critical areas.

> We actually had a total of three days of demonstrations here by EMS, the winning company, and we went up there for 2 days, the Selection Team did, to Milwaukee. . . . We controlled the demonstration, not them. . . . We wanted to see what it would do on our problems, not how pretty the screens were. . . . They came in for 3 days. . . . The demonstrations were basically, . . . "Show me how this is done. Show me how that is done." . . . But we did not turn them loose and say, "Show us your system," because we did not want to see a lot of these other things. We wanted specifically to see how are we going to do this if we install this system. (VP of Information Systems)

Keller also used site visits and calls to vendor references as other means to evaluate the functional capabilities of the software. According to the VP of Information Systems, various members of the Acquisition Team visited certain vendor reference sites that had purchased the technology Keller was interested in. They also called the various references that the vendor had provided.

> We then had site visits—and I say we, it was not the entire group, it would be various ones of us—I think [the Corporate Materials Manager] and I went to Memphis to look at a SYMIX operation; I think 4 of us went to Jasper to look at a SYMIX operation, for instance. We called a lot of people, a lot of references, before the site visits. In fact, that was one of things that we asked the rep for, "Tell us who is doing, with your software, what you understand that we want to do." That was quite revealing, right there, because many times, they could not come up with someone that they wanted us to talk to.

> For all 3, we did site visits, did a lot of phone conversations with customers, did a lot of work in the office short of demonstrations, where their people (technical people) would come in and say, "Yes, we can do this and this is how we do it; and we can do that and this is how we do it." We evaluated that. (VP of Information Systems)

7.4.3   Evaluation Tools

During the Planning process, in preparation for the different stages of the Evaluation process, Keller developed questionnaires, the demonstration scenarios, and evaluation matrices using the functional and vendor criteria that they had established. The Acquisition Team assigned weights to each of the criteria and ranked them in the order of their importance.

One of the matrices that was developed (what we would call a Critical Requirements Score Card [CRSC]) was used during the Selection process for evaluating the RFI responses. This "score card" contained 14 high-level criteria for evaluating the vendors and the functional aspects of the software packages. According to the VP of Information Systems:

> We had a very structured method of ranking—but we had a ranking right at the top, "financial stability," and we had some facts there—their profitability, their annual sales, which we got off of the D&B. . . . We had the 14 critical requirements, and down at the bottom of the page, we had "evaluation" as a final summary evaluation—usually, that came out as a negative or a positive [in the ranking of 1 to 10, the closer the

ranking was to 1, the less likely the vendor/product would meet Keller's needs; the closer the ranking was to 10, the more likely the vendor/product would meet Keller's needs]—one or the other.

This team of 5 then evaluated those, literally around the table, to where each man did his own evaluation independently and then we discussed each evaluation. We would go to point number 1, and we would look at each one of these people and ask, "What did you evaluate?" and it was a ranking of 1 to 10. Then, along with that ranking, we had the comments that anyone wanted to enter into the record, so-to-speak, as far as the capability of this company to do this one specific requirement. . . . Then we literally averaged those rankings and that was the number that was put in the box. . . . We then totaled them . . . and we looked at whether we would consider this company further or not.

7.5   CHOICE PROCESS

The Acquisition process culminates in the Choice process and consists of the final choice or recommendation. In Keller's case, a final choice or recommendation of the software solution was arrived at by the Acquisition Team. The responses to both the first and the second RFIs, meetings with the vendors, calls to vendor references, site visits, and standard/"canned" software presentations—all contributed information that enabled the Acquisition Team to narrow their lists of potential vendors to a primary choice. Then, for the purpose of confirming their choice, Keller invited the primary vendor in-house to do a scripted demonstration. According to the VP of Information Systems:

So, when EMS came in to demonstrate, and this was a demonstration not to compare them to other companies as much as to confirm our decision—"Are you really the right one, or should we continue to look?," because at that point, we had selected them as number one, though we had not made the firm decision yet. So they were trying to confirm that selection.

According to the Plant Manager, the Acquisition Team chose this particular vendor's software solution because it was the one (in the price range that Keller was looking at and for the size of company that Keller is) best able to meet Keller's current and future requirements, not only on the manufacturing side, but also in other areas of the company:

We arrived at EMS because they had a strong shop floor system that followed all the operations, all the detail on the shop floor—labor, material numbers—that was the big draw there. Plus, they did have everything else, too. We were looking for something that was enterprise-wide so we would not have to tie several companies [products from different vendors] together, because we saw problems there—if you start tying them together and something's not quite working, well, hey, he's not tied right, or he's not tied right. We wanted to remove that, too. That was another thought process we used.

In addition to the "score card" that was used during the Evaluation process, a meeting was convened of all of the Steering Committee and Acquisition Team members to see if there was a consensus on which technological solution was the most appropriate for Keller. Input from the shop floor users who had participated in the Evaluation process was also factored into the final choice.

So, after the demonstrations, the Selection Team, these 5 men, got together and canvassed, essentially, the opinions and went back to the 12 and said, "This is what we recommend." Of course, we had made the selection but we wanted the other 12 or the others on the 12-member team to buy-in to it, which they did, and at that point, the selection process was basically over. We started the negotiations and the actual implementation. (VP of Information Systems)

Although the final recommendation, as stated earlier, rested with the VP of Information Systems, it was "a group process" (VP of Personnel) and he (the VP of Information Systems) "looked at all of us as having to agree on it."

7.6   NEGOTIATION PROCESS

Within this case, we observed two types of negotiations that transpired during the course of Keller's Acquisition process: business (characterized as informal) and legal (characterized as formal). As the "primary negotiator," the VP of Information Systems conducted Business Negotiations with the vendors throughout the whole process on such things as cost and modifications:

We do not pass up an opportunity to negotiate as we're going along, and we would come up with something that they would say, "Well, there's going to be a number of modifications to do this," and we'd talk about the price of the modifications and they would say, "Well, it's $100 per hour," to which we'd reply, "That's too expensive. We couldn't do that." Then they would come back. This was while they were still trying to make sure their foot was staying in the door.

He also conducted Legal Negotiations on the pricing and fine contractual details leading to the signing of the contract with the vendor. According to the VP of Personnel, they entered formal negotiations with their vendor of choice, EMS, after the final choice (recommendation) was approved by the Board of Directors.

In addition to being an informal process, it is worth noting here that the Business Negotiations, as well as being informal, could be characterized as "fluid." As per the VP of Information Systems, Keller did "not pass up an opportunity to negotiate as they went along."

7.7   *INFLUENCES ON THE ES ACQUISITION PROCESS*

Several influences were noted in the Keller case. They are presented as to the principal targets of their effects. Hence, the influences are categorized according to their effects on the acquisition process, the final choice of ES solution or the Acquisition Team.

7.7.1   Influences on the Process

The following items had varying influences on Keller's ES Acquisition Process:

- Strong management commitment
- User community
- An aging system
- Project management techniques

Strong Management Commitment

The strong commitment to this acquisition project by Upper Management was another influence that was noted in Keller's case. According to the Plant Manager:

> . . . probably the strongest commitment by Upper Management to anything I've seen. I've been with the company 20 years. It was [the President's] commitment in saying [to the VP of Information Systems], "Here it is. We need it—go do it."

User Community

A significant amount of influence on the process came from the users. It was important for Keller that the user community have input and participate in the ES Acquisition Process. Users participated in the requirements definition (during the Planning process) and in the Functional Evaluation process. As stated earlier, the EAC is an example of user participation in the Acquisition process and, although they were not directly involved in the decision process, they nevertheless had an influence on the process as well as on a decision that impacted the implementation of the software solution. According to the Plant Manager, the EAC's input was instrumental in the Acquisition Team's decision to implement workstations on the shop floor:

> . . . they were very instrumental in one major thing we did and that has to do with using workstations on the floor. Our thought in the beginning was to use just a little digital readout machine that would just, basically, give you numbers and maybe small messages. And, we went toward that, but this group—and thank goodness they did, they were right—this group said, "No, no. Why not give us the whole workstation where we have a computer out there to access to everything." And, that was probably the smartest thing we did. And, that was a huge impact, I mean, that's unbelievable. It would not be nearly what it is today without that.

An Aging System

An aging AS400 was a factor that played a minor role in Keller's decision to start from "ground zero" technologically. Hence, with no platform constraints to worry about, Keller chose the ES solution that was best suited to its needs and decided (in the course of doing the Acquisition process and after talking to references) to implement it on DEC Raid 5 servers in a Windows NT environment.

Project Management Techniques

Project management techniques were used to structure the Acquisition process that Keller's Acquisition Team followed. As noted by the Corporate Materials Manager:

> I think one of keys to this project's success was that it was very structured. We were very methodical about what we did and we were very thorough.

Since these techniques are commonly used by MIS/IT, Engineering, and other areas in an organization to structure projects, they are familiar tools that were relied upon to provide a structure for this process.

7.7.2   Influences on the Final Choice

The following items had varying influences on Keller's final choice of ES:

- Economic factors
- Single vendor solution
- User buy-in
- Business process reengineering
- Vendor demonstration

Economic Factors

In the very early stages of the process, in the midst of the Information Search for the different manufacturing ES solutions that were available in the market-place, economic factors had an influence on the process and necessarily, Keller's final choice of ES solution. Given the size of the Keller organization, Keller was limited by cost to seeking a software solution from a smaller vendor. According to the VP of Information Systems, when he contacted SAP to inquire about their product, in no uncertain terms, SAP rejected them based solely on the size of their organization. (There is an implied correlation between the size—in terms of annual sales volume—of an organization and the size and thereby cost of the software solution that they require.)

Single Vendor Solution

Another influence arose from the desire, by Keller, for a single vendor solution. According to the VP of Information Systems: "We wanted a company that could do the whole thing—an enterprise system."

User Buy-In

An important factor that influenced Keller's Acquisition process and conse-quently, the final choice, was user buy-in. To achieve buy-in and the notion of ownership, weekly information notices were published and distributed to the employees to keep them abreast of the situation regarding the selection of the software. Thus, each employee was informed as to where the Acquisition Team was in the process.

> We did give them special information, and you'll see that in those his-tory documents, the KIS (Keller Information System) Bulletin. We tried to have something on the bulletin boards no less than every 30 days. We tried to get something out every 2 weeks just to keep it in front of

them—that, "Hey, this is happening . . ."; "Here's what's happened now"; "Here's what's going on . . ."—to keep them informed. The big thing, though, was getting them involved early on and having them a part of the process, trying to make the process theirs. (VP of Information Systems)

In addition, the active seeking of user input and the formation of the EAC were both instrumental in getting the users to "buy-in" to the process. As attested to by the VP of Information Systems:

The big thing, though, was getting users involved early on and having them a part of the process, trying to make the process theirs. Definitely, the supervisors—our production managers feel that this is their system, it's not something that MIS has pushed down on them. I also think that our employees, even though they would not feel ownership to that extent, I think that they feel that they had a good input and that they were listened to.

Business Process Reengineering

Though not directly stated, another factor that appeared to have influenced both the Acquisition process and the final choice was BPR. There are several elements in the case that point to this factor. As an anticipated benefit of buying a software solution, Keller was hoping to gain the advantages of an improved information flow in their organization:

They [the IBMTC] could not see how we could do that because of our lack of information, that we had absolutely no information, that compared to most people our systems were very archaic. (VP of Information Systems)

Besides the improved flow of information within the organization, another benefit that Keller wanted to achieve with the new technology was improved efficiency over the levels that were being attained with their existing modus operandi. Since Keller was in the market for a "best of breed" manufacturing software solution, the software would, in all likelihood, impose or, at the very least, outline the processes that they would need to adopt. In short, Keller would be introducing BPR into the organization with (and by way of) the new software solution. For Keller, the consequence of implementing this type of solution would necessarily entail a redesign/reengineering of the processes that were in place prior to the acquisition and implementation of the software. Their existing processes, involving a mix of manual procedures and automated systems, would be replaced (reengineered) or significantly modified (redesigned) commensurate with the requirements of the new technology.

As seen in the following quotation, one example of process redesign that would be done would involve Keller's shipping schedules:

> We had to put shipments together from all three plants. When a customer placed an order—might be a truckload or might just be one dining room suite, for instance, but there could be product that comes from each of the three plants. We have to dovetail that together so that all that gets on the same truck and it gets to him [the customer] on roughly the delivery time that he is expecting. That is what we were having trouble doing. Of course, as far as controlling cost, and reducing frustrations in the shop, helping our people, these were all secondary things that we expected to get out of the information system. (VP of Information Systems)

In other words, what the VP of Information Systems was saying (based on our own knowledge and experience in manufacturing and shipping) is that while Keller's shipping schedules were being prepared, the status of the products-on-order that were to be shipped was unknown (for whatever reason). This lack of knowledge about the order status caused disruptions in all phases of the production process and left little time to plan for schedule corrections. It also looks as though the volume of information that the employees need access to in order to meet the demands of Keller's growing business exceeds the ability of their existing processes/systems to deliver. The new technology would, thus, either modify the existing processes or create new ones, and would also provide Keller's employees with immediate access to time-critical information.

7.7.3   Influences on the Acquisition Team

The following items had varying influences on Keller's Acquisition Team:

- Leadership
- Interdisciplinary nature of the Acquisition Team
- Cohesiveness of the Acquisition Team

Leadership

Leadership was a driving force in Keller's Acquisition process. The leadership exhibited by the VP of Information Systems drove the process. The impact of the VP of Information Systems' leadership skills was apparent on all of the processes within the Acquisition process. The following quotes illustrate the confidence that the President and members of the Steering Committee (and hence the Acquisition Team) had in the leadership ability of this individual:

> I can't say enough about what [the VP of Information Systems] did. He really set it off on the right foot and I guess it was our President having the vision to say, "I want to take this one guy and I want to take everything else away from him and let him focus on this and this is his number one job"—where [the VP of Information Systems] was our Vice President of Engineering and he covered, I mean, just a huge span. And, I think it was pretty smart of our President to say, "This is the guy for the job." (Plant Manager)

> [The VP of Information Systems] is such a great person as far as organizational skills and focus, but also having a vision. As far as a team leader, task force leader, it probably would not have gone as smoothly without him, so I think that was a key influence—it was a huge influence. (VP of Personnel)

Interdisciplinary Nature of the Acquisition Team

The Steering Committee and the Acquisition Team were interdisciplinary. With members from Personnel, Finance, Marketing, Engineering, Production/Manufacturing, Operations, Information Systems, and Quality Control, "it was a very cross-functional team." (VP of Information Systems)

Cohesiveness of the Acquisition Team

The Steering Committee and the Acquisition Team were very cohesive and worked very well together.

7.8 *CHARACTERISTICS AND CRITICAL SUCCESS FACTORS (CSFS)*

Several factors about Keller's Acquisition process were critical to its successful outcome.

- **Formal process:** First, the process that the VP of Information Systems developed for this acquisition was very formal. As per the Plant Manager:

> I think it was well structured and formal. [The VP of Information Systems] was given the task and he brought everything together. Then he laid it out for us and then he led the group in discussions. . . . I think it was well laid out and very professional.

- **Structured process:** Another CSF of the Acquisition process for Keller is that it was a structured process. According to both the Plant Manager (in the previous quote) and the Corporate Materials Manager:

> One of keys to this project's success was that it was very structured. We were very methodical about what we did and we were very thorough.

- **User-driven:** Another CSF of the Acquisition process is that it was user-driven. This was considered by each of the participants to be very important to the successful outcome of Keller's Acquisition process. The overall effect of user involvement in the process helped to ensure that the chosen software solution would be more readily accepted. According to the Plant Manager, they wanted to have full user buy-in to ensure the success of the acquisition and hence, they involved the users early in the process:

> Yes, oh yes, that was one thing [the acquisition being user-driven], I think, why we've been very successful, I feel, with the implementation. That was because I did not have somebody give me something and tell me, "This is for you. This is going to be good. You go use this." I feel like I was in on looking at what it could do for me, so that I felt like this was something that I could work with, my people could work with, and it would give the information I want, understanding that there would have to be things developed. I don't think you can get any canned software anywhere that you're not going to have to develop for, and there were a few things that they're working on as we go, but it's doing exactly what we want, and that's why it will succeed.

Moreover, with the exception of one individual (the IS person), all of the members of the Acquisition Team were users.

- **Partnership:** Similarly, another CSF of the process was the "sense of partnership" that the Acquisition Team tried to achieve both internally and externally. Keller's Acquisition Team worked to establish a "sense of partnership" not only with the various user communities within the organization, but also with the potential vendor.

In addition, some of the influences that were discussed in the previous section can also be classified as CSFs. The following list includes all of the CSFs for Keller's ES Acquisition Process:

- Formal process
- Structured process
- User-driven
- Partnership
- Strong management commitment
- Leadership
- Interdisciplinary nature of the Acquisition Team
- Cohesiveness of the Acquisition Team
- User buy-in

7.9 LESSONS LEARNED

For the Keller organization, the ES Acquisition Process was an incredible "learning experience." As described by the VP of Information Systems:

> All of us learned unbelievably from this experience. There was continual learning. We were running into phrases and statements that we'd never heard of before, especially since none of us were really trained MIS people.

Among the lessons that this experience taught them was that:

1. **They could do it!** Even though they took the long route in doing things, they learned that they could do it, on their own, without the help of outside consultants.
2. **They could adapt** and accommodate a lot of new information about technologies that they knew little or nothing about. This information was not always easy for them to understand nor was it always "cut 'n dry."
3. **They had to develop new procedures for dealing with ES software acquisitions.** Since they had never previously undertaken a process for this type of software nor did they have in-house expertise in this area, the Acquisition Team had to "construct" ("design") the process as they went along. While there were some fundamental purchasing processes (minimal) in place for the Acquisition Team to follow, in large part (say 99%), procedures had to be developed ad hoc to deal with this "new" buying situation. This really was a "learn as you go" process for Keller.
4. **They had to modify their existing purchasing procedures.** Since Keller's standard purchasing procedures were inadequate, they had to be substantially modified to suit the complexity of this acquisition. With this being a first-time purchase of packaged software of this complexity and

magnitude, beyond the standard practice followed for the issue of a purchase order, Keller did not have any buying procedures in place that the Acquisition Team could follow for this type of purchase.

The VP of Information Systems carefully documented the new procedures as well as this process so as not to lose what the organization had learned. Since this was a new experience, the VP of Information Systems wanted to leave behind some documentation explaining the rationale that was used and the decisions that were made for choosing this (the EMS software) technology over another. As a result, the Acquisition Team contributed a documented history of what transpired during this Acquisition process to the organizational memory.

7.10   CONCLUSION

As a final note on this case, for Keller's size, its needs, and its budget, the whole organization contributed to finding the right fit of ES. Not only would it meet Keller's immediate manufacturing needs, but it would also fit with Keller's future objectives for implementing integrated software into its other functional areas, that is, enterprise-wide. For a small- to medium-sized company, such as Keller, that had no existing technological infrastructure to speak of, and that had no prior "success" in the way of implementing complex software systems, there was substantial risk involved with their decision to begin at the shop floor level. This decision by Keller's senior management defied convention.

The "traditional approach to information systems," as referred to by Keller's VP of Information Systems, that was recommended in the "Impact Assessment Report" by the IBMTC as well as by other sources (not named) would have had Keller begin with a general ledger, then proceed to order-entry, then expand a little further, and eventually get down to the shop floor. But, as stated by Keller's VP of Information Systems:

> We saw "eventually" as being a very long word with a very long time span, and we did not want to wait because we needed it on the shop floor right away. So, we essentially jumped into the frying pan right away and put it in, in the most difficult area, which was the shop floor itself.

Keller took the risk and, fortunately for them, it paid off.

8

Information Search

If you have come to this chapter as the logical "next step" from Planning, and your Acquisition Team is actually in the midst of the Acquisition process, then we can say that you have already begun your search for information with the definition of requirements, since this task was undertaken during the Planning process. The Acquisition Team will have sat with key users from the various departments and at the various levels of the organization (entry-level to executive) who will be directly impacted by the new ES to determine all aspects of their daily job/system-related functional needs. OK then. So far, so good. The Team will have also established the criteria it wants to use to select/evaluate the software products and vendors. Super!! Now you have come to the point of doing the Marketplace Analysis—another major task covered in the Planning chapter, but still you are left with questions about where and what to look for. First, where do you look for information on ESs? Magazines? Journals? The Web? Consultants? And what about available products and vendors? Who are the major players out there?

First, let us talk a little bit about the Information Search process proper and the commodity that you will be working with. As you may have already begun to notice, information obtained by means of "searching and gathering" feeds the Acquisition process. However, information might also come unsolicited from any number of sources (such as in casual conversations with colleagues or through the media). In such instances, you have no control over "if and when," during the course of the Acquisition process, you will receive the information or what its value will be to the decision process. You may also have begun to notice (and if not, then it will become clearer to you as the Acquisition process goes along) that activities that might be considered part of the Information Search process (such as the Marketplace Analysis or obtaining information from referrals) are not limited to a specific juncture point in the scheme of the Acquisition process. What does this all mean? In short, it means that the Information Search process is not a "one time only, go out and get all you can in one fell swoop" type of effort. Although many of the search and gather activities/tasks are concentrated in or occur concurrently with the Planning process, there are many others (examples of which can be found in this section) that could, and even should, be planned for throughout the entire Acquisition process. Hence, you will note that the Information Search process will occur in stages and is reiterative. As to the process itself, it is quite simple: search, screen, discard or keep; repeat.

   In this section, we will be focusing on the types, sources, and quality of information that are needed as well as the levels of screening that will need to be done in this process. Then, in the next section, we will discuss the Selection process and its role as an intermediate step toward the final choice.

8.1   *INFORMATION SEARCH AND SOURCES*

Information is a critical element in the Acquisition process and hence, the Information Search process plays an important part in the ES Acquisition Process. This process yields information for all of the different processes within the ES Acquisition Process, from the Planning process right through to the Negotiation process. It is during the Information Search process that information is gathered and screened from all available sources. An important factor in the Information Search process is the information "source." As with other types of acquisitions, the nature and source of information are important to the process of choosing an ES solution. We distinguish two principal sources of information: internal and external.

   Internal sources of information come from within the organization. Information can be obtained from:

- Scanning the organization's existing memory (human, paper, and/or databases)
- Documented processes
- Reports such as internal evaluations, feasibility studies, needs assessments, current resource analyses, cost-benefit analyses, return-on-investment (ROI) analyses, feasibility analyses, vendor analyses (history, litigation, financial, and performance); and IT planning reports
- Organizational mission statement

- Strategic performance objectives (these would include the overall operational and long-term goals and requirements of the organization)
- Formal research/environmental scanning groups
- Acquisition team members
- Users
  Other sources

External sources of information originate from outside the organization and can include the following:

- Advertisements from vendors
- Sales literature
- Promotional items
- Periodicals
- Conferences
- Trade shows
- Outside consultants
- Outside references
- Research services such as Gartner Group, Meta Group, Yankee Group
- Solicitations from vendors (salespeople)
- Seminars given by vendors
- News publications
- Market surveys
- Trade associations
- Industry or government product rating services
- Outside business associates
- Personal networks
  Other commercial sources

Many of these external sources can be consulted as part of the Marketplace Analysis (part of the Information Search process that is embedded in the Planning process) to research available products and vendors that are most likely to meet the organization's needs. As discussed in Chapter 4, the purpose of the Marketplace Analysis is to produce a short long-list of vendors (and their technologies) that will be based on high-level requirements definitions and selection and evaluation criteria established earlier in the Planning process. As in Keller's case, Keller made initial contact with 63 vendors following their review of the marketplace, after which they reduced their list first to 30 vendors and then to a shorter long-list of 15. As for International Air, their Marketplace Analysis in conjunction with their vendor information/awareness session enabled them to arrive at their long-list of 7 vendors. Both ESC and Telecom International came up with shorter long-lists of 3 and 5 vendors respectively as a result of their Marketplace Analysis findings.

Both types of information sources will need to be used to meet the needs of the different parts of the ES Acquisition Process. As mentioned earlier, one internal source of information is users and in each of the cases, the Acquisition Teams consulted the users for information on their functional requirements. This information was then used in the RFP (which was sent out to the vendors following completion of the Planning process) and for developing evaluation questionnaires and grids/matrices (which were subsequently used in the Evaluation process). Other internal sources of information that we noted were the Acquisition Team members themselves and, in the case of International Air, in-house consultants that were brought in to be part of the Acquisition Team.

While some information regarding vendors of possible technological solutions will come from internal sources (based on prior experience), the greater source of information on this subject will be external. In the Marketplace Analysis that your Team will conduct, concurrently with the Planning process, some of the information that will be gathered will be used in part for the Planning process, the result of which will be the shorter long-list of vendors that the RFP will be sent to. As part of this analysis, information from various external sources will be gathered to find out, among other things, what types of technological solutions are available and who the major players are. The external sources of information that were consulted in the four cases included trade publications, professional journals, referrals, conferences/seminars, stockbroker, RFI, competitors and professional network.

One of the most notable sources of information used in three of the cases (International Air, Telecom International, and ESC) was the professional research groups, and these included Gartner Group, Meta Group, CSC Index, Yankee Group, and TRI. These groups identified the vendors and products available in the marketplace and provided in-depth information on each. Keller, on the other hand, established contact with a professional association (MESA) that provided them with a list of vendor-members. Keller subsequently used this list to extend their initial short long-list of vendors.

Another external source of information can be the Internet and it was used in three of the four cases (the exception being Keller). A word of caution though— do not use the Internet as your only source. As with any source of information, it is necessary to find and distinguish the credible, reputable, or factual sources from those that are fraudulent or less than truthful about their products. It is also important to be able to separate the facts from the "marketing fluff," which cannot always be easily done. As our study indicates and as will be discussed later in this section, the credibility of the source of information is an important factor in the decision process. Hence, if you are unable to differentiate between "hearsay, rumors, and marketing fluff" and "factual" information, then your final decision for this acquisition is in jeopardy.

Following is a list of some of the internal information sources that can be consulted during this process:

- Users for requirements definition
- Users as a general source of information
- Acquisition Team members
- In-house consultants
- Strategic Planning Group
- Reengineering Task Force (group)
- Employee Advisory Committee
  Feasibility analysis

Next is a list of some of the external information sources that can be consulted during this process:

- External consultants
- Trade publications
- Trade shows
- Training seminars
- Professional journals
- Conferences such as: CEBIT, ERP World, Sapphire, Comdex, Government & Technology
- Seminars
- Competitors
- Magazines
- Online magazines such as: www.techweb.com, www.datamation.com, www.dmreview.com, www.interex.com/erpnews/index.html
- Professional Research Groups such as: Gartner Group, Meta Group, Yankee Group, CSC Index
- Vendor via RFI
- Stockbroker
- Professional associations
- Professional networks
- Marketplace surveys
- Referrals (references supplied by vendors)
- Dunn & Bradstreet financial reports
- Internet
  ERP Web sites such as: www.erpfan.com, www.erpsupersite.com, www.erpworld.com, www.erpcentral.com, www.erpassist.com, www.interex.com, www.phptr.com/crp/crp-index.html

It is a good idea for the Acquisition Teams to designate an individual(s) to collect, document, and disseminate information from internal and external sources. Once the information about available ES solutions is disseminated, it can be used to confirm or disconfirm any assumptions that the Team has about particular products and/or vendors.

In the search process itself, some consideration should be given to the type or nature of the information that you will be gathering. What do we mean by *type* or *nature*? Among other things, positive and negative information. That's right, negative information. This is something that most people do not think about when seeking information on a product. We go out looking. We ask questions about all of the gadgets, the buttons, "What can it do? How fast can it go? What can it handle? What does this button do?" etc., but we rarely think to look for instances or cases where the product fails. Well, this is what you want to do here. In addition to asking all of the positive questions, ask some negative ones. Actively seek out organizations where the ES solutions, which you are or will be seriously considering, have failed, or are not working out as well as they had hoped, or that were difficult to implement. The information that is obtained may provide your Team with some valuable insights, such as:

- Another perspective on the technological solution.
- What it is like dealing with a particular vendor.
- Alerting you to problems or limitations of the software that might not otherwise be discovered, say, until your organization is 6 months into using it, and then what do you do?
- Alerting you to issues or factors that your organization might want to subsequently include in its negotiations with the vendor. One example of this can be seen later in this section in the paragraph on "professional network" that has to do with information that was obtained by International Air regarding an ES's performance.
- Alerting you to why a particular ES implementation failed—was it the technology itself that failed or were there other factors involved in the implementation process that caused the failure, such as:
  - Was it the wrong technology for that organization?
  - Was it due to a lack of skilled personnel—too few, skilled personnel or insufficiently skilled personnel?
  - Was it due to poor planning on the part of the organization?
  - Was it due to weak project management?

  Be aware that it is not always the vendor's technology that is the cause of the failure. Do not let the first answers that you hear lead you to jumping to the wrong conclusion—do some digging to find out the "real" reason(s) for the failure.

Should the information that is obtained be sufficiently compelling, it could lead your organization to decide not to purchase a particular ES. If anything, a search for negative information is likely to result in a clearer, more balanced perspective of the ESs and the vendors. Then, when the final decision is made and the ES solution is chosen, your organization will have the sense of knowing that its decision was soundly based, with as little as possible left to chance.

Also in the search process, it will not only be necessary to look at the types of information that will be gathered, but it will be equally important to consider the credibility of the sources as well, whether internal or external. While not an absolute guarantee, the odds are better of obtaining reliable information when it comes from a reputable and credible source. Hence, the reliability of the sources of information is also an important factor in the Acquisition process. An example of this comes from the ESC case. One of the consultants from the professional research group working with ESC's Acquisition Team highly recommended a particular vendor over another. Based on the information the Team had gathered and this consultant's recommendation, the Team was ready to discount the vendor that the consultant was not recommending (which eventually became the Team's primary candidate). However, in the process of gathering more information (again, to reduce the level of risk and uncertainty), the Acquisition Team found out that the aforementioned consultant was previously employed by the vendor that he or she was recommending and this cast doubt on the credibility of the source (the consultant) and hence the reliability of the information he or she was conveying. With the exception of this incidence, each of the three cases that used professional research organizations considered them to be an important and, more often than not, reliable source of information.

When gathering information from internal sources, specifically users, it would be best to obtain information from the key users in the areas that would be affected by the incoming technological solution. For many reasons, key users have more experience with regard to their daily functional needs and would, thus, be able to provide the most complete (dare we say credible) information to the Acquisition Team. They could also provide information as to what they think the current software that they use lacks in the way of functionality and what they would see as a solution or fix to those shortcomings.

As previously mentioned, the Information Search process is important for ES acquisitions, and the types and characteristics of the information that is obtained influence all of the other processes within the ES Acquisition Process. Due to the complexity of ES, Acquisition Teams should seek out information to help them reduce the uncertainty associated with these types of acquisitions. One way of doing so is to obtain details from others (outside references), who are using or have acquired the same or similar solutions.

Outside references, and more importantly, individuals who have been directly involved in the evaluation of this type of technology, will have a higher impact on the Acquisition Team's decision to acquire the same (or different, if the experience of the outside reference has been negative or less than desired) ES, and might subsequently impact the Acquisition Team's current choice of vendor. Acquisition Team members might thus be able to more accurately assess the capabilities of the technology based on the information obtained from these outside references as well as use it as a measure against the performance, experience, and feedback on vendor(s) from previous installations. This information could further assist the Acquisition Team, which may itself be uncertain about information it had previously obtained, about the sources of information that exist, and about which sources have the most credibility.

The Team might be equally uncertain about the advice given by salespeople (vendors) or about the claims made in advertising, so much so that it might doubt even valid claims. The Acquisition Team might improve its chances of making a more sound ES acquisition decision if it could learn from other organizations' experiences; carefully screen and rank the information its Team's members have found, and subsequently, develop and implement a very concise set of evaluation criteria that includes both a set of general factors and a set of factors that are unique to its organization.

Generally speaking, the more sources that are used, the greater the amount of data that is retrieved, and the greater the probability of collecting conflictual reports, all of which may result in confusion and information overload. The uncertainty that then arises is due to either knowledge uncertainty, which is uncertainty regarding information about alternatives or that is conflictual, or choice uncertainty. While choice uncertainty appears to re-open and broaden the search, knowledge uncertainty has a weaker, though more negative effect. Both of these, however, are reduced during the Information Search process. This process, in effect, serves to increase the level of certainty that a satisfactory software solution can be selected and purchased, and to decrease the negative consequences should the purchase be unsatisfactory.

It is, therefore, in the best interest of the organization that the Information Search process be completed for the acquisition of ES.

8.1.1   Information Screening

Finally, there is no search for information without, at the very least, some high-level criteria against which to filter or screen the information. Screening is a necessary part of any search for information. It is used first to reduce a large amount of information and is invoked when a search is expected to generate more information than can be intensely evaluated. This is often the case when searches are completed for information on complex software solutions. While it is true that Acquisition Teams are often faced with a lack of information on a desired solution, they are just as likely to find too much and too diverse information. When this occurs, a careful screening of the information needs to be done.

There are several different levels of screening that will be done with information during the ES Acquisition Process. For example, there are first-level screenings that will be done as part of the Marketplace Analysis by the individual(s) responsible for that task to filter out irrelevant information and information that does not meet the Team's basic pre-established criteria. Second-level screenings will then be done by the Acquisition Team as a whole to arrive at a short long-list of vendors to whom the RFP will later be sent. Both the first- and second-level screenings are fairly high-level and occur concurrent with the Planning process. Following these high-level screenings, a third and more detailed level of screening will be performed on the RFP responses that are received from the vendors. Screenings, at this level, go hand-in-hand with the review that the Acquisition Team does during the Selection process of the RFP responses to determine which of the vendors' proposed software solutions most closely matches the Team's established criteria. This third level of screening results in the Acquisition Team narrowing the short long-list of vendors to a short-list of two or three vendors. Then a fourth level of screening will be performed during the Evaluation process, hand-in-hand with the evaluation of the software demonstrations, to arrive at the final choice of vendor and solution.

So, while it is commonly understood that information screening is done throughout any process, for our part, we view screening as an integral part of the Information Search process that is looped back to several times throughout the ES Acquisition Process.

8.2   SUMMARY

Information gathering is an important endeavor in the Acquisition process. The credibility and reliability of the sources of information, regardless of the type of source and type of information, are critical to the process. Incorrect, doubtful, or unreliable information could have a major impact on the final outcome of the process. As shown, this might have been the case with ESC if they had relied solely on the word of the aforementioned consultant and discounted ORACLE in the early part of the process. Rumors and/or hearsay are other types of information that the Acquisition Team can encounter. While they are not always valid, requiring confirmation from other sources, in more instances than not, vendors are discounted or not even approached because of what a Team has heard about them regarding service, performance of their technology, reliability, etc.

One example of a source that was considered credible and reliable was the professional network. International Air's Project Manager for Technology consulted his professional network of peers regarding certain performance aspects of PeopleSoft's solution in a client-server environment. The information that he obtained led his Team to investigate further into the matter and resulted in the inclusion of a "performance" clause in the contract, which they eventually used.

Client referrals from the vendors could also be considered credible sources. In each of the cases, information that they provided to the Acquisition Team weighed heavily in the ES Acquisition Process decision process. Information that they provided helped all of the teams in their evaluation of the vendors and the technology. A more specific example comes from the case of Keller—the information that was obtained from these referrals allowed Keller's Acquisition Team to refine their requirements. As a final note on client referrals, be aware that there are referrals (clients of vendors) who are given incentives by the vendors to supply positive references for them—hence, the importance of obtaining several references from a variety of reputable and credible sources.

As a final note, there are a few other factors that should be mentioned about the Information Search process—first, it does not occur linearly, meaning that information is not a "one-time only" or single effort. Several different activities will yield information for the ES Acquisition Process and these occur at various stages of the process. This process is also often plagued with delays, dead ends, and search routines that loop back to previous routines. One example of this is with searches done on the Internet. These can often be extremely frustrating and time consuming, especially when search patterns result in several thousand hits or web site links that lead nowhere. Another example is with requests made for information from various vendors—when these are slow in responding to the Acquisition Team's request, the Team can experience delays. Another factor to be aware of during this process is the role that different sources of information have in channeling information to the Acquisition Team and it is important that the Team be aware of these and regard the information that is obtained with a critical and discriminating eye.

As we can deduce from this section, one of the objectives of the Information Search process is to create a memory base of information regarding the technology that the organization previously acquired, as well as the technology that they are about to acquire. The Selection process, which is the next major step, makes use of this and other information that was gathered during the Information Search process for the selection of both a product and a vendor.

9

"Investigate, Investigate, Investigate" The Case of Energy Systems Corporation (ESC)

In this chapter is the case of Energy Systems Corporation (ESC), a holding company that completed the purchase of a well-known ES solution in March of 1997. The chapter begins with a presentation of ESC's corporate profile and is followed by a background description of the circumstances that led to the decision to buy a packaged ES solution. Subsequent to that, an overview of the ES Acquisition Process that ESC went through to arrive at its final choice is presented.

9.1   ORGANIZATIONAL PROFILE

Energy Systems Corporation (ESC) is a holding company for a gas and electric utility and non-utility energy business, ESC Energy. One of its subsidiaries, ESC Plus, supplies natural gas and electricity to about 628,000 customers in Kentucky. The utility's service area covers approximately 700 square miles in 17 counties and includes Fort Knox Military Reservation. Another of its subsidiaries, ESC Energy Systems, owns co-generation projects and independent power plants in the U.S. as well as in Argentina and Spain. The company markets energy and related services to customers across the U.S. through high-revenue, low-margin ESC Energy Marketing.

9.2   *BACKGROUND*

In the early part of 1996, an internal study was conducted during which it was determined that some major enhancements were required to ESC's financial systems. ESC's financial systems consisted of four separate and distinct general ledger systems, and separate "feeder" systems and modules such as accounts payable and budgeting. None of these separate systems were linked in a manner that enabled effective reduction in the monthly closing cycle duration, nor did these systems enable the Finance and Accounting Organization to deliver value-added analysis to management in a fashion that was consistent with the strategic direction of the company. Further, these systems and processes relied heavily on manual effort to gather and interpret much of the available information. Most often, human rather than automated processes bridged the gaps between critical components of the financial reporting value chain.

9.2.1   Potential Y2K Disaster

ESC's financial system was IBM mainframe-based and was not Y2K compliant. Their financial systems were, in many cases, antiquated; they relied on disjointed, outdated, and technologically cumbersome software and hardware platforms that would, within the next 5 or 10 years, be unable to support their business growth. While these systems supported their existing business needs, they did so in a manner that was neither efficient nor functionally responsive to user needs.

Evaluation of these findings showed a need to implement Y2K solutions throughout the entire organization. Given the urgency and magnitude of this task, management set a deadline of September 30, 1996 to determine the plan for bringing the Financial Management Information System (FMIS) and its related systems into compliance. This plan entailed the hiring of consultants and programmers and the development of a timetable to bring these systems into compliance in order to avoid a potential disaster.

9.2.2   The Most Expedient Solution

A team was assembled. After a more extensive review of the situation, the team concluded that failure to replace the existing FMIS within the following 18 to 24 months would result in an inability to migrate to a new financial system for another 4 to 5 years. The existing systems would need to be replaced by 1998. The team also concluded that the timing of this system replacement was pivotal to orchestrating ESC's other Y2K compliance initiatives. Given the restricted time frame to replace this system, the team decided that the most expedient way to do so was with the acquisition of a packaged solution. Hence, in late summer of 1996, a project team for the acquisition of a packaged software solution was formed to look at replacing the current financial system.

9.2.3 The Cost of Change versus the Cost of Doing Nothing

For this project, ESC's management stipulated that all costs associated with the Y2K compliance initiative be expensed in the year incurred. They felt that this one-time capital expenditure would substantially increase the value and functionality of the financial systems as well as their ability to manage by providing more timely, accurate, and meaningful information. ESC's management also realized that the ongoing expenditures associated with the existing legacy system would remain the same. The benefits associated with replacing the systems, however, significantly outweighed "the cost of doing nothing" in terms of both tangible dollars and intangible costs related to lost productivity, lost business opportunities, and decisions based on untimely or inaccurate information.

The costs that were expected to be incurred over the next 4 years if the status quo was maintained could be broken down as follows:

- Estimated cost of making FMIS and related systems Y2K compliant: $1,000,000 (H$)[1]
- Cost of updating FMIS related Focus programs to be year Y2K compliant: $1,000,000 (H$ & S$)
- Version upgrade to Platinum G/L, A/P systems: $10,000 (H$)

ESC's management speculated that if they had decided to invest the effort needed to make FMIS Y2K compliant, ESC would in all likelihood have remained on the FMIS for at least 4 more years. Moreover, certain Single Business Units (SBUs) would have probably ended up spending money on new financial systems that would nevertheless have been replaced in an eventual company-wide initiative to adopt a common platform. They estimated that the cost of continuing to operate the existing systems would be approximately $1,300,000, while the cost of operating the new systems would be approximately $3,310,000. The cost of replacing the existing systems was estimated at

---

1. H$ denotes hard dollars that will flow out of the organization. S$ indicates soft dollars expected to be incurred in the form of productivity losses and inefficiencies, labor spent on non-value-added activities, etc. However, some departments would have needed to employ temporary labor or pay overtime to absorb the incremental workload. Therefore, there would have been a mix of hard and soft dollars incurred to make the Focus programs Y2K compliant and the mix was unknown at that time.

$6,500,000 over 4 years. When all was "said 'n done," they estimated that the new systems' cost would result in net savings of approximately $3,400,000.

In addition to these tangible monetary benefits, they also saw that there would be qualitative benefits associated with the new systems, benefits including:

1. Improved ability to manage business as a single enterprise
2. Enabled quantification and evaluation of risk across consolidated business enterprise
3. Improved query capabilities and timeliness with drill-down functionality for all SBUs
4. Better adaptability/flexibility in combining, realigning, or restructuring businesses
5. Reduced risks with the reduction of the number of systems experts needed to maintain the existing four separate systems
6. Improved future merger integration plans with the new platform
7. Elimination of the need to pay premium prices for increasingly scarce expertise to maintain obsolete software and hardware platforms
8. A better managed disaster recovery plan/process
9. Training that would be performed in a consistent and standardized fashion thereby reducing cost and increasing "bench strength" and inter-SBU staff movement flexibility.

They also realized that there were potential technology-enabling synergies that would benefit the organization and these included:

- Consolidation of certain elements of the accounts payable functions throughout the organization (of which there were a total of six separate functions) and combining the cash disbursement function into a common shared services environment.
- Reduction of the costs associated with materials management information systems (MMIS) and elimination of the need to ensure that the linkages between the new MMIS system and FMIS are Y2K compliant. Also, accounts payable (A/P) module would stand on its own rather than as a component of an MMIS system.
- Improved relationships with vendors through combined A/P and cash disbursement systems. Improved management of payables and reduced risk of duplicate payments.
- More value added to resources spent on maintenance and training for a single system than for four separate systems.

ESC felt that no added value would be gained from the continued use of their existing systems, as per status quo, relative to the significant costs that would be incurred due to:

1. Loss in productivity
2. Lack of improved functionality
3. Lack of increased capacity
   (a) Respond to changing business needs
   (b) Improve the speed with which information is moved from source to user

ESC decided, therefore, to keep the existing hardware systems for no other reason than the ability to continue their use in other capacities beyond the year 2000.

So it was that in the early part of 1997, ESC gave the final approval to acquire an enterprise-wide solution for its general ledger, accounts payable, budgeting and forecasting, and miscellaneous sundry billing, work orders, and projects systems. This integrated enterprise-wide solution would replace their existing independent systems.

9.3   *ESC's ES Acquisition Process*

Although ESC had previously purchased packaged software, such as a general ledger package, buying a fully integrated packaged solution such as the financials was a first-time experience. In this case, ESC was looking to replace not only the general ledger package, but also budgeting, work orders, and projects, etc., and with the exception of the general ledger package, these were all software systems that had been written in-house.

9.3.1   Getting Outside Help

In early October 1996, a high-level planning meeting was scheduled during which several issues were discussed and general plans laid for undertaking the acquisition project. Shortly thereafter, the Acquisition Team's Project Manager–Financial System realized that the Team would require some outside assistance to complete the acquisition for an ES solution. Hence, ESC engaged the services of Arthur Andersen Business Consulting to help with the Acquisition process. Together, Arthur Andersen and the Acquisition Team planned the various tasks and milestones necessary to choose the financial package that would best meet the needs of ESC. This plan would need to be carried out within the constraints of a very tight timetable. At subsequent planning sessions, the list of requirements to be included in the RFI was drawn up, the schedule for vendor demonstrations was set up, and the various evaluation criteria were established. These planning sessions were completed by late November of 1996.

In conjunction with Arthur Andersen, ESC also engaged the services of Meta Group to find out who the major vendors of financial systems were in the marketplace and which of these would have a product suitable for the needs of ESC. Meta Group supplied the ESC Planning Group (formerly, Research & Development Group) with the names of 15 vendors considered to be the best in the industry for financial package software. By way of discussions with other consulting firms and some reference checking, ESC narrowed that list further to 7 vendors—Hyperion, Coda, SQL Financials, Computron, PeopleSoft, Oracle, and Lawson.

9.3.2   Evaluating the Vendors

At this point (January 1997), each of the 7 vendors was invited to give a 2-hour information session about their product, and at approximately the same time, each vendor was also sent an RFI. When two of the vendors opted not to present a 2-hour demonstration to ESC (for unknown reasons), the list was further reduced to 5 vendors.

After each of the presentations by the 5 remaining vendors (Computron, SQL Financials, PeopleSoft, Oracle, and Lawson), the vendors were evaluated, first, according to a preliminary set of criteria which was established during the planning sessions. From the results of these evaluations and the evaluations of the vendors' RFI responses, a short-list was made consisting of 3 potential candidates—Lawson, Oracle, and PeopleSoft.

Each of these 3 vendors was then sent an RFP. Following the return of the RFP responses and their evaluation, ESC's final short-list of 2 vendors was determined—Oracle and PeopleSoft.

Each of these vendors was in turn invited to give a 2-day demonstration based on scripted scenarios that were provided by ESC. A group of 50 users was brought in to participate in both demonstrations. Each user evaluated (on a scale of 1 to 5) the technology based on the functionality of the system and how it performed based on the scripted scenarios. A technical evaluation was also conducted on the various architectural elements of the software and scored.

After these demonstrations, an addendum with additional questions and requirements was sent to each vendor. Following the replies from the vendors, the Acquisition Team completed their evaluation and made their final choice of vendor. A multi-voting technique was devised where each team member had an equal vote. The evaluation scores from each of the 50 users were also factored into the final analysis as were the scores from the technical evaluation. For the final calculation, each of the areas of evaluation was assigned weighted scores which were then quantified. The final result clearly indicated Oracle as the packaged solution of choice.

The Acquisition process that ESC began shortly after the decision to buy an ES was made took approximately 6 months and was completed with the signing of the final contract. The final choice that resulted was for Oracle's packaged ES at a cost of $6.5 million.

In the next chapter, the ES Acquisition Process that ESC used will be looked at more closely. Each of its constituent processes will be broken down and the activities that ESC undertook for their acquisition will be discussed.

10

Detailed Analysis of The Case of Energy Systems Corporation (ESC)

This chapter presents a detailed account of the processes and activities that ESC completed for the acquisition of Oracle's software solution. The case of ESC provides yet another example of the rigor that needs to be given first to the Planning process, with the determination of the organization's requirements and the establishment of evaluation criteria, and subsequent to that, to the Evaluation process for the vendors and the packaged software solutions.

This case also demonstrates the need to verify sources of information. As will be seen later in this chapter, Oracle had been discounted as a possible supplier based on information that ESC had obtained from what they considered to be a credible source. Later, though, Oracle was returned to their list for further consideration. As we saw in the previous chapter, it was Oracle's Financial software solution that was determined to be the best choice for the ESC organization.

10.1 ESC'S PLANNING PROCESS

The initial stage of the Acquisition process that was completed by ESC correlates with the Planning process. For ESC, "planning" marked the beginning of the Acquisition process. Planning encompassed all of the activities that ESC deemed necessary to pursue this endeavor. In global terms, "planning" included meetings to determine schedules, priorities, participants, resources that would be required, activities and tasks that would need to be completed, types and sources of information to be sought, and so forth.

According to ESC's Project Manager–Financial System,

> We did have kind of some high-level planning sessions. We had one, I think it was in early October of last year (1996) where we had a cast of thousands attend. It was an all-day offsite meeting and we just talked about, "Okay, how do we get started? What are the steps that we need to go through?," and we kind of came up with this process that I just described to you, although again, at that time, it was still fairly high-level and we had to rely on Arthur Andersen to help us kind of fill in the blanks using some of their templates and some of their tried and tested methodologies.

> We defined scopes, some scopes, again at a high level, which basically included, "these are the things that we do intend to do, these are the things that we do not intend to do." We talked about things like basic platform, basic architecture. We talked about the size of the team and resources that will be required, time frames to implement, the cost constraints that we were under.

> Many of the objectives came out of that earlier project that I was telling you about, in order to put some consistency around "Why are we doing this?," "Why do all these things make sense?"—the business asked for them and here are the things that they asked for; "Now, what are we going to be able to deliver on?," "What does all of this mean?," and, "How do we proceed?"

As we see, within the case, a Planning phase was completed by ESC's Acquisition Team. What can also be deduced from the case is that while some high-level planning was done, it was not until the services of Arthur Andersen were engaged that a more detailed and extensive level of planning was conducted by ESC for every stage of the Acquisition process. As per the Project Manager–Financial System:

> We really did not get to that level of detail, milestones and checkpoints, at that point. It really wasn't until we engaged Arthur Andersen to come in and then we had some actual diagrams, process flows, things that you mentioned earlier here, that said, "Here are the different phases of this project. Here's the estimated duration. Here are the resources that we require. Here are the things that we are going to go through in each of these phases, and then here are the milestones and checkpoints and deliverables." Those were all things that we covered once their resources got here.

A review of ESC's Planning process shows that it covered a series of issues that included:

- Participants: Who would participate in the different phases of the acquisition?
- Acquisition Strategies: How would the organization approach/deal with the vendors?
- Establishing Evaluation Criteria: How would we evaluate the software and against what criteria?
- Establishing Requirements: What are our organizational needs in each of the areas that would be affected by the software?
- Present Status Assessment: What resources do we currently have? Where are we deficient?

10.1.1 Participants

The Manager of IT Projects was responsible for the acquisition project. Responsibility of the overall process was given to the Project Manager–Financial System. Individuals were recruited to participate in the Acquisition process from the functional areas (lines of business) within the organization that would be immediately affected by the new technology (and that were identified during a previous project when the decision to buy a packaged software solution was made). As per the Project Manager–Financial System:

> We have Wholesale Electric Business—I have an accounting manager out of that business; Forecasting & Budgeting—I have a senior analyst out of Forecasting & Budgeting; we have a representative who is a senior budget and accounting analyst representing the retail business which is Retail Gas and Retail Electric at the Utility; I have a sundry billing accountant out of the General Accounting department of [ESC]; I have a senior accountant out of our non-utility business out of our [ESC] Power Group; myself, of course—my position prior to taking this on a year ago was Manager of Financial Planning & Accounting for [ESC] Corp. which included most of our SEC (Securities and Exchange Commission) reporting, a lot of internal management reporting, consolidation, business development, things like that. I have an accountant out of the General Accounting Group for the Utility and I have an accounts payable clerk out of the holding company. Then, of course, I've got a number of people out of our IT development group.

As one can see from this and the following quote, users from various functional areas played an important role in ESC's decision process:

> . . . seeing what the needs were from every department in this company and how this project is going to impact the entire corporation top to bottom. This company's 3,000 people—we had to consider each one of those people in the process. How's this application going to impact them on a daily basis? (Technical Team Leader–Financial System)

So, whether as members of the Acquisition Team, as sources of information for determining system requirements, or for their input during the Evaluation process, it was apparent in this case that user involvement in the process was important to ESC. By inference, user buy-in to the new technology was also important since each functional area (line of business) was either represented or had some input into the process. This is supported by the Technical Team Leader–MMIS:

> Certainly we want end-user ownership of the system, and one of the ways you obtain that is to get their buy-in early on in the process. It needs to be very much their decision because they will be living with the system and they'll be working with it, more so on a daily basis than the IT Group will be—at least we certainly hope so. So, that's pretty much the standard practice, and for my time at [ESC], that's certainly been the way that they've done that.

By design, many of the individuals that were part of the Acquisition Team were also part of the implementation project. As the Project Manager–Financial System stated, it was "not coincidental" that "a lot of the same people [that participated on the Acquisition Team are those] we have on the implementation team." Participant continuity (team members and users) for the acquisition through to full implementation would ensure user buy-in of the chosen solution.

ESC's Steering Committee also had a role in this Acquisition process—they oversaw the project, providing direction as needed, and were the final authority for approval of the acquisition. According to the Project Manager–Financial System:

> Our Executive Committee, or our Steering Committee, had the authority to do whatever it took to spend up to that limit and essentially fulfill the objectives that were set out in that business case.

The Steering Committee was composed of "a cross-functional group of officers" and "a couple of additional officers were added to the group, just to make sure that we were fully represented" (Project Manager–Financial System).

The Purchasing department, in this particular case, had a limited role in the Acquisition process. According to the agent of the Procurement Group, they have a "formal bidding process for everything including software," and as mentioned by the Project Manager–Financial System, "in instances where we had specific procurement guidelines that had to be adhered to, I did follow them." However, even the procurement guidelines were modified to accommodate the special considerations needed for the packaged software. As explained by the agent of the Procurement Group:

> The only difference I would think would be the fact that, because it is of such a technical nature, the IS department has much more influence on the decision simply because there are things there that they can detect and understand that the Purchasing people don't have knowledge of. We have a more general knowledge of purchasing as opposed to technical aspects of the software package itself. . . . [Then, speaking with reference to the MMIS project] This whole idea of client-server versus mainframe, I mean, we eliminated a couple of companies based on that. I mean, I just had to accept their word that that was a good reason to eliminate people as opposed to not.

However, many of the standard practices within ESC that are "normally" followed were not adhered to for this acquisition. According to the Project Manager–Financial System:

> I would say that we do have all of those formalized procedures—[formally documented IT acquisition strategies, business practices, standards and/or acquisition procedures], and I would say that we did not apply a lot of them in this case, . . . if they were required and if I was going to get us into a lot of trouble for not following them, we would have been following them. And in instances where we had specific procurement guidelines that had to be adhered to, I did follow them.

> But some of the things, in terms of the development of the business case and the depth of the analysis, etc., I did not think we did nearly as much as we would have otherwise or if other people had been doing it. Not that I'm special or anything, but we recognized early on that because of our year 2000 problems and because of the well-known issues that come up with doing implementations of packaged software, we could not let a lot of grass grow under our feet in fooling around with a lot of bureaucracy and procedures and things like that—we had to get on with it.

10.1.2   Acquisition Strategies

The "Acquisition Strategies" that ESC employed impacted their Selection and Evaluation processes.

One strategy that ESC used was to have their shorter long-list of 5 vendors (Computron, SQL Financials, PeopleSoft, Oracle and Lawson) come in and do "high-level, half-day, overall 'look 'n feel' demonstrations" (Project Manager–Financial System). These high-level demonstrations allowed ESC to narrow their shorter long-list to a short-list of 3 vendors.

ESC also had their final 2 short-listed vendors do on-site scripted demonstrations over a 2-day period of their proposed technological solutions. For their presentations, each vendor would be required to use predetermined scenarios supplied by ESC. According to the Technical Team Leader–Financial System:

> We created a test script of what we thought were some highlights of our processing needs from a functional aspect and sent those to the vendors and asked them to come and do a 2-day scripted demo, trying to simulate our chart of account information, our work-order information as best they could.

10.1.3   Establishing Evaluation Criteria

Establishing evaluation criteria was very important to the Acquisition process for ESC and much time and effort went into establishing the evaluation criteria for the technological solution. ESC's Acquisition Team established criteria for three distinct types of evaluation: vendor, functionality, and technical. Vendor evaluation criteria included size, financial stability, reputation of the vendor, etc. Functional criteria dealt with the features of the software and included functionalities specific to front-end interfaces, user-friendliness, and so on. Technical criteria dealt with the specifics of systems architecture, integration, performance, security, etc.

ESC established all of the evaluation criteria (with very few exceptions) for all three areas early in the Acquisition process (during the Planning process) because the majority of it was needed for incorporation into the RFP that would be sent to the vendors. This document would inform the vendors of the criteria against which they and their software solutions would be evaluated. ESC also used these criteria to develop scripts for the in-house demonstrations that were prepared for the short-listed vendors to use. According to the Project Manager–Financial System:

> Arthur Andersen assisted us in taking the requirements criteria, developing scripts from them.

For the technical evaluation criteria, according to the Project Manager–Financial System:

> We defined scopes, some scopes, again at a high level, which basically included, "these are the things that we do intend to do, these are the things that we do not intend to do." We talked about things like basic platform, basic architecture.

The Technical Team Leader–Financial System elaborated more on the minimal technical criteria that they were looking for:

> I had to look at more of the vision of the company, the history of the software development and how that fit into the architecture plan at [ESC]. Initially, we were constrained by going to the client/server development environment. We had been trying to standardize on Microsoft NT with SQL-server and that was one of our primary selection criteria up-front with Meta as well. We said, "These vendors have to fit into this category. They've got to support Microsoft NT SQL-server."

10.1.4 Establishing Requirements

Given the wide-sweeping range of areas that the software solution was expected to cover, ESC had to determine exactly what requirements would need to be met by the technology as well as what their own business requirements were. They looked at their current resources—what they had, what was lacking. They determined what they wanted that was not being met by their current systems. In addition to looking at the requirements that would need to be met by the new technology, they also ascertained the resources that would be required in order to acquire and implement this technology. Hence, they assessed their staffing resources, considered the time requirements, looked at the financial requirements (how much it would cost to add more staff), examined their own systems architecture (would it be sufficient to support the new technology), and so on. In this way, they covered all areas of the organization. As per the Project Manager–Financial System:

> We defined scopes, some scopes, again at a high level, which basically included, "these are the things that we do intend to do, these are the

things that we do not intend to do." We talked about things like basic platform, basic architecture. We talked about the size of the team and resources that will be required, time frames to implement, the cost constraints that we were under.

It really wasn't until we engaged Arthur Andersen to come in and then we had some actual diagrams, process flows, things that you mentioned earlier here, that said, "Here are the different phases of this project. Here's the estimated duration. Here are the resources that we require. Here are the things that we are going to go through in each of these phases, and then here are the milestones and checkpoints and deliverables." Those were all things that we covered once their resources got here.

10.1.5   Present Status Assessment

As has already been presented, ESC closely examined their existing status prior to the acquisition to determine the staffing requirements (i.e., human resources) that were needed in order to successfully complete the Acquisition process. They also looked at their information technology requirements (i.e., their infrastructure from both a software and hardware perspective) to assess what would be needed to support (and interface with) the new technology.

10.1.6   Recap of the Planning Process

In preparation for the other stages of the Acquisition process, ESC completed a fairly rigorous Planning process during which several key issues and activities were addressed and completed. The deliverables that resulted from the Planning process were:

- RFP (the primary deliverable)
- Long-list of 7 vendors
- Definition of the various organizational requirements (which includes a current status assessment)
- Determination of the selection and evaluation criteria
- Formation of the Acquisition Team
- Determination of acquisition strategies

10.2   INFORMATION SEARCH PROCESS

ESC obtained information from both internal and external sources for the Acquisition process. As to the internal information sources, ESC availed themselves of information from various sources within the organization that included individual users, team members, and internal consultants. These internal sources provided information primarily on the organization's requirements (existing) at all of the levels and in all of the areas that the technology would impact (see Section 10.1.4).

As to external sources, these were sought to provide information about the software solutions that would best meet their needs. According to the Project Manager–Financial System, ESC engaged the services of two professional research groups, Meta Group and CSC Index, to conduct a marketplace search:

> We began by talking with Meta and CSC Index, two consulting outfits that we do business with, to ask them who are the premier packaged software vendors for financials.

In addition, ESC also gathered information from such varied sources as external consultants, publications, trade shows, conferences, references, and the Internet. Many of these sources are referred to in the following quotation from ESC's Technical Team Leader–Financial System:

> Information gathering came through the Meta Group, from external contacts (the Internet and personal networks), and from the internal company employee network.

One particularly interesting source of information that ESC used was their competitors (the reference being to companies in the same business as ESC, but not necessarily in the same geographical area). As references, ESC found them to be a useful source of information. According to the Technical Team Leader–Financial System:

> From each vendor, we pretty much demanded that they give us a list of references and we wanted them to be in the same industry and the same size company as we were, if they could. Again, Oracle seemed to have a few more references for us to contact in that respect. . . . They were able to provide us with utility customers that were using their product. So when our functional business leaders were talking on the phone, they were talking journal transactions, budgeting process, work-order, how to generate electricity, and the reference checks were saying, "Ya, ya, ya, we do all that. The software supports it."

It is worth noting that for the Information Search process, the credibility of the source of information stood out as being very important to the Acquisition Team. For the amount of readily available and oftentimes unreliable information that one has access to, the credibility of the source can play a significant role by providing the seeker with a more reassured sense that the information that has been provided is both accurate and reliable. According to ESC's Technical Team Leader–Financial System, they found Meta Group to be a credible source of information:

> . . . Meta. They came back at one point, told us that the Lawson people were pretty much the "Boy Scouts" in the industry, if you will. They [Lawson] were the most up-front and honest. And, we found that to be very true, that they didn't have to tell us that they could not do certain things, but they came in and said, "We're going to have to back out. We can't do this." When they did that, as soon as they left, we all looked at each other and said, "Boy, those Meta people sure called that right!"

This process also involved the screening of information. Concurrent with the Planning process, several iterations of screenings were done on information from all sources to determine the long-list of vendors. Using high-level selection and evaluation criteria pertaining to both vendors and technologies that ESC's Acquisition Team had determined early in the Planning process, vendors were screened to determine who could supply the type of software solution that ESC was seeking. According to the Project Manager–Financial System:

> We started out with probably 14 or 15 companies that mainly Meta recommended and through kind of a process of discussion, some reference checking, and discussions with other consulting outfits, we probably narrowed that down to about 7 that we thought we should talk to: Hyperion, Coda, Computron, SQL Financials, Oracle, PeopleSoft, and Lawson.

Various levels of information screenings were done by the Acquisition Team throughout the ES Acquisition Process and these corresponded to the stage of process at which the Team found itself.

10.3 SELECTION PROCESS

ESC's Selection process was conducted in two phases—the first with high-level demonstrations by the vendors on their shorter long-list and the second upon receipt of the RFPs responses from the vendors. According to the Project Manager–Financial System:

We scheduled high-level, half-day, overall "look 'n feel" demonstrations with these vendors. Two of the vendors, Hyperion and Coda, were
either unable to or unwilling to fit this into their time schedules, and so
we eliminated them right off the bat. So, that narrowed it down to 5 and
we ended up doing those overall "look 'n feel" demos, those half-day
demos with the 5 that were remaining.

The high-level demonstrations allowed ESC to narrow the shorter long-list of 5
vendors to a short-list of 3 vendors.

Concurrent with these high-level demonstrations, as part of their Planning
process, ESC (with the assistance of the consultants from Arthur Andersen
Business Consulting) was defining the list of requirements/criteria that they
would use in their RFP.

We started to develop at that time the list of requirements, but also were
in the process of scheduling these high-level demos which were conducted—I believe they were wrapped up by Thanksgiving of last year.
So, we did them in a fairly tight time frame. (Project Manager–Financial System)

Then, working with the detailed list of requirements, ESC and the Andersen
consultants put together a RFP document which they sent to the 3 vendors on
their short-list. As per the Technical Team Leader–Financial System:

After the 2-hour demos when we had shortened the list to our top 3, we
created a detailed RFP for each of those areas and from the technical
side and sent those to the vendors to try to give us a preliminary look
at—"Okay, what can they do?" What we were really looking for were
"show stoppers"—could we identify any of those without wasting 2
days sitting in a demo? And then we sent those out and got those back
and graded each vendor on the RFP documentation.

Then, with the RFP responses in hand, an evaluation was done during which
ESC came up with additional questions to the vendors for clarification on cer-
tain items. Again, the 3 vendors were contacted and following their responses,
ESC was able to narrow the list further leaving just 2 vendors—Oracle and
PeopleSoft.

For the most part, we see the Selection process as having begun at the point
when the Acquisition Team received the RFP responses back from the vendors.
However, the sequence of activities that ESC performed during their Selection
process was somewhat unusual. While they only sent the RFP responses to the 3

vendors on their longer short-list near the end of the Selection process, they did perform "Selection"-like activities earlier with all 5 of the vendors from their longer list.

As for the tasks themselves that ESC undertook during the Selection process, ESC evaluated the vendors' high-level demonstrations based on general criteria that they (ESC) had defined. ESC conducted a "paper" evaluation of the 3 short-listed vendors' packages based on their RFP responses. During their evaluation of the responses, more questions were formulated by ESC for clarification by the vendors. At this point, ESC asked the 3 vendors to re-submit certain parts of their responses, requesting that clarification be made on some items. As indicated by the Project Manager–Financial System:

> We evaluated them, came up with an additional list of questions and additional requirements, after looking at the responses [the initial replies to the RFP], for clarity, and had them go through a clarification process which they did before we narrowed it down further.

Once the responses were received from the vendors and ESC had reviewed them, ESC proceeded to invite the remaining 2 short-listed vendors to do on-site presentations of their software solutions.

10.4   EVALUATION PROCESS

There were three distinct types of evaluation that were conducted by ESC: vendor, functionality, and technical. Evaluation criteria for all three types were developed in the Planning phase of the Acquisition process.

10.4.1   Vendor Evaluation

In this case, the Vendor Evaluation was conducted only after ESC had selected their short-list of three vendors. Criteria such as vendor strength and/or reputation, financial stability (based on the vendors' financial statements), long-term viability, and the vendor's vision and corporate direction were factors that were considered during the Vendor Evaluation. As per the Technical Team Leader–Financial System:

> . . . only after we were down to our top 2, top 3. . . . We also had our General Ledger person go do whatever that financial term is, but it was looking at their financial statements and seeing what kind of shape the company was in. Again, Oracle came out on top there because the

application side of their business is only a tenth of their overall business. They're not going to go under. PeopleSoft's not going to go under either but their application is 75% to 80% of their total revenue, which made us think long and hard. Oracle's been in the software business a long time. They can bring some pretty savvy technical resources to bear when there are issues. And we know their CEO has a stated direction and all those factors were weighed.

While it is standard practice for ESC to evaluate vendors using D&B reports, they decided not to do so for this project. According to the Project Manager–Financial System:

> We did not do a Dunn & Bradstreet. If it had been anybody other than PeopleSoft and Oracle, we probably would have done a D&B on them I can almost assure you, because I've done these evaluations for other people when I was in the Finance group, helped them with these things and have insisted that we get D&B's on them.

Information for the Vendor Evaluation was also obtained from copies of the short-listed vendors' annual reports, Securities & Exchange Commission (SEC) filings, and lists of references. Also, as stated by the Project Manager–Financial System, "both of them [Oracle and PeopleSoft] had a lot of information available in the public arena for helping us to evaluate them." Lastly, as part of the Vendor evaluation and relative to the price of the software solutions, ESC's Acquisition Team also requested and received a cost proposal (an RFQ) from both short-listed vendors. The information that they received in the RFQ was factored into the Acquisition Team's final recommendation to the Steering Committee.

10.4.2   Functional Evaluation

Responsibility for the evaluation of each technology's functionality rested with the entire Acquisition Team and the users who attended the demonstrations, while responsibility for the evaluation of its technical aspects rested with the Technical Team Leader–Financial System and his team. The Functional Evaluation proved to be an important process for ESC, carrying 42% of the overall evaluation weighting. It was during the Functional Evaluation that users participated in the decision process. As per the Technical Team Leader–Financial System:

We brought in our core team which consisted of the functional business leads and they were asked to invite 3 to 4 key users from their area. So, we had for each session 25 to 30 people looking at each functional section of the . . . software . . . and we even provided breakout rooms after sessions were done for the key users to go meet one-on-one with the presenter and do even more probing questions and analysis of the software.

Functional criteria that were established as well as questionnaires and scenarios that were developed during the Planning phase of the Acquisition process were implemented during this process. Short-listed vendors were invited to participate in a 2-day demonstration of their technological solution. According to ESC's Project Manager–Financial System:

We did 2 full-day scripted demos with Oracle and PeopleSoft, which is probably less than we might have done otherwise, but it was still a fairly rigorous process.

10.4.3   Technical Evaluation

In addition to the Functional Evaluation, ESC also had their technical team (led by the Technical Team Leader–Financial System) look at the technical aspects of the software. Most of the technical criteria that had been established during the Planning stage and included in the RFP were now tested with the technology. According to the Technical Team Leader–Financial System:

. . . looking at the RFP responses, you know, I had my detailed questions. I had to look at more of the vision of the company, the history of the software development and how that fit into the architecture plan at [ESC]. Initially, we were constrained by going to the client/server development environment. We had been trying to standardize on Microsoft NT with SQL-server and that was one of our primary selection criteria.

10.4.4   Evaluation Tools

As part of their Evaluation process, ESC developed matrices and assigned weights and scores to the various areas of evaluation. The following quote from the Project Manager–Financial System describes what they did:

We developed evaluations, with a 1 to 5 scale, 1 being poor, 5 being excellent or meets all the requirements, and then compiled all those evaluations and said, "Okay, who's the winner on functionality based on what we saw during that period of time?" We also developed a list of other criteria that were important to us. Those criteria—functionality was one, integration with other applications was another, cost was one, ease of implementation was one, and vendor strength and/or reputation. Those were the 5 main categories of criteria.

We also went through a process or tool (continuous improvement tool) called, "Consensus Prioritization Matrix," where we went about weighting those criteria, and then assigned teams to come up with their assessment along each of those lines, and then applied that weighting . . . and ultimately coming up with our final selection.

It was also noted that ESC used an external consulting group to assist them in evaluating the software (Arthur Andersen Business Consulting helped ESC develop the list of requirements, the evaluation matrices, etc.); they did not, however, forfeit control of this process to them. As stated by the Project Manager–Financial System:

There are some companies, like there was one of the reference calls—this would be an interesting study in and of itself, I think—who engaged the consulting firm . . . to come in and develop a vision of their financial systems, you know, "How did they see the best practices?" and "What are a lot of the trends in the industry?" and "Where is this company headed?" and "What do they need to enable them to get there?" and essentially handed them this report, made presentations, and said, "Oh, and by the way, we think the best solution for you is Oracle."

They did not go through the process we went through and they accepted that recommendation. They said, "Oracle and you need to implement activity-based cost management in that process." So, they took all of that, they used the consulting firm to do the implementation and, low-and-behold, 2 years later and countless millions of dollars later, they were the proud owners of a bouncing baby Oracle system.

I could not imagine going through a process like that, essentially, having somebody else tell you what system you ought to be on and just accepting that. And that's probably overly simplified, but when we conducted this reference call, this was exactly how they characterized it.

10.5   CHOICE PROCESS

The Acquisition process culminates in the Choice process and consists of the "final choice" or "recommendation." In ESC's case, a "final recommendation" of software solution was arrived at by the Acquisition Team. It was based on the sum of the weighted scores for the five main categories of criteria: functionality, integration with other applications, ease of implementation, vendor strength and/or reputation, and cost. For the last category, cost, the Acquisition Team requested and received a cost proposal (an RFQ) from both short-listed vendors. As explained by the Project Manager–Financial System while referring to the scoring matrix that was used, the scoring of the functionality was based, in large part, on the 2-day demonstrations of the software by the vendors, from which they (ESC) "wound up getting to the choice on the functionality component." Evaluation of the technical aspects of the software, covering issues such as the ability of the software to integrate with other applications and the ease with which it could be implemented (both among the main categories of criteria) were also scored, and a final "choice" was arrived at for each of these criteria. A final "choice" was also arrived at regarding vendor strength and/or reputation. As stated by the Project Manager–Financial System:

> To come to the point of making our final selection [after they had evaluated and scored functionality, integration with other applications, ease of implementation, vendor strength and/or reputation], we had received a cost proposal from both vendors.

> Each X [with reference to the table/grid] was worth a score of 1, so we would simply multiple 1 by that value [the assigned weight] and put their score over here. Integration, Oracle won out. Ease of implementation, PeopleSoft won out. Cost, PeopleSoft won out. Vendor strength, Oracle won out. So, we summed them, and Oracle came out ahead.

The Choice process that was noted in the ESC case consisted of one element, a final recommendation or choice. This recommendation was subsequently conveyed to a body outside the Acquisition Team (the Steering Committee) for final approval. We noted within this case, that although ESC had previously acquired Human Resource and Payroll software from PeopleSoft and were considering the PeopleSoft ES solution, the issue of PeopleSoft being a "former" supplier to ESC did not appear to have had much (if any) impact on their final choice of software solution. As per the Project Manager–Financial System:

There were some people in the company that were familiar with PeopleSoft because we had implemented their HR modules and we were in the process of implementing their Payroll module. So we did have some conversations with some of that team, but they were very, very, very focused and could not really speak to the Financial applications side of it, and so, we really did not find that much value out of that. Initially, we had some conversations with people in the IT organization that worked on the PeopleSoft implementation, but really did not get much value beyond the initial conversations.

Additional information on this issue was supplied by the Technical Team Leader–Financial Systems. As we can see in the following quotation, the technical issue of "integration" outweighed the influence that PeopleSoft, as a "former" supplier, might have had in the Acquisition Team's final recommendation:

We have PeopleSoft HR in-house and there was some pressure from that group to go ahead and go with the PeopleSoft Financials, because of the integrated solution that would provide, and that was one of our key things on our evaluation matrix, was integration with other packages. Well, one of the things that I found during the technical evaluation was that there was no integration between PeopleSoft HR and PeopleSoft Financials. They don't have it, it's not there yet, even though they claim it. It does not exist. It might exist today, but six months ago, it was not there in a commercially purchasable product. And those things went into my report, the technical report, saying these are the reasons why.

10.6 NEGOTIATION PROCESS

Two types of negotiations transpired during the course of ESC's Acquisition process: business and legal. The Business Negotiations were informal, while the Legal Negotiations were very formal.

There were different things that we were trying to negotiate as we went along, but they weren't really formal. . . . Again, just talking in generalities, not really keeping tabs on each other. So, it was more informal, but then once we got to them getting their people here and me getting our people here and sitting face-to-face and trying to hammer out the contract, was when we really started to get down to the real negotiations.

As part of the Business Negotiations, the Project Manager–Financial System also felt it important to establish executive-level relationships between ESC and both short-listed vendors. One of the reasons for this, he explains, is that in the event of problems that might arise during the Acquisition process, those issues could be dealt with "at the right level."

> There were other aspects to the business discussions as well. One of the things that I asked both vendors, this was before our final recommendation, was I told them that I thought it was very important that we establish some executive relationships here, because if there were conflicts that were to arise or if there were opportunities that were to arise, I would want to make sure that we both have the kind of relationship where we could take advantage of either exploiting those opportunities or dealing with those issues at the right level. And, if I have to take them up to whomever in their organization or vice versa, those relationships exist to do that.

> Oracle was a lot more willing, I think, to set those things in place, but we did have some executive meetings prior to ultimately signing on the dotted line. They sent in some of their headquarters brass to meet with some of our folks when we were doing the final negotiations just to smooth everything over and make sure that we understood that we were an important client to them. (Project Manager–Financial System)

According to the Project Manager–Financial System, ESC entered formal negotiations with their vendor-of-choice, Oracle, after the final recommendation was approved by the Steering Committee. At that point in the Acquisition process, the Project Manager–Financial System set up a negotiation team that consisted of individuals from three different departments (Legal, Procurement, and IT) within ESC. Together, they assisted the Project Manager–Financial System during the final stage of the Negotiation process leading to the signed contract.

> I set up a negotiation team which consisted of somebody from our Legal department, somebody from our Procurement department, myself, and somebody from our IT department. All of these people had different roles on the team. The Procurement people were trying to keep me from "committing suicide" with regard to all of our policies and procedures. The attorneys were there to, essentially, scrub down all the language and make sure it contains all of the "Now therefores" that we require. The IT people were there, again, to make sure that we included everything from a technical perspective that needed to be there. And then, I was there just to make sure that the deal got done and pull it all together. (Project Manager–Financial System)

It is worth noting here some of the issues that were negotiated as described by the Project Manager–Financial System:

> The formal negotiations took place . . . and we were still talking about final pricing: . . . about pricing of the actual licenses; . . . about pricing of the support, . . . about trying to put caps on support; . . . about year 2000 language, making sure that we had no holes in that process; . . . training and education credits and getting what we thought was a reasonable price for that and a reasonable level of those; ability to buy additional licenses up to a certain point and still maintain the discounts that we had secured; the time value of money—this is really kind of a strange issue, but I learned that they were offering some financing, Oracle was, and they had been talking with some of our other database users about this, and when I got wind of that, I said, "Well, what kind of financing here?" Well, it was basically the same kind as no interest for 12 months or 3 years or whatever, and you just make 3 equal payments and that's fine with us. And I was like, "Well, hey guys, I'll take that every day." And they said, "Okay."

> So they started to write out an agreement to do that, and then I said, "Well, wait a minute. You know, being a finance guy, there's a present value calculation that I need to do here, and since I don't really need to borrow money from you, why don't we just reduce the price of the software for that discount." That was something that they weren't really happy about when I kind of sprung that on them, but I was like, "Hey, this is a business deal." So, we were kind of jockeying over that particular issue right up until the end, until we got down to our final pricing.

As to how this process could be characterized, it appeared to us that the Business Negotiations were fluid throughout most of the process. When asked to characterize the Negotiation process, in his reply that "there were different things that we were trying to negotiate as we went along," the Project Manager–Financial System was describing the ongoing or continuous nature of this process and that the negotiations were "fluid" throughout the Acquisition process.

10.7 *INFLUENCES ON THE ACQUISITION PROCESS*

Several influences were noted in the case of ESC. They are presented as to the principal targets of their effects. Hence, the influences are categorized according to their effects on the Acquisition process, the final choice of ES solution, or the Acquisition Team.

10.7.1 Influences on the Process

The following items had varying influences on ESC's ES Acquisition Process:

- Y2K
- Obsolete systems
- Well-known issues that arise during implementation
- Organizational IT objective
- Business and technological reasons
- Economic factors
- Outside consultants
- Project management techniques
- User community

Y2K

A factor that influenced ESC's Acquisition process was Y2K. The Technical Team Leader–Financial System commented that:

> Year 2000 problems with our legacy system were also a driving factor in looking at getting a new system.

Obsolete Systems

The issue of obsolete systems influenced the decision to buy a packaged ES solution.

Well-Known Issues That Arise During Implementation

Another influence that appeared to have had an effect on the process pertained to the "well-known issues that come up with doing implementations of packaged software" (Project Manager–Financial System). As explained by the Project Manager–Financial System, this issue coupled with the Y2K issue were cause for the abbreviated nature of this Acquisition process. As per the Project Manager–Financial System:

> We recognized early on that because of our year 2000 problems and because of the well-known issues that come up with doing implementations of packaged software, we could not let a lot of grass grow under our feet in fooling around with a lot of bureaucracy and procedures and things like that—we had to get on with it. So, I would say that it was done in a more hurried-up fashion than our IT management would have cared for—well, some of our IT management—some thought we did not do it fast enough.

Organizational IT Objective

An influence that affected the Acquisition process came from the ESC's organizational IT objective to move to an NT client/server architecture. As explained by the Project Manager–Financial System:

> The whole notion of going from mainframe to client/server is another change that some people are probably—well, I know a lot of people are not comfortable with, but it's tough.

Business and Technological Reasons

However, this objective, which had the Acquisition Team gravitating toward a "client/server, NT SQL-server platform," was subsequently altered and this was influenced by "business" reasons and technological limitations inherent to the NT technology (categorized as an "Environmental" influence). As stated by the Technical Team Leader–Financial System:

> The information technology architecture constrained us to client/server, NT SQL-server platform, although we kind of missed that target, we had to for business reasons. In the end, we selected a UNIX/Oracle database solution. Our IT architecture plan called for an NT/SQL Server solution and the project team originally limited its search to those products that would run on that platform—this was a target objective. That is why I said we kind of missed that one. I realized and finally convinced management that a corporate-wide financial system would not efficiently run on an NT Server. UNIX is capable of handling 100's of users, NT is not.

ESC's organizational IT objective to move to a client/server architecture affected the Acquisition process. However, "business reasons" (such as the need for a large number of users to be able to access the server simultaneously at any given time—"UNIX is capable of handling 100's of users, NT is not" [Technical Team Leader–Financial System] and that architecture's technological limitations "forced" the decision to be otherwise.

Economic Factors

Economic factors in terms of the various costs that are associated with this type of acquisition influenced the process. Since this project was allocated such a "high budget," according to the Technical Team Leader–Financial System, ESC's upper management saw the need for a Steering Committee to oversee it:

This one had such a high budget that we had an executive steering committee that was brought together to oversee the project.

Outside Consultants

Outside consultants also exerted their influence of ESC's Acquisition process. The outside consultants brought their experience to bear on Acquisition process, as explained by the Project Manager–Financial System:

> We, then, decided to engage Arthur Andersen to help us with the software selection process. This project was something that our senior management wanted me to head up and it was also something that I knew very little about in terms of the actual process. . . . Having a very seasoned consultant to assist, and consultant could be either internal or external consultant, but in our case, I don't think that there was anybody in our company that had the breadth of experience with selecting packaged software or implementing packaged software as Arthur Andersen—and this isn't Andersen Consulting, this was Arthur Andersen Business Consulting.

> I asked for some very specific resources from Arthur Andersen and got them and we were very lucky. If I had not had some of those specific resources, I'm not sure where we would have ended up, but these people were very good at holding our hand through the process, helping us understand the implications of our actions, and being very frank and not just telling us what we wanted to hear.

While their experience in software acquisitions did influence ESC's process, they were careful not to influence ESC's choice of software, however. As noted by the Technical Team Leader–Financial System:

> Arthur Andersen, after it was all said and done, they were very good about not showing who they thought was the best choice for us, because we asked them not to. In fact, we told them, "If you start recommending one over the other, we're going to kick you out of here. You're here to help us choose who we think is the best." When it was all said and done, we went back to them and, in confidence, said, "What do you guys think?" And they said, "Based on what we saw, we agree with your choice. Based on what we know from other companies, you probably would have been better off with somebody else."

Project Management Techniques

Project management techniques were also found to have influenced the structure of the Acquisition process. Based on the explanation provided by the Project Manager–Financial System, we could see that the Arthur Andersen consultants used these techniques to structure the Acquisition process for ESC:

> We really did not get to that level of detail, milestones and checkpoints, at that point. It really wasn't until we engaged Arthur Andersen to come in and then we had some actual diagrams, process flows, things that you mentioned earlier here, that said, "Here are the different phases of this project. Here's the estimated duration. Here are the resources that we require. Here are the things that we are going to go through in each of these phases, and then here are the milestones and checkpoints and deliverables."

In this case, with Arthur Andersen consultants becoming part of ESC's team, providing guidance on the different phases of process and the various tools to be used, these techniques influenced the structure of the Acquisition process that resulted at ESC.

User Community

ESC's users also influenced the Acquisition process. Their buy-in was considered an important factor and hence, there was heavy user involvement in the process, not only as participants in the evaluation of the software, but as members of the Acquisition Team since the team was composed predominantly of users.

10.7.2   Influences on the Final Choice

The following items had varying influences on ESC's final choice of ES:

- Capped budget
- Single-vendor solution
- Integratibility of the software
- Business process reengineering
- Vendor demonstration
- Ease of adaptability of the ES
- Technological preference
- User buy-in

Capped Budget

It also appeared that the Steering Committee was firm on the ceiling of the budget that was set for this project and the Acquisition Team was made well aware of this. According to the Technical Team Leader–Financial System, "they [the Steering Committee] set the budget—by golly, we had to live to that budget."

Single-Vendor Solution

The desire for a single-vendor solution had an influence on the process.

Integratibility of the Software

Integration was also a technological factor that influenced ESC's final choice. Although ESC already had two of PeopleSoft's modules in-house (Human Resources and Payroll), one of the reasons that they did not choose PeopleSoft's Financial software was because, at the time of the acquisition project, they were not integratible products.

> One of the things that I found during the technical evaluation was that there was no integration between PeopleSoft HR and PeopleSoft Financials. They don't have it, it's not there yet, even though they claim it. It does not exist. It might exist today, but 6 months ago, it was not there in a commercially purchasable product. (Technical Team Leader–Financial System)

Business Process Reengineering (BPR)

Another factor that influenced the Acquisition process was Business Process Reengineering (BPR). By replacing their existing financial software with a "best of breed" solution, ESC would, in effect, be reengineering many of their existing processes. Although their existing software used to be "best of breed," the software no longer was due to several series of customizations that were effected to it in order to match their own processes. While the "systems we had in place, that we are replacing now, have been in place for some time and . . . have been customized to the point where they work for everybody," the Manager–Inventory Management (who was also a member of the Reengineering Group) explained that, "you can take upgrades," which we interpreted to mean that there are still things that they could be doing "better." Deficiencies in their existing software, though, were brought to light by the Project Manager–Financial System. Apparently, the software was no longer meeting ESC's reporting needs and as a result, "a lot of manual processes" were required in order to "get the information that we need." Moreover, their existing financial systems could not supply them with activity-based cost information nor were drill-through capabilities available. As explained by the Project Manager–Financial System:

> We used to customize the hell out of every application that we would implement even if it was packaged software and then figure out ways to make it interface with all the other systems, and we're just not doing that here. So, it's a radically different approach.

This was further corroborated in a statement by ESC's Technical Team Leader–MMIS concerning this issue:

> So, it was kind of a "one size fits all," and as such, companies either took one of two approaches: they would modify their processes to fit a generic system, or modify the system to fit their processes. Most of the companies took door #2.

> [ESC] took one of them, and that was one of the reasons why, given the number of customizations that were put in on the system, when companies go out to look at packaged software now, they look back and say, "Look how our other system wound up in 5+ years, it became obsolete and we got entangled in this customized system that we have." So, there's more of a tendency now for software companies to market their products as "best case scenarios" ["best of breed"], and companies are more reluctant to go in and modify the systems that they now get.

> So, there's more of a theme, we found, where business will try to modify their processes because, true or untrue, the packages today are being presented as "best in class" and you're better off modifying *your* processes. And, companies are saying, "You bet, because I got burned when I modified my system 10 years ago, and it outlived its usefulness a lot sooner than I thought it would."

What we deduced from this was that ESC would be modifying some of their processes (doing BPR) according to the demands of the new software that they were buying. This would entail, in some areas, a complete reengineering of some processes (doing away with entire processes) and modifications to others. As explained by the Manager–Inventory Management, speaking more in his capacity as a member of the Reengineering Group, this would be appropriate when existing processes (*modus operandi*) become outmoded and are no longer efficient. Benefits could then be achieved by designing new processes that would be directed to their future needs:

> I am of the opinion that we will be growing out of any system that we implement right now and what is that time, I do not know, if it is 3 or is it 5 years, some point in the future we will grow out it. So, . . . do you buy a big bulky system now for a lot of money that you may only be using 50, 60 or 70% of it in a period of time? . . . Or do we have a reasonable level of investment now that may not give us everything that we are doing now, but maybe we are not going to do those things in the future anyway. So you give up some of the functionality short-term to match the investment.

In so doing, ESC was aware of how this new "best of breed" solution would be accepted by their user community. With regard to this issue, the Project Manager–Financial System expressed the following:

> I said when I began this process, when I began as the project manager, to our executives and to a lot of my constituents, there are going to be people that love me for what I've done, and there are going to be people that are going to hate me, and I doubt if there's going to be anybody that's just going to feel neutral about it. Because we're either going to give people a lot of the things they've been looking for, or we're going to take away some stuff that they had—because we used to use a "best of breed" solution.

Hence, BPR had both a positive and negative influence on ESC's decision to acquire a "best of breed" software solution.

Vendor Demonstrations

Another factor that influenced the final choice of ES was the 2-day vendor demonstration. The demonstrations that were done by both short-listed vendors had an impact on ESC's decision process and hence, final choice:

> Based on what we saw, really, it was the 2-day demo, I've got to admit. . . . It made a huge difference. (Technical Team Leader–Financial System)

These demonstrations highlighted, for the Acquisition Team and for the other participants, the ease of use (among other functionalities) and the flexibility of each vendor's software solutions to meet ESC's needs. Moreover, as recounted by the Technical Team Leader–Financial System, the Arthur Andersen consultants commented that, "It looks like the Oracle team sent in their 'A' team to sell you their product, and it looks like PeopleSoft sent in their 'C' team to sell you their product."

Ease of Adaptability of the ES

Another influence came from the software itself, namely the ease and flexibility with which the software could be adapted for the 2-day demonstrations. According to the Technical Team Leader–Financial System, these factors also appeared to have played a significant influence on the final choice:

> Based on what we saw, really, it was the 2-day demo, I've got to admit. . . . It made a huge difference. When the PeopleSoft experts were having trouble navigating through their own product and finding where things were and unable to answer some questions. The Oracle team was able to navigate smoothly. They incorporated our data elements in their presentation, which PeopleSoft didn't. PeopleSoft said it was going to be too hard to change their software, that for a 2-day demonstration, to do that, it wasn't feasible. Oracle did it. And then, in everybody's mind, they were thinking, "Well, if it's too hard for the PeopleSoft experts to change their software for a 2-day demo, and Oracle can do it . . . " we're looking for that ease and flexibility. So, I would have to say that it was the 2-day demos.

Technological Preference

Another influence on the choice was the technological preference (or perhaps bias) of the Technical Team Leader–Financial System toward the UNIX platform. This preference, apparently based on technical reasons, had an influence on the platform of the software solution that was chosen. As noted earlier and in the following quotation, although the IT objective was to move to an NT-based client/server architecture, the Technical Team Leader–Financial System was able to convince ESC's management on the merits of having a UNIX server within their hardware architecture.

> I realized and finally convinced management that a corporate-wide financial system would not efficiently run on an NT Server.

> That was a battle I had to fight. Other groups had tried to get UNIX in here before and I basically went to the mat and said, "It's something we've got to have. If we're going to have a successful project, we've got

to go this route." As much as our Operations Group hated the idea of supporting UNIX—it was a new platform for them—we'd wanted to keep it out of here. I felt like my hands were tied because I'd requested, from the get-go, "Can we chose a 'mainframe' solution?" "No, no, no. It's got to be a client/server."

Well, . . . you can have a mainframe in a client/server environment, but some of our managers don't realize that yet. So, what we ended up doing is buying "a server" to fit the client/server model, but our server is—the production box that we buy will be as powerful as any mainframe that's out there today. So, we'll be there, but they'll say, "Oh, you made a client/server." "Ya, ya, ya." It could have been easier for us because we have a mainframe down there with excess capacity that we could have used, but . . . "

User Buy-In

User buy-in was also an important influence on the final choice. To obtain user buy-in, heavy user involvement was encouraged in the process. Not only was there a predominance of users on the Acquisition Team, but a large group of users participated in both 2-day vendor demonstrations. The feedback and scores from their evaluations of the software contributed to the decision for the final choice of ES.

10.7.3   Influences on the Acquisition Team

The following items had varying influences on ESC's Acquisition Team:

- Leadership
- Y2K
- Interdisciplinary nature of the Acquisition Team
- Competency of the Acquisition Team members

Leadership

The influence of leadership was a driving force in the Acquisition process. The leadership exhibited by the Project Manager–Financial System drove the process. The impact of his leadership skills were also apparent on all of the processes within the Acquisition process. Moreover, the confidence that ESC's upper management had in his leadership abilities is reflected in the following comments:

> This project was something that our senior management wanted me to head up. (Project Manager–Financial System)

> I, as the Project Manager, and our Executive Committee or our Steering Committee, had the authority to do whatever it took to spend up to that limit and essentially fulfill the objectives that were set out in that business case. (Project Manager–Financial System)

> Once we made our recommendation to the officers and they accepted it, they approved of me proceeding with negotiations with Oracle. (Project Manager–Financial System)

As a group, ESC's Steering Committee also took a leadership role by removing several administrative obstacles that were part of ESC's standard administrative procedures. As stated by the Project Manager–Financial System:

> One of the things that I asked for, in one of those first meetings with our Executive Committee was that I, personally, was probably going to need a lot more authority to make decisions in order for us to move quickly and put this thing on the right track. They all recognized that we were on a very tight time frame. "

The Steering Committee did provide ESC's Project Manager–Financial System with the "ability to move quickly and not add a lot of bureaucratic policies and procedures," and hence, the Acquisition Team was able to proceed rapidly through the Acquisition process.

Y2K

The rapidity with which the Project Manager–Financial System and the Acquisition Team were able to proceed with the Acquisition process was greatly influenced by the Y2K factor, as noted in the following quote:

> Again, this was probably a little bit unique from the standpoint that we were working up against the year 2000 problem, having to move very, very quickly.

Hence, Y2K was not only an influence on the process, but it was also a "motivational" influence on the group for completing the Acquisition process for the financial system in as short a time as possible.

Interdisciplinary Nature of the Acquisition Team

The Acquisition Team was interdisciplinary, composed of highly motivated professionals, and each team was very cohesive. As stated by the Project Manager–Financial System:

> We worked very well together as a team: free exchange of ideas. . . . A real professional desire to get the job done. Highly motivated. People excited about the project.

Competency

The competency of the various individuals that were on the Acquisition Team was another factor that influenced the process. This factor is a testament to the skill of the Project Manager–Financial System in selecting team members for the acquisition project. As stated by the Project Manager–Financial System about the Technical Team Leader–Financial System:

> He was integrally involved in the software selection process. In fact, from an IT standpoint, he was my right-hand man who was very instrumental in getting a lot of things done.

10.8   CHARACTERISTICS AND CRITICAL SUCCESS FACTORS (CSFS)

Several factors about ESC's Acquisition process were critical to its successful outcome. In addition, some of the influences that were discussed in the previous section were also CSFs of the process and these are included later. The following list includes all of the CSFs for the case of ESC:

- Planning
- Evaluation—Vendor, Functional, and Technical
- Formal process
- Structured process
- Rigorous
- User-driven
- Partnership
- Leadership
- Competency/skills of the Acquisition Team members
- Interdisciplinary nature of the Acquisition Team
- User participation

Various elements from the Planning and Evaluation processes were critical to ESC's ES Acquisition Process. Their omission would have resulted in a less-than-optimal outcome for the ESC organization. For ESC, what stands out the most from them is as follows:

- **Planning:** The most outstanding CSF of the ESC's ES Acquisition Process was that it was planned. Its successful outcome can be attributed in large part to the level and rigor of planning and preparation that the Acquisition Team did with the assistance of their outside consultants.
- **Evaluation:** Another CSF of ESC's ES Acquisition Process was the detailed manner in which the evaluation criteria were established and the care with which the evaluations of the ES vendors and software solutions were carried out. This was also critical to their determination of the right ES fit for the ESC organization.
- **Formal process:** According to the Project Manager–Financial System, parts of the Acquisition process that the Acquisition Team followed were formalized while others were not:

  > I would say that we do have all of those formalized procedures that you just mentioned (formally documented IT acquisition strategies, business practices, standards and/or acquisition procedures), and I would say that we did not apply a lot of them in this case, strictly because I'm not familiar with them—not really, because if they were required and if I was going to get us into a lot of trouble for not following them, we would have been following them.

  > And in the instance where we had specific procurement guidelines that had to be adhered to, I did follow them, but some of the things, in terms of the development of the business case and the depth of the analysis, etc., I did not think we did nearly as much as we would have otherwise or if other people had been doing it. . . . So, I would say that it was done in a more hurried-up fashion than our IT management would have cared for.

  This lack of formality appears to have been influenced by the Y2K issue.
- **Structured process:** Another characteristic of the Acquisition process for ESC is that it was "structured," although, according to the Project Manager–Financial System, "it was not as structured as it might have been otherwise if we had more time, but it was not unstructured." The process that the Acquisition Team followed for this acquisition was structured based on some of the processes and methodologies that

were introduced by the consultants from Arthur Andersen Business Consulting. According to the Project Manager–Financial System:

> It really wasn't until we engaged Arthur Andersen to come in and then we had some actual diagrams, process flows, things that you mentioned earlier here, that said, "Here are the different phases of this project. Here's the estimated duration. Here are the resources that we require. Here are the things that we are going to go through in each of these phases, and then here are the milestones and checkpoints and deliverables." Those were all things that we covered once their resources got here.

Further to this, the Technical Team Leader–Financial System added the following:

> . . . it was semi-structured. Again, having the Arthur Andersen people come in and they had their base templates that they kind of recommended that we follow, and for the most part, we did follow them, but business need kind of tore it apart in places. They said we had to be at this point at this time. Well, guess what? Half the team got pulled off to close the books for year-end. Well, they're off doing their real work, who's going to be doing this new financial project? Well, it had to wait. And [the Project Manager–Financial System], the project team, we were doing some acquisitions in Argentina, he got pulled off and sent to Argentina for a few weeks, and that delayed the project.

- **Rigorous:** Although the Acquisition process that ESC's Acquisition Team completed was done in a "rushed" and "abbreviated" manner, a significant effort was still put in to do as thorough a job as possible in identifying the different types and levels of organizational needs and establishing the criteria for evaluating the vendors and the ES solutions. An example of this was noted by the Project Manager–Financial System regarding the 2-day demonstrations:

> So, we did 2-full day scripted demos with Oracle and PeopleSoft, which is probably less than we might have done otherwise, but it was still a fairly rigorous process. Arthur Andersen assisted us in taking the requirements, developing scripts from them. [We then] gave the vendors the scripts a couple weeks in advance and then asked them to come in and do a presentation, do a demo.

- **User-driven** – Another CSF of the ESC's Acquisition process was that it was "user-driven." The overall effect of user involvement in the process helped to ensure that the chosen software solution would be more readily accepted. Whereas past acquisition projects were driven by the IT department, acquisition projects are now being driven by the users with the IT department assuming the role of support and service. As per the Technical Team Leader–MMIS: "IT is a service organization towards the lines of business." This is further supported by the Manager–Inventory Management, again, speaking more in his capacity as a member of the Reengineering Group:

> The other big difference, I think was, these decisions have normally been solely made by the IT organizations. These current projects have been managed by non-IT personnel, so that is a little different.

- **Partnership:** Yet another CSF of the process was the "sense of partnership" that the Team had with its user community. On another front, the Acquisition Team also developed a "partnership" with the consultants that they were working with for this acquisition project as well as in a previous project:

> Arthur Andersen had assisted with our original project and we felt comfortable that they could do a good job with our software selection project. (Project Manager–Financial System)

> Working with Arthur Andersen as a selection partner, they helped guide us using their templates, whatever those were. (Technical Team Leader–Financial System)

There was also a "sense of partnership" that was developed between ESC and the short-listed vendors with the goal of establishing the foundation for a long-term relationship with the vendor-of-choice. The Manager–Inventory Management stated it thus:

> I see the purchasing philosophy going forward . . . more on the strategic partnership aspects as opposed to a one shot deal. . . . We are trying to go more towards partnerships in terms that we are in this together for a number of years. So that is a little different than on traditional purchasing.

The Project Manager–Financial System commented on his strong belief in the importance and role of relationships with the vendors. He believed in establishing high-level relationships between the organization and the vendor that could assist the process when necessary.

> I'm a firm believer that relationships are everything. People do business with people they like, people who have credibility, people who stand behind what they say, they do what they say, and who have a

good reputation in the marketplace. I felt like both of these vendors had a lot of credibility with us.

PeopleSoft probably had more credibility with us as an organization and that was an influence that got them into the final 2, I'm sure . . . but the relationship that our team had with the PeopleSoft representatives, I don't think was nearly as good as with the Oracle folks.

The Oracle people brought way more resources to bear. They were significantly stronger in terms of doing what they said they were going to do. If they said, "We're going to get two or three people in here to help you understand this issue," by God, they were here in spades and they were there on time. They gave us the answers that we were looking for and they seemed to be relatively well-balanced in terms of presenting the good with the bad, whereas PeopleSoft's attitude seemed to be, for everything, and you can go out there and ask anybody on my team, "We can do that." That was their response to everything, "We can do that. We can do that." But when it got down to actually seeing it, putting your hands on it, and understanding it, it was a lot harder to—sometimes, even they would get lost.

So, I felt like we developed a real good relationship with the folks at Oracle, but again, with respect to my relationship with the account executive and the other people at Oracle, I did not let that influence or carry over to the rest of the team, you know, how I felt about them. I just kind of kept that to myself until we were done and then I said, "Phew! Boy, I'm glad we're done with that because those PeopleSoft people were really getting on my nerves." And then, a lot of the people on the team said, "We're glad you feel that way, because that's exactly how we felt!" (Project Manager–Financial System)

The following factors that were noted in the previous section as influences were also CSFs of ESC's ES Acquisition Process: Leadership, Competency/skills of the Acquisition Team members, Interdisciplinary nature of the Acquisition Team, and User buy-in.

10.9   LESSONS LEARNED

The Acquisition process for complex packaged software was not a "new experience" for ESC as an organization. ESC had previously acquired packaged software for Human Resources and was in the midst of acquiring a packaged software solution for Payroll. However, while the members of those acquisition teams had experience buying packaged solutions, their experience does not appear to have been conveyed to the members of the Acquisition Team for the Financial System. Thus, for the members of the Financial System Acquisition Team, this was a new experience.

Among the lessons that this experience taught was that:

1. **They had to develop new procedures for dealing with ES acquisitions.** As we can see for ESC, their consultants played a large part in the development of new procedures for dealing with ES acquisitions. As stated by the Project Manager–Financial System:

> Yes, I would say that that is probably a very good way to character- ize it [that it was constructed as we went along] because I've used those words several times, for example, "Folks, not that I'm mak- ing this up as I go along, but I have a vision of how we need to do this. We know kind of what the endpoint is, when we need to make the decision, and so I'm going to need some help distilling some of this high-level vision into action items and deliverables," and that's where some of our IT people and Arthur Andersen were able to help that all congeal.

> Some fundamental processes or guidelines were in place, however, that the Acquisition Team followed for proceeding with certain aspects of the buying task, such as some "specific procurement guidelines." In large part, though, various procedures had to be developed ad hoc or were "borrowed" from the Arthur Andersen consultants to deal with this "new" buying situation.

> Also, no formal process for acquiring complex ES appeared to be in place in the IT department at the time of this acquisition, because if there had been, the Technical Team Leader–Financial System would, in all probability, have brought it to the attention of the Project Manager– Financial System. Thus, it was necessary for ESC to engage the services of outside consultants to assist them with the task of acquiring a financial software package.

2. **The ES Acquisition Process is very complex**. As noted by the Technical Team Leader–Financial System, "even with all the variables known, the magnitude of a project like this is complex. There is no way around it." The Project Manager–Financial System added the following comments on what he discovered about the complexity of this type of decision process:

> It was a lot more complex than I ever would have imagined. You know, there are a lot of things that have changed in terms of the way we view what the vendor told us in the pre-sales or sales cycle

going to the implementation, just because I don't think you ever have enough time. It's like so many things—you never have enough time, you just have to make a decision based on gut feel sometimes and just go with it based on the information that you've got, and we did that.

I'm sure that, you know, we could have . . . spent a year and a million dollars and probably been no closer than we are today, but might have uncovered some things. At least we would know a little bit more about what we were dealing with going in. But, I'm not convinced there's enough benefit in spending that sort of time and money.

As you know, my background is in accounting and auditing, and I have always worked around these kinds of implementations. I had a number of clients when I was in the auditing business that implemented packaged software, but I never really understood the complexity of the software or the complexity of the decision until going through what I'm going through right now.

The Project Manager–Financial System was careful to document the Acquisition process that they followed:

I could go back and look at the minutes because I would prepare an agenda for each meeting and then fill in on the agenda what the responses were to each of the agenda items and any new items, and then distribute that out. So, I could probably tell you about when we made that decision as to how we were going to make decisions or who was going to have authority.

Hence, although the Acquisition process was done in a "rushed" and "abbreviated" manner, the Acquisition Team still contributed a documented history (meeting minutes/agendas, RFP document, lists of requirements, final report and recommendation, etc.) of what transpired during this Acquisition process to the organizational memory.

10.10 SUMMARY

This case demonstrated, among others, the need to verify and cross-check information that is obtained from various sources. While reputation and credibility may speak to the accuracy and reliability of the information that is obtained, these should not always be taken at "face value"—it does not hurt to inquire about the background of the consultants that you work with. As we saw in this case, the consultant's former ties with one of the ES vendors biased the information that he provided to ESC's Acquisition Team and resulted in ESC dropping the vendor (Oracle) from their long-list. Although ESC later chose Oracle's software package, the biased information from the consultant could have resulted in a very costly mistake or a less than optimal choice for ESC. While PeopleSoft was among the Acquisition Team's final 2 choices, and its HR software already in use by ESC's Human Resources department, the Acquisition Team felt that Oracle's Financial package, a "best-of-breed" software in the utilities industry, would provide them with the best fit for their needs.

11

The Halfway Mark: Selection

Now that you have completed the Planning process, with the Marketplace Analysis, and the Information Search process (although this latter process will really continue intermittently through to the end of the Acquisition process), you have your shorter long-list of vendors and you are ready to narrow down your list of contenders. How many should you select? While one vendor/solution may not be enough, 5 may be too many. During the Selection process, you should be able to narrow your shorter long-list to 3 or 4 potential ES vendors/solutions. If you have more than that, you will not have done your "homework" well enough; that is, you will have either insufficiently defined your requirements or not established sufficiently refined selection and evaluation criteria, or both. As it is, you will find that making your final choice from a short-list of 3 or 4 vendors/products will be difficult enough.

11.1   THE SELECTION PROCESS

During this process, the Acquisition Team will investigate the feasible alternatives (ES solutions/vendors) and select a course of action. The selection from among alternatives does not indicate the end-point of the ES Acquisition Process, however. It is rather an intermediate phase in the overall Acquisition process that results not in the final choice or recommendation, but rather in the final short-list of 2 or 3 primary vendors. Hence, the term "selection" refers to those activities that contribute to the ultimate choice, including the precursory steps of recognizing or delimiting and evaluating alternatives, as well as the final selection (as in "group" or "short-list") of 2 or 3 technologies/vendors.

As to the process itself, we view the Selection process as beginning with the activities following the return of the RFP responses from the vendors. This process, as you will find, is an iterative process not only in itself, with the Teams repeating certain steps as needed, but also between the Acquisition Team and the vendors.

11.1.1   Reviewing the RFPs

We noted from the cases that, upon receipt of the RFP responses, the Teams reviewed these to see if all of their requirements had been addressed and to make certain that enough information from the vendors was provided concerning the proposed technological solutions. In instances where the initial RFP responses were not complete or lacked sufficient detail, the Teams in each of the cases rejected them immediately. In instances where the RFP responses were properly completed but were unclear on certain points, the Teams went back to the vendors for clarification on those points. In all of the cases (except Keller[1]), the functional and technical requirements from all relevant sections of the RFP were categorized with the appropriate evaluation criteria (pre-established in the Planning process).

11.1.2   Arriving at the Final Short-list

Each team member then entered the results of their review of the RFP responses, function-by-function, criteria-by-criteria, into the pre-established grids/matrices (in the case of International Air, the responses were entered into a software called "Decision Pad"). The scoring results suggested which of the vendors would be retained for further consideration. Only those vendors whose solutions met all functional and technical requirementswere retained for further consideration. A list of those vendors was then drawn up and a further review was done to arrive at a final short-list of 2 or 3 vendors.

At least one reiteration of this process was done by International Air. Working from their short-list, International Air asked each of their vendors to re-quote on pricing using the same breakdown structure. Since International Air's initial RFP did not include precise instructions on how they wanted costs to be broken down, each vendor responded with their own method of costing—some vendors costed on the number of users, some on the size of the mainframe, etc., and each response was different enough to make valid comparison impossible. Hence, International Air went back to their top candidates

---

1. In the case of Keller, as they gleaned more information on the various technological solutions, they were able to refine their list of critical requirements. The more information that they received, the more they learned about what they needed. Since this was a new experience not only for the VP of Information Systems, but for the organization as well, they "learned as they went along."

and asked them to redo their costing according to very specific guidelines and thus, International Air was provided with a consistent view that enabled them to do a "true" comparison.

In all of the cases, each Acquisition Team used a grid/matrix. The Team's members first evaluated each of the RFP responses individually using a grid/matrix tool and then met as a team to compare their individual results.

From the results of this two-stage ranking process (first individually, and then as a team), the Acquisition Team built a short-list of vendors which was then presented to the Steering Committee for approval to continue to the next phase of the ES Acquisition Process. As for Telecom International, they were asked by their Steering Committee (or more precisely, the CIO) to add 2 more vendors to their short-list, bringing it from 3 up to 5 vendors.

At this point, each of the cases proceeded to implement various evaluation strategies (strategies that were appropriate to this phase of the ES Acquisition Process) that they had developed during the Planning process (discussed in Chapter 12). In the cases of International Air, ESC, and Keller, the short-listed vendors were invited to do in-house presentations of their technologies. In Telecom International's case, they proceeded to visit each of their short-listed vendors to view their technology.

11.2 SUMMARY

The objective of the Selection Process is to reduce the shorter long-list of vendors to either a short-list of 2, 3, or 4 vendors maximum. This process begins following the return of the RFP responses from the vendors and proceeds with an intensive review of those responses.

12

Enterprise Software Evaluation Process: Vendor, Functional, and Technical

With the groundwork completed (i.e., the organizational [business, procedural, etc.], user, functional, and technical requirements defined) and the foundation laid with the establishment of selection and evaluation criteria, work can get underway with the Evaluation process. This process represents the fourth critical piece of the Acquisition process "puzzle." It is for this phase that much of your planning and advance preparations have been done and where you will be able to see a lot of your hard work pay off.

While as many evaluation criteria as possible were established during the Planning process, you can expect that more criteria may and, in all likelihood, will be added during the Evaluation process, even if only a few. You can also expect that additional information will feed the process. Because of this, the Evaluation process is evolutionary in nature and you can expect that as new information is obtained, this process will evolve and decisions will have to be adjusted. Since there is a large amount of information that feeds this process, the tools (questionnaires, grids/matrices) that were developed by the Acquisition Team during the Planning process will help to manage this process.

There are three types of evaluation that should be carried out during this phase of the ES Acquisition Process and hence, three different types of selection/evaluation criteria that need to be established during the Planning process:

1. Vendor
2. Functional
3. Technical

First, *vendor evaluation criteria* need to be established that are commensurate to the levels of screening that will be conducted during the Marketplace Analysis, the Selection process, and then in the final Evaluation process. The Vendor Evaluation process, in most instances and for the most part, is conducted primarily by the Purchasing department. (More information on both vendor criteria and the Vendor Evaluation process is provided later in this chapter.)

Second, *functional evaluation criteria* also need to be established that are commensurate to the different levels of screening that will be conducted. These will be established with the help of the users and will be used in the RFP that is to be sent to the vendors. These criteria will also be used during the Selection process for the review/evaluation of the RFP responses from the vendors, and for the Functional Evaluation of the software during the product demonstrations. Functional criteria and the Functional Evaluation process are discussed later in this chapter.

Third, different levels of *technical evaluation criteria* will also need to be established for use during the Acquisition process. Among others, these will be used within the RFP and then, to evaluate the RFP responses during the Selection process, as well as for the Technical Evaluation of the software. Technical criteria will be established primarily by the IT department. So, too, will they conduct the Technical Evaluation of the software. (More details on technical criteria and the Technical Evaluation process are provided later in this chapter.)

12.1 EVALUATION PROCESSES AND TOOLS

The rigor with which the definition of evaluation criteria and the three different Evaluation processes are carried out should be proportionate to the size or type of purchase that your organization wants to make and the potential effects it could have on the organization in terms of strategic benefits. The rigor with which these tasks/processes were carried out is evident when comparing the cases and it appears to have been proportionate to the organizations needs.

Between the cases, the Evaluation processes took on slightly different twists depending on the technological solution that was desired, the internal customers, the culture of the organization, and even the approval process that needed to be followed to get funding.

The Acquisition Team will want to develop tools (questionnaires and matrices or grids) during the Planning process, based on their Selection and Evaluation criteria, that they will use to assist them with the three different areas of the Evaluation process. These evaluation tools should have both quantitative and qualitative attributes. The following excerpt from the interview with International Air's Project Director illustrates two different types of tools that they developed for the Evaluation process:

We had a very "scientific" approach to it. We broke it down into major categories and within each one of those categories, we had multiple questions. We also used an evaluation tool to do pair-wise comparisons for each functionality or each characteristic, and gave it some weighting so that we had a quantifiable assessment on how they met our requirements in the different categories that we had defined, whether it was functionality, technology, support and so on. What we did was, we established weighting for each one of those categories. In each category, we had a breakdown in detail. We had over 400 elements to evaluate, function-by-function, or characteristic-by-characteristic, and they were grouped into 7 or 8 major categories, and each of those categories carried a different weight so that we had a quantifying bottom line.

As will be seen in the next three sections, the Evaluation process is an iterative process. The Vendor Evaluation that occurs concurrently to the Planning process is, in part, embedded in the Marketplace Analysis. As more information is obtained during the course of the Acquisition process, from client referrals and other sources, the Vendor Evaluation process is again revisited. Similarly, the processes for evaluating functionality and the technical aspects of the technology are reiterated. Preliminary evaluations in both areas are carried out during the Selection process during the review of the RFP responses. Then, during the formal evaluation, more in-depth investigations are conducted.

12.1.1   Vendor Evaluation Process

In the early stage of the Planning process, during the Marketplace Analysis, each of the teams conducted a cursory evaluation of potential vendors. During this cursory evaluation, an initial screening was carried out using pre-established high-level or general criteria. The end result of this evaluation was a long-list of vendors.

Some of the basic screening criteria that were used to evaluate potential vendors were the size of the vendor and the vendor's reputation, market share, and global presence.

An exception to this was done by Telecom International. As with International Air and ESC, the size of the vendor was a criterion that Telecom International's Acquisition Team had used to weed out vendors. It was only when the Team presented their short-list of 3 vendors to the Steering Committee at the end of the Selection process that the exception came about. More precisely, Telecom International's CIO (a member of the Steering Committee) asked the Acquisition Team to add 2 more vendors that he knew of to their list for consideration, one of which was a small vendor. The reason for this was that the CIO did not want the Acquisition Team to discount any new technology that might come from a smaller vendor simply because of their size. (This vendor was soon eliminated from further consideration, though, due to their limited product scope.)

As the teams received more information, their long-lists were further reduced to an acceptable number of vendors. As previously noted, one of International Air's strategies to evaluate the vendors on their long-list was to bring all of their potential vendor candidates together, which they did, in a vendor awareness session. Though uncertain of the results of this strategy (some organizations prefer to keep the vendors "in the dark" about whom they are competing against), it proved to be useful in that:

1. It served as a natural weeding mechanism to reduce the number of potential candidates—one of the vendors[1] bowed out once they saw who they were competing against and realized that they would not be able to meet International Air's criteria for an integrated solution.
2. It allowed International Air to get a feel for who could do the work for them.
3. It gave vendors the opportunity to team or partner together in order to provide the full scope of applications that International Air ultimately wanted.

To reiterate, as more information was received and their long-lists shortened, the teams then conducted more in-depth vendor evaluations. Each of the teams did financial evaluations of each vendor for which they obtained D&B reports. These reports allowed the teams to verify each vendor's financial stability and viability. Given the cost of the proposed ES solutions and the long-term commitment with the vendor that would be required to maintain the system, any sign of financial difficulty was cause to further investigate the vendor.

In addition to this, we would like to add that the financial viability of a vendor should not be the sole criteria for either evaluating or eliminating a particular vendor from consideration. It should, rather, be looked at in conjunction with and relative to the size and longevity of the vendor. For example, in 1999, several ES vendors experienced major downturns in their sales and as a result, suffered significant losses. This, however, does not mean that these vendors will continue to experience financial losses. Consideration of their size and a review of their growth over the past several years would provide a historical perspective of the vendor and show what their track record has been up to this point. Further to this, an investigation into their future plans, what their vision is, whether

---

1. It is to be noted that other vendors bowed out shortly afterwards when they realized that International Air was seeking an integrated solution preferably from a single vendor.

theirs is an "up and coming" technology, etc., will provide you with an indication of whether or not they are on track and have a plan for turning their current situation around. These, together, would provide a more complete picture of the vendor. This is also one of the reasons to request that the vendor provide a "vision statement" in the RFP.

Single- or Multiple-Vendor Solutions

Another criterion that was important for all of the cases was that the solution be from a single source. That is, was the proposed technology developed in-house by the vendor-candidate or would the vendor-candidate have to outsource part of the application to another vendor? A single-vendor solution would reduce or eliminate the risk of a potential fallout between partners or of one of the partners no longer being in business, which could result in problems regarding the long-term responsibility for the overall solution. A single-vendor solution would also avoid any shifting of responsibility for the technology ("passing the buck" or "finger pointing").

A single-vendor solution may not be the "best" solution for your organization, however. As it so happened for each of the cases in this study, it was, and so it will be for many others. Meanwhile, for those organizations that determine otherwise, a multiple-vendor solution is another alternative. A multiple-vendor solution is a solution for which several vendors have come together to do a bid, because no one of them, alone, can supply the desired product. For example, a vendor who is only able to supply a portion (consisting of one or more modules) of a required solution partners with one or two other vendors who can supply the remaining portion(s) of the solution that your organization needs. This type of vendor partnership is an example of a temporary alliance that is formed to meet a client's immediate need. Again, depending on your organizational needs, this may be acceptable.

A multiple-vendor solution or, rather, the modules that constitute it may or may not qualify as examples of "best of breed," however, and we want you to be aware of that, especially if this criterion is important to your organization. This applies equally to single-source ES solutions. While a single-source ES solution may be considered "best of breed" (because of the overall quality and performance of the ES solution), not all of the modules within that solution will necessarily be "best of breed" for their particular areas. For example, the two or three principal modules of the ES solution (where the vendor is especially strong) may be "best of breed," while lesser modules (modules that are not the "heart" of the package, but that are rather the "nice to have for convenience sake" type of modules) are not. Hence, if this is a criterion that your organization deems important, it will be necessary that your Acquisition Team determine for which areas/modules this criterion of "best of breed" is *most* important. So, for example, if your most important needs are in materials management, then you will want to select the vendor whose particular strengths lie in materials management. Or, it may be determined that there are two or more areas within your organization for which "best of breed" modules are desired. There, again, you will want to pick the vendor that is strong in those areas.

While the ultimate, for an organization, would be to "cherry pick" the products that are considered "best of breed" for each of its different areas and have them all be able to "talk to each other," the reality, at least at this point in time, is that certain products do not integrate well. Nevertheless, your organization may decide that this is the route to go—to have a multiple-vendor solution that consists of several "best of breed" products. If it does not, that is, if your organization decides not to go "best of breed" all the way (100%), your Acquisition Team will still need to determine whether a single-vendor or a multiple-vendor ES solution will best meet your organization's needs.

Once again, it comes down to Planning—doing your homework and investigating things well. This is why the Planning phase is so critical in the acquisition of an ES. We can not stress this enough.

Other Vendor Evaluation Criteria

In addition, we noted that the vendors were also evaluated according to:

- Their ability to assist the organizations with the implementation of their packaged software solutions
- Their association with or the availability of third-party vendors/partners to assist with local support
- Their vision, that is, their future plans and trends regarding the direction of the components of the proposed solution (both technical and functional)
- Their strategic position

Below are all of the criteria that we identified from the cases against which the vendors were evaluated:

- Financial strength
- Market share (sales volume, size)
- Annual growth rate
- Customer support
- Product recognition
- Range of products/Ability to meet future needs
- Reputation
- Vision and/or strategic positioning of the vendor

- Longevity of the vendor
- Qualifications, experience, and success in delivering solutions to organizations of a similar size, complexity, and geographic scope
- Quality of the vendor's proposal
- Demonstrated understanding of requirements, constraints, and concerns
- Demonstrated understanding of the need to solve the hardware platform constraint and "Year 2000" problem
- Implementation plan that properly positions the proposed solution to achieve the maximum level of business benefits
- Implementation services
- Implementation strategy
- Support services
- Business process reengineering
- Ability to provide references
- Costs
- Training
- Risks
- Time frames for the project
- Guarantees or warranty
- Financing
- Single supplier
- Single integrated solution

12.1.2   Functional Evaluation Process

The Functional Evaluation of the packaged software is also an important facet of the Acquisition process. In the case of ESC, the functional requirements that drove their selection accounted for 42% of the overall weighting, and in the case of Telecom International, functionality accounted for 60% of the overall weighting. For International Air, as well, the functionality of the packaged software was the prime consideration and received the most weighting. According to International Air's Technical Project Manager,

> Although technology was also part of it, I think we have to look at applications and functions. Functions have got to be there. If a function is not there, it doesn't matter if you have the best technology in the world, it won't satisfy the objectives. . . . Essentially, the functionality drove the decision, although other factors, including technology, were included.

Several different methods were used to accomplish the Functional Evaluation:

1. Canned demonstrations
2. Scripted demonstrations
3. Reference site visits

Two of the cases, International Air and ESC, used the strategy of a scripted demonstration. At the completion of their Selection process, International Air and ESC developed demonstration scripts, based on their defined requirements, that would be used to:

1. Verify the contents of the RFP responses—"Can the software do what they claimed it can do?"
2. Simulate tasks—from simple to very complex
3. Clarify issues and areas that were unclear or were not addressed in the RFP responses

These scripts were then sent to each of the vendors on their short-lists a couple of weeks prior to the demonstrations and were the basis for the functional demonstrations of the vendors' proposed solutions.

For International Air, the Functional Evaluation consisted of intensive three-day in-house demonstrations by each of their top vendor-candidates, and for ESC, two-day demonstrations. Keller, on the other hand, received standard or canned demonstrations from the vendors they had invited in-house. Keller then asked their top vendor-candidate to return for an intensive two-day in-house "scripted" demonstration where Keller had them perform a multitude of simulations of tasks with the software. For all three of these cases (International Air, ESC, and Keller), user participation at these demonstrations was considered very important. Thus, in addition to the Acquisition Team, users from all levels and from various departments attended the functional demonstrations. The number of users involved varied according to each of these three organizations, but overall, 12 to 50 of the same users participated at each of the vendor demonstrations.

Telecom International's strategy was quite different from the others on this point. They decided to visit the vendors on their short-list. In addition to the Acquisition Team, Telecom International had some of their key end-users and technical people attend these visits, individuals "who knew exactly what their needs were and what they were looking for" (Project Manager). Their intent during these visits was to collect more information on both the vendors' products and their companies, to look at the software (canned demonstrations), ask probing questions, and to see the concept behind the vendors' packaged solutions.

In each of the four cases, feedback was obtained from all demonstration participants to determine their impressions about the proposed software solutions. Both the users and the Acquisition Team members completed matrices/grids and/or questionnaires to report their impressions and score the appropriate categories for the demonstrations.

Prior to inviting their primary short-listed vendor to do a scripted demonstration, Keller conducted reference site visits as a means of obtaining information and doing high-level evaluations of the vendors and software that they were considering. The Acquisition Team's assessment of how well the software performed in manufacturing environments similar to Keller's helped it to further narrow the field of vendor-candidates under consideration.

Functional Evaluation Criteria

The following list presents a few examples of general categories and questions that could be part of the Functional Evaluations:

1. Definition of Business Functionalities that are in the Proposed Vendor's Solution

Examples of ES Functionalities for such business needs as:

Customer Invoicing
- Can each location produce a bill in the organization's name?
- Can the system bundle bills for a client from different organizational billing locations with a summary statement?
- Does the user have the ability to choose the invoice medium (paper, diskette, CD-ROM, or other) and format per customer and/or product?
- Does the system have the ability to determine the language of correspondence of the customer?
- Can the system:
  - Maintain a customer account balance from current period and have prior periods balance forward?
  - Apply automated credit and/or adjustments?
  - Apply general credits and/or process specific adjustments to the current invoice (representing changes with the invoice month)?
  - Apply general credits and/or specific adjustments to prior invoice items (minimum 3 months)?
  - Specify an absolute dollar amount?
  - Specify the rate for a particular product/destination?
  - Combine the billing on the charges for multiple products?

Accounts Payable

- Vendor Information
  - Can the system provide one-time vendor payments without setting up a vendor record?
  - Does the system allow a record to contain both "Buy from" and multiple "Remit to" addresses?
  - Can all invoices for a specific vendor be put on hold?
  - Can the system put selected invoices on hold?
  - Does the system provide a tracking ability by supplier code?
  - Can the system validate a vendor by zip code?

Accounts Payable Entry and Distribution

- Does the system allow for online entry of P.O. and Non-P.O. payments?
- Can the user input invoices when manual checks are typed?
- Can the system:
  - Process forms with electronic routing and approvals?
  - Uniquely identify different voucher types (besides P.O. or non-P.O.)?
  - Generate recurring payments?
  - Carry forward account numbers from a P.O. when a voucher is added?
  - Distribute invoice amounts among multiple companies?
  - Validate account numbers online?
  - Add one invoice for multiple P.O.s and not lose the reference for each?
  - Support inter-organizational payables requirements?
  - Distribute invoice line item amount or invoice total amount by percentages or dollars to one or multiple companies?

Electronic Payment/Invoicing

- Can the system:
  - Make electronic payments and receive invoices?
  - Support electronic imaging of AP documents?
  - Support 2-way, 3-way, and 4-way matching?
  - Forward employee payments to payroll rather than print a check?
  - Support multiple checking accounts?
  - Support flexible selection of invoice payment based on discount dates, invoice due dates, user defined, and based on vendor?
  - Consolidate several vendor invoices into one check?
  - Support EDI?

Budgeting and Forecasting
- Does the user have the ability to:
  - Enter budgets at the Manager/Supervisor Levels?
  - Roll-up budgets to a higher level?
  - Provide responsibility reports at multiple levels of management?
  - Develop budgets at a resource and responsibility level?
  - Prepare and enter budgets at remote locations for corporate utilization?
  - Provide multi-organizational reporting?
  - Change the organizational chart?
  - Generate applicable reports during the Budget Development process?
  - Generate ad-hoc reports that provide "drill-down" capabilities?
  - Generate exception reporting with e-mail notification (e.g., When a project or responsibility budget is within "x"% of budget authority on a project, an automatic notification is sent via e-mail)?
  - Generate internal "Management Based" reports that differ from external reporting formats?
  - Roll information from different companies under different methods for management and legal reporting?
  - Generate reports that compare actual to commitment and to forecast amounts?
  - Provide year-to-date/year-to-go reporting?
  - Electronically route budget information for approval (e.g., authorization of capital expenditure/business case)?
  - "Lock" budgets at a functional and corporate level?

2. Improvement over Current Systems
This is where the Acquisition Team would determine the fit-gap between the proposed system's functionalities and the organization's current systems' functionalities. This is also where your process model and the ES process model that is supplied by the vendor come into play. Do the differences, in effect, constitute improvements or shortcomings in the proposed ES solution?

3. Global Business Requirements
- Can the proposed ES support:
  - Multiple currencies?
    (a) Can it handle multiple currencies at the transaction level?

  (b) Can the system maintain the transaction amount in the local country currency (settlement currency) as well as the U.S. equivalent at the time the transaction was made?
- Multiple languages?
  (a) Are Customer Support services provided in more than one language, and if yes, explain how this support is done?
  (b) Does your system support upper- and lowercase characters, including accented characters used in the, e.g., French or Spanish character sets? If yes, explain how your system handles sorting sequence with fields, such as Name, which may contain both English and French characters?
  (c) Are alphanumeric data items stored in upper and lowercase, in the fashion in which they were entered?
  (d) Are application update releases distributed in more than one language at the same time? If not, what is the normal lag time between, e.g., the English, the French and the Spanish releases?
  (e) What other languages can your system support?
- Multiple corporations?
  (a) The Organization has a need to create and track individual and distinct companies under the Organization corporate "umbrella." Explain how your system supports this requirement.
- Government compliance?
  (a) Define which countries your system will not support for any possible legislative requirements.
  (b) Explain the process of how any new legislative requirements for a country would be added to the system.
  (c) Does your system meet data retention requirements as mandated by federal or local legislation?

4. Customization
Here, the vendor would need to explain how their proposed solution will support and control the customization and/or development of data and processes.

- Is there a Systems Development Kit (SDK) or an Application Programming Interface (API) to customize or extend the solution?
- How easily can the system be customized?
- Can all customization be done by the organization? If not, explain what are the limits to the customization?

- Can the menus and panels be modified by a system administrator? or User?
- What happens to customization when a new release is issued?
- Can the proposed system allow users to create new or modify existing reference and control tables that are used during processing?
- Can calculations and formulas used for processing be modified by an authorized user or are they hard coded?
- Does the proposed system support a testing environment? If yes, how are changes migrated from the test environment to the production environment?
- Does your licensing agreement allow for the creation of a testing environment to the production environment?
- How are application changes distributed to remote platforms or workstations?

5. User Interfaces

This is where the system is evaluated with regard to its user-friendliness and its intuitiveness. The organization may require that the proposed system have an intuitive, user-friendly Graphical User Interface (GUI).

- Does the proposed system follow generally accepted standards for a Windows type GUI interface?
- Does the proposed system use drop-down selection lists for all table-driven data fields?
- Is a Web browser interface available?

12.1.3   Technical Evaluation Process

The last of the three types of evaluation that are conducted during the Acquisition process is the Technical Evaluation. Criteria for the Technical Evaluation will need to be defined in the Planning process and included in the RFPs to the vendors. These criteria should include the definition of the technical prerequisites and co-requisites, or more specifically:

- The platform that the proposed solution should ideally operate on
- The DBMS (Database Management Systems) that should be used
- The hardware requirements—request that the vendor inform your organization as to whether the capacity of the existing hardware that the solution will be installed on is sufficient or whether new hardware will be required

- The integration requirements of the proposed solution into the organization's existing environment
- The required capacity of the proposed solution: number of users, number of transactions, etc.
- The required performance objectives of the proposed solution
- Internationalization/localization requirements
- Extensibility and openness requirements
- Systems management requirements
- Reliability requirements
- Security requirements

In short, criteria for the Technical Evaluation should include all of the standard things that are normally looked at when designing systems. Consequently, this will also mean that the Acquisition Team will look at the functionality of the proposed solutions from the technical perspective.

The Technical Evaluation itself consists of a series of tests to assess the rigor, capacity, and performance of the software and all aspects of the technology supporting the applications, including the platforms, the operating systems, the database management systems, and all of the systems management aspects (availability, security, etc.). While these issues will have been addressed in the RFP (with the defined technical pre- and co-requisites) and reviewed during the "paper" Technical Evaluation, the "live" Technical Evaluation will provide physical evidence of the software's ability to actually do what the vendor claimed. Hence, the Technical Evaluation will provide answers to such questions/issues as:

- Is the platform that the organization intends for the proposed solution to operate on ideal for optimum performance?
- Is the organization's existing DBMS compatible with the proposed solution?
  - What are the redundancy capabilities of the system, in terms of server clustering, data mirroring, DBMS replication, etc.?
  - Explain/demonstrate the system's data retention, archival, and retrieval processes by system.
- Can the proposed solution integrate into the organization's existing environment?
  - Can the system operate acceptably within the organization's existing hardware architecture?
  - What is the recommended configuration (not the minimum) for the proposed system?
  - Does the proposed system provide an import/export facility to accommodate ASCII data file transfers?

- Can the proposed system import/export data and reports to PC based software (e.g., spreadsheet, word processing, etc.)?
- What is the architecture of the proposed solution: client/server, 2-tier, 3-tier, other?
  - If client/server, does the vendor have a development strategy for this architecture?
  - If client/server, what are the percentages (relative to workloads) on both the client and the server processors for typical system usage?
  - Outline the system's batch versus online processing. Identify those processes that can be run in either mode with a breakdown by system (e.g., General Ledger, Accounts Payable, etc.).
  - Describe the modularity of the architecture.
- What is the capacity (minimum and maximum) of the proposed solution?
- Scalability of the system
  - Is the system scalable?
  - To what extent is it scalable regarding the number of users, transactions, etc.?
  - Is the existing hardware that the solution will be installed on sufficient or will new hardware be required?
- Performance
  - If the organization's intent is for users to access the system from remote locations, have the vendor explain/demonstrate the system's performance over a LAN, WAN, etc. under the following circumstances:
    - (a) The capability of users making file queries without the involvement of the systems administrator and using technologies such as the Internet.
    - (b) Users working unconnected from the corporate networks who need to input and download data.
  - Response time—in situations where there is high traffic over the network (LAN, WAN, etc.)
- Extensibility and Openness
  - Is there an SDK or API to customize or extend the solution?
  - If your organization has many unique processes and data requirements, there may be a need for additional customization in the way of a large scale development of missing components. In such instances, you will want to ask the vendor to explain/demonstrate how the proposed systems will support and control the customization and/or development of data and processes.

- Demonstrate the recommended development environment including all necessary components (e.g., hardware, software, development tools, testing and debugging tools, configuration control tools)?
- Will the organization receive source code?
- Can all customization be done by the organization? If not, explain/demonstrate the limits of the customization that can be done by the organization.
- What happens to customization when a new release is issued?
- Can the menus and panels be modified by a systems administrator? An end user?

• Systems management
- What tools and utilities within your solution can be used for the management of the production environment in order to lessen operator or system administrator intervention?
- Does the proposed system have an automated job scheduler (e.g., for reports, financial period processing, etc.)?
- Can backups be done while the application is online?
- Does the proposed system have a security administration function to monitor and manage data and process access?
- As to reliability, can some parts of the system function even if others are "down"?
- Does the system include a monitoring utility that provides notification of outages?
- What tools and utilities within your solution can be used in order to achieve close to 100% availability?
- What third-party systems management tools may be required or desirable?

• Internationalization/localization
- Does the GUI support multiple languages?
- European Character Support—Does the proposed system support upper- and lowercase characters, including accented characters used in the, e.g., French or Spanish character sets? If yes, explain how the system handles sorting sequence with fields, such as Name, which may contain both English and French characters?
- Asian Character Support—Is there support for multi-byte character sets?
- Are alphanumeric data items stored in upper- and lowercase, in the fashion in which they were entered?

• Security Features
- Is there access protection through the use of a User ID and password and to what levels can it be applied?

- Are user groups supported?
- Can a master user customize a unique user group or are there only standard groups that have to be used?
- Is security applied at the data level for add/change/delete/view authority, and to the processing level for execution authority?
- Does the security system extend controls to the reporting and query tools?
- Does the proposed system maintain an online activity log for auditing purposes?
- Can security be specified according to date and time?
- Are users allowed to change their own passwords?
- Can access to data be defined to the level of a subset of a data population?
- Can a single sign-on be used to log into the network and application (i.e., the user doesn't have to log in more than once to reach the desired application)?
- Is there support for 30-day or 90-day password change policies?
- Recovery
    - Describe/demonstrate your existing "Disaster Recovery" process from strictly a software and data point of view.
    - How easily can the system be brought back to consistency if it fails?
    - Does the proposed solution have the capability of providing data backup which supports disaster recovery at a "hot-site"?
    - Is there any product licensing condition which applies to the recovery and operation of the system at a "hot-site"?
    - Can the software run in a "high availability" architecture such as clusters?
- Strategies for the support and utilization of:
    - Web/Internet/Intranet/Extranet
    - Electronic commerce and EDI
    - Document imaging and document management
- Implementation
    - Tools available for implementation
    - Risks involved with the implementation of the proposed solution
    - Implementability of the proposed solution

The Technical Evaluation will be carried out in a three-phase process (much the same as the Functional Evaluation was carried out):

1. Paper evaluation of the RFP responses
2. Vendor presentations and demonstrations
3. In-house demonstrations

The first phase will happen subsequent to the return of the RFP responses from the vendors (i.e., evaluation of the paper responses). The second phase will take place either before or following the in-house vendor demonstrations. It is conducted at the vendors sites or at reference sites. The third phase will occur as part of the in-house vendor demonstrations. The Technical Evaluation process is also an iterative process. As the Acquisition Team learns more about the vendors' solutions from the RFP responses, it will be able to adjust, add, or remove criteria, benchmarks, etc., in its Technical Evaluation process.

All of the cases in this study conducted a Technical Evaluation of their proposed ES solutions. However, the Technical Evaluation that Keller's Acquisition Team conducted was considerably different from those done by the other three cases. Since Keller was incorporating a manufacturing/production software solution into their operations, they were really starting from "ground zero" as far as using IT on the shop floor. Hence, they had no existing hardware environment per se to consider in their choice of packaged solutions. Keller's approach to the Technical Evaluation consisted of drawing on the experience of the referrals they spoke with. In the course of inquiring about how the software worked for these companies in their manufacturing environments, the reliability of the vendor, etc., Keller made inquiries about the platform that these reference sites were running the software on, their reasons for selecting that platform, the benefits, the drawbacks, and so on. After considering all of the input that they had received, Keller then made their choice of platform and infrastructure.

Business Processes

As to the cases of International Air, Telecom International, and ESC, the Acquisition Teams used the information they had gathered during the Planning process about their organizations' current functional and data/information needs, their existing systems architecture, and their existing (or future) technological infrastructure as the basis by which to evaluate the vendors' solutions. From an evaluation of the information they gathered on their current functional and data/information needs, they gained a high-level understanding of:

- Their organizations' business processes and needs
- The key functions that were supplied by their existing applications (and that would necessarily be required of the new applications)
- The minimum data that they needed to keep track of
- The types of interfaces that were used (and would be required of the new software solution)

From both a business perspective and a technical perspective, this was important because of the existing relationships and interdependence of the applications that were to be replaced by the proposed ES solution and those that would remain in place. Integration of the new applications might necessitate modifications to their organizations' existing processes (business and technical) and data models in order to conform with the new software. Modifications to the business processes were an issue of BPR and were of concern to the organizations. International Air, ESC, and Keller viewed the replacement of their current systems as an opportunity to reengineer the way they do business in those areas. However, from a technical perspective, each of the organizations voiced that a conscious decision was made on their parts to be as flexible as possible with regard to changes that they might have to make in order to accommodate the ES solution of their choice into their technological environment. So, although it was important for them to understand the internal workings of their current applications as well as the proposed ES solutions, they found it more important that the new software meet their base requirements regarding business processes, key functionalities, minimum data, and visual (front-end) interfaces. These issues will be equally important for your organization to consider, except if it is in a situation similar to Keller's prior to this acquisition—starting from ground zero with no existing systems to integrate with.

To facilitate their Technical Evaluation, International Air's Technical Evaluation team used a system design methodology based on IBM's SDMM World-Wide Application Development and System Design Method (WSDDM). This methodology enabled them to define the required key characteristics of the proposed system, not only from a technical standpoint, but also from a functional or user standpoint.

Implementation

From a support and implementation standpoint, International Air, Telecom International, and ESC each did a high-level analysis of the proposed ES system architecture during their initial Technical Evaluation. Here, once again, they began by referring back to information that they had gathered during the Planning process when they were defining their system requirements and gathering information on their infrastructure for inclusion in the RFP, information such as:

- Who the users were
- What processes and data the systems would be handling
- What the availabilities were
- Service-level requirements
- Platforms they were on
- Type and number of hardware systems
- Network
- DBMS

They compared their requirements with the information that was supplied by the vendors on:

- The major components of their solution
- Its architecture
- Its process and data models
- Integratibility with the organization's systems
- Infrastructural requirements
- Their implementation services and strategies

During this initial evaluation, they were able to assess the appropriateness of each vendor's solution for their organization; that is:

- How it would fit with their organization's current technological environment
- The ability of the organization to support it (in-house technical expertise, etc.)
- What the processing requirements were—online, batch, synchronized, central, distributed
- Its scalability
- Its openness

It also gave the teams an indication of:

- What type of performance they could expect
- What the loads would be on their networks based on their volume of data
- The volume of processing that would be required
- Whether the traffic would be significant
- What the impact would be
- What the response times would be on a local area network (LAN) versus a wide area network (WAN)

Further, they looked at:

- What systems management tools would have to be procured (if any)
- What systems management processes would have to be executed if they needed to have software data distribution across the network, etc.

They also looked at:

- The ability of their whole infrastructure, end-to-end, to support the availability feature of the software if someone lost a terminal, or a line, and/or a router, and/or a server:
  - What would happen with the software?
  - What mechanisms, if any, were built into the software to deal with these types of situations?
  - What would the organization's IT department have to do to be able to maintain the availability of the system for the users?

Security and access were also important concerns, and so they looked at how these were defined and managed. Disaster recovery was yet another issue that was addressed.

Altogether, the information provided in the RFP responses from the vendors enabled the Acquisition Teams to more accurately assess the total cost of the acquisition, including its full "Total Cost of Ownership." These assessments were made by taking into account not only the software costs (one time and ongoing [maintenance, upgrades, support, etc.]), but also the costs arising from the consequent acquisition of new hardware (if any) as well as network and manpower costs.

For the second and third phases of the Technical Evaluation, which consisted of evaluating working versions of the software solutions at reference sites and during the in-house demonstrations, International Air and ESC used benchmarks that they had established earlier in the ES Acquisition Process. They had benchmarks to evaluate the server capacity, the capacity of the network components, and the size of workstations that would be needed. The Technical Evaluation teams also validated benchmarks that were supplied to them by the vendors as well as those that came from external sources to assist them in evaluating the capacity of the software.

The Technical Evaluations that were conducted in these cases were found to differ somewhat from those that are conducted as a part of software development. In software development, each step or module is evaluated and tested as the software is developed. In the cases here, however, the organizations were evaluating a "finished" product and hence, the Technical Evaluation that was done of the packaged software took a significantly different approach. In fact, the Technical Evaluation that was described in three of the four cases appeared to have been an "outside-in" approach (not to be confused with "reverse engineering"), where they began with the finished product and examined its architecture, design characteristics, and how the proposed solution integrated with their existing systems; tested load capacity and speed on their networks, response time, availability, security, and so forth (see the list that is in the following paragraph).

Role of the Technical Evaluation Team

Lastly, let us touch on the role of the Technical Evaluation teams. As we noted from the cases, their role was to:

- Establish (during the Planning process) Technical Evaluation criteria, some of the general categories of which were:
  - Integration with current systems
    - (a) Database integration
    - (b) Solution integration
    - (c) System interfaces
    - (d) Improvement over current technical environment
    - (e) Systems architecture
    - (f) Technology infrastructure
    - (g) Process and data models
    - (h) Data requirements
    - (i) Performance
    - (j) Benchmarking
    - (k) Security
    - (l) Expertise of the vendor
    - (m) Technical assistance (support services)
    - (n) Implementation services
    - (o) Implementation strategies
- Contribute to the comparative weightings of the different evaluation categories
- Evaluate all aspects of the software from a design (architecture) perspective
- Assess the ability of the proposed system to meet their organizations, business objectives
- Determine the impact and suitability of their existing technology infrastructure
- Assess the integratibility of the packaged software into their existing environment
- Determine the cost of the acquisition

12.2   SUMMARY

All three types of evaluation were conducted by the four cases and of the three, the Functional Evaluation carried the most weight.

The Vendor Evaluation process was carried out, in part:

- During the Planning process (as part of the Marketplace Analysis)
- Was ongoing throughout the rest of the ES Acquisition Process during the:
  - Selection process—with the review of the RFP
  - Evaluation process—with client referrals and input from other sources
  - Business Negotiations process—ongoing dealings with the vendors throughout the ES Acquisition Process.

As for the Functional Evaluation, it was carried out:

- First, at a very high level during the Marketplace Analysis
- Then at a more detailed level during the Selection process
- Most intensively during the Functional part of the software Evaluation process

The Technical Evaluation, for its part, was carried out, in part:

- During the Selection process
- More intensively, during the Technical Evaluation process.

Criteria that were established during the Planning process were used to conduct all three types of evaluations.

13

"Down to the Wire and Then, No Dice" The Case of Telecom International

This chapter presents the case of Telecom International, an international telecommunications organization that began but did not complete the purchase of a packaged ES solution. The chapter begins with a presentation of Telecom International's corporate profile and is followed by a background description of the circumstances that led to the decision not to buy an ES solution. Subsequent to that, an overview of the ES Acquisition Process that Telecom International partially completed is presented.

13.1   ORGANIZATIONAL PROFILE

Telecom NA is a North American based overseas carrier which maintains commercial relations and operates facilities that allow domestic network operators and other service providers to exchange telecommunication traffic with 240 countries and territories. Telecom NA,[1] with its extensive telecommunication networks, owns and operates three earth stations in North America with a total complement of 37 satellite antennas, has interests (co-ownership) in both INTELSAT[2] and INMARSAT[3] satellite systems, as well as access to satellites

---

1. INTELSAT and INMARSAT are international treaty organizations established to provide international and marine fixed and mobile satellite telecommunications services and Telecom International is designated as the sole signatory for Canada.

2. INTELSAT was founded in 1964 and it was the first organization to provide global satellite coverage and connectivity, and continues to be the communication provider with the broadest reach and the most comprehensive range of services. It owns and operates a global satellite system which provides voice/data and video services to users in more than 200 nations, territories, and dependencies on every continent.

3. INMARSAT was set-up in 1979 to provide worldwide mobile satellite communications for the maritime community. Today is has 82 member countries and is the only provider of global mobile satellite communications for commercial, emergency, and safety applications on land, at sea, and in the air.

owned by Panamsat, Intersputnik, and Telesat, and approximately 100 submarine cables which operate, by means of fiber-optic links, facilities that are connected to Telecom International Inc. switching centers. It is through these facilities that Telecom Inc. offers intercontinental telecommunications services to carriers, resellers, multinational corporations, and consumers around the world.

Telecom International was founded in 1995 and currently has 200 employees worldwide. Its headquarters are located in the Washington, DC area and it is the global carrier subsidiary of Telecom Inc. With offices established in the major cities of the United States, Germany, the United Kingdom, South America, the Middle East, Asia, and other areas of the world where the highest density routes are found, Telecom International has established its presence in the global market. It is one of the world's leading intercontinental telecommunication companies, offering other carriers and businesses information services.

13.2   BACKGROUND

In December 1996 and January 1997, Telecom International began looking for one or more software packages that would support its billing needs and would integrate with their current systems architecture. The billing software package would have to be sufficiently flexible for Telecom International to rapidly address the changes imposed by a telecommunications environment in constant evolution.

The packaged solution that was required had to support the notion of multi-billing for the various Telecom NA subsidiary companies and cover all the services offered by these subsidiaries, such as:

- Call record collection
- Rating capabilities
- Discounts and promotions
- Multi-level customer hierarchy
- Invoicing for a variety of services (e.g., International Direct Distance Dialing [IDDD], international toll-free service, international private lines, indirect access, country direct, inbound direct, broadcast services, card products, etc.)
- Payment options
- Taxes
- Controls and error corrections
- International settlement, etc.

If no one solution was available, a combination of several software packages would then be needed to address all of these requirements.

The ES system would also need to integrate with Telecom International's existing computing environment, which included both operational systems (related to the management of Telecom International's communications infrastructure) and administrative systems. The administrative systems were comprised of a LAN connected to several UNIX servers. The e-mail system was Beyond Mail (and Banyan Mail for remote access). In addition to the Banyan file and communication servers, the LAN was connected to a number of UNIX database servers (Sequent hardware) running Oracle database technology. The major database application was the Oracle Financials package that included General Ledger, Accounts Payable, and Fixed Assets modules.

The primary client workstations of the LAN were Pentium-based machines with 16 to 24 MB of RAM, running DOS 6.2/Windows 3 and common applications such as WordPerfect, Lotus 1-2-3, and Microsoft Office. There were no plans to install Windows 95. In fact, the decision had been made to migrate the desktop environment to Windows NT.

13.3   TELECOM INTERNATIONAL'S ES ACQUISITION PROCESS

The decision was made that Telecom International would acquire one or several packaged solutions that would enable it to handle Telecom International's growing needs. There were several phases in the Acquisition process. Given the areas/services that were to be addressed by the software solutions, this would not only be an expensive acquisition, but it would also be a strategic one—for Telecom International, the billing system was considered of strategic importance. Telecom International provided telecommunication services to a variety of customers, each of whom needed to be adequately billed and its present billing systems were no longer able to accommodate all of the features that were required in a competitive global environment.

13.3.1   Putting Together an International Team

In the initial phase, the participants of the acquisition team were selected. Individuals from various areas of the organization were chosen to be part of the Acquisition Team. While the purchase was initiated in Canada, the billing system was for the Telecom NA subsidiary, Telecom International, located in Washington, DC. Therefore, not only did the team's composition include individuals from Telecom NA corporate headquarters, it also included members from the international division (Telecom International) located in the United States. From the corporate headquarters of Telecom NA, team members were selected from the IT department (the project manager), Procurement, Finance, and Products, and from Telecom International, Marketing, and Finance.

Each of these individuals was responsible for specific tasks in the initial phase. For example, the individuals representing Marketing and Finance were responsible for making certain that the Acquisition Team had access to key individuals in the organization on the user side. Another individual was responsible for finding out which software packages were available on the market. This person also served as the main contact with the various vendors. Yet another individual represented the legal side of the organization, and so on.

13.3.2 Lots of Vendors, But Only a Few Real Contenders

During the planning phase, the Acquisition Team engaged the services of a consulting firm (TRI) that provided them with a report of the various products on the market. They found the report to be a valuable tool because it targeted every major vendor and described their products in detail. This report was a very good source of information, providing information on each vendor's revenues, major customers, past activities (sales, product development, etc.), and their vision for the future. This report was supplemented with additional information provided by individual team members who went to various conventions and trade shows. Trade magazines, specialized documents, and the Internet were other sources of information that were also used. Based on all of the information that was gathered, the Acquisition Team was able to put together their long-list of vendors, which comprised 40 companies.

From this point, they proceeded to formulate a RFI based on the information from the TRI report, information provided from interviews with the key users, and the information that they had gathered. This RFI was less detailed and less formal than the RFQ which was issued later in the process.

Upon receipt of the responses from the various vendors to the RFI, the Acquisition Team evaluated each of them based on a set of established criteria. From this initial response, the Team rejected several potential vendors. A shorter long-list of vendors was then created.

The Team subsequently contacted the vendors based on this list and visited their sites. In conjunction with this, the Team also sent out a RFP to these vendors, which was more complex and detailed than the RFI. Within the RFP document, Telecom International went into great detail about what they wanted in terms of business needs and technical requirements. Upon receipt of the RFPs, each team member proceeded, individually, to evaluate them using a grid that they had to complete. Following the individual evaluations, the Team, as a whole, completed the grid. It is from this grid that the Team was able to construct the short-list of 5 vendors who were then invited to give demonstrations of their products.

13.3.3   One Solution Stands Out Above the Rest

After the visits to the various vendors and the evaluation of their responses, the Team proceeded to choose a finalist based on a weighting factor or scoring. In the end, a primary vendor (Keanan) was chosen for its package as it was the software solution best suited to meet Telecom International's needs.

13.3.4   But Wait, There's a Problem!

Business negotiations were then begun. However, it was very shortly after this point that the Acquisition process came to a halt. While Telecom International was able to reach agreement with the primary vendor on several issues, an impasse was reached. Since this acquisition was considered strategic, Telecom International regarded "code ownership" as a key issue in the negotiations. The cost of $10 million over 3 years was another key issue. As to the issue of code ownership, Telecom International's upper management felt very uncomfortable with the fact that Telecom International would be bound to a single vendor and their proprietary system for the next decade, a decision they felt would be tantamount to relinquishing control over an area of strategic importance to the vendor. Hence, Telecom International decided to break off negotiations with the vendor. They reversed their initial decision to purchase a packaged solution and decided instead to develop the system in-house.

In Chapter 14, the ES Acquisition Process that Telecom International partially completed will be more closely examined.

14

Detailed Analysis of The Case of Telecom International

Thishis chapter presents a detailed account of the processes and activities that Telecom International completed in its efforts to purchase an ES solution. Though unable to complete the Acquisition process, this case lends further support to the importance of rigorous planning for the process. It also illustrates the influence of new management on the overall Acquisition process.

14.1   TELECOM INTERNATIONAL'S PLANNING PROCESS

For Telecom International, planning marked the beginning of the Acquisition process. "Planning" encompassed all of the activities that Telecom International deemed necessary to pursue this endeavor. However, Telecom International's "planning" was not extensive. It was, however, very aggressive. According to the Project Manager–Technical:

> There was a global plan and at every phase, we reviewed it. We tried to follow it. It was very aggressive. . . . We also had some milestones in the plan and at every milestone, we reviewed our progress. Even before that, every week we had a little review, but at the milestone, we would review our progress and see if we had to change our plan. Concerning the time frame, we could say that it was like we had planned, although we did have some adjustments to make, but overall, it was good.

Their plan included meetings to determine schedules, priorities, participants, resources that would be required; activities and tasks that would need to be completed; types and sources of information to be sought; and so forth. Various tasks and activities needed to be accomplished such as the development of a list of requirements and meetings with internal customers that would be affected by the new systems. Additionally, studies were conducted to assess the strengths and weaknesses of Telecom International's existing legacy system, an RFI was created and sent out, and information was obtained from various sources:

> First of all, we analyzed the needs that we had within the company by meeting with key people who could give us information about our own requirements. We studied what we had already done. Since we already own some in-house legacy billing systems, we studied their weaknesses and their strengths. Briefly, we studied our own actual situation concerning the billing software and our billing needs. After that, we tried to get as much information as possible from specialized documentation, magazines, as well as key people and specialists, conventions, and so on. (Project Manager–Technical)

Though the level of planning may not have been as extensive as it could have been, according to the CIO, "there was some planning" and "it was not random." The Planning process as completed by Telecom International encompass the following issues:

- Participants
- Acquisition strategies
- Establishing evaluation criteria
- Establishing requirements
- Present status assessment

14.1.1   Participants

Individuals responsible for the Planning process had to identify who would participate in the Acquisition process. Participants were recruited from within the organization. These individuals were from the various departments that would be immediately affected by the new technology. Responsibility of the overall process was given to the CIO who had joined Telecom International after the decision had been made to purchase a software solution. The CIO, in turn, had to select the various managers, leaders, and individuals that would participate in the process. A primary concern of the CIO was to select individuals who would be responsible for designing the architecture of the new system.

There was some planning. I [CIO] basically selected the team who should do the project. I emphasized on having architects, software/hardware architects, because I believe only in one thing: system architecture (could be hardware architecture, software architecture), and if this is good, then you will have a good system. If the architecture is deficient at the beginning, whatever you ask later on, you will run into problems.

Telecom NA's Procurement department was also given a role in the Acquisition process. Although they did not participate until near the end of the Planning process, they assisted in analyzing the RFI and preparing the RFQ.

Towards the end of that process [planning], we got involved, here in Procurement, and we assisted them in finalizing the analysis of the RFI. From that information, we prepared a formal request for quotation having identified the potential companies that were likely to respond to such an RFQ. (Contract Administrator)

According to the Contract Administrator, Telecom NA's Procurement department customarily gets involved very early in an Acquisition process. However, in this case, they were not able to.

Initially, our internal architecture group prepared and issued an RFI. We, in Procurement, like to be involved in that process. We're not always successful in doing that because our internal customer will usually get the ball rolling initially. In this case, they did that. They also prepared the RFI and tested the market to see if there were companies out there that were prepared and capable of fulfilling an eventual request for quote.

Unbeknownst to the Acquisition Team, earlier involvement in the Acquisition process of Procurement would have enabled them to identify prospective vendors who did not meet some of Telecom International's organizational requirements, that is, who were not ISO 9000 certified vendors. According to the Contract Administrator:

We're ISO certified, so all the suppliers are required to be ISO certified as well, and this type of check should be done very early in the stages. Unfortunately, this was not done originally. While the companies that were eventually short-listed were very renowned companies—although, it comes to mind that one of them was rather small and there was a risk, and this came out more at the request for quote stage—it could have been identified as early as the RFI stage if Procurement had been involved a little earlier.

14.1.2   Acquisition Strategies

One strategy that Telecom International used was to limit access of the Acquisition Team members to the vendors. All access to the Team was channeled through one or two specific individuals who acted as the primary contacts:

> We also had an individual who was a specialist in searching for software packages available on the market. This person was our main contact with the vendors. We have a protocol that we followed. We also had someone from the legal side involved. At the RFQ stage, we considered that we needed to be very formal. At the RFI stage also, but it was less formal than the RFQ. So, at the RFQ stage, we involved someone from the legal side and we made certain that they understood our requirements and also our planning. At this point (the RFQ stage), we asked all the vendors to only call that person if they had any questions or anything else that they wanted from us.

One reason that they chose to use this strategy was because of their past experience in which some vendors targeted specific team members involved in previous projects and sent them "gifts." According to the Project Manager–Technical:

> Some vendors called us and they asked for the name of the team member to whom they wanted to send some gifts, and so on. Myself and [the Contract Administrator] decided that it was not a good idea, and so we never gave the name of the team members. We also asked the vendors not to send gifts to anyone, that it would not help them and might in fact hinder them.

Another of Telecom International's strategies was to visit the vendors' sites. According to the Project Manager–Technical, visiting the various vendors would enable them to further reduce the list of potential vendors and thus eliminate incompatible vendors and/or technologies/solutions early in the process. As to the benefits of having "face-to-face" meetings with the vendors, the Senior Adviser–Information Systems expressed the following about site visits to the vendors' locales:

> You get a very good feel face-to-face which you do not always get in an RFI. Some vendors are very, very good at responding, but face-to-face when you're dealing with them, you may find out that perhaps there are certain things you do not like about that vendor, not quite so much that you do not like, but that are not appropriate or makes them inappropriate for your particular need.

The site visits also provided another means for Telecom International to gather more information. As per the Project Manager–Technical:

> We decided to go and see the vendors even before they had time to respond to our RFQ. In our case, it was a good way of doing things because we collected a lot of information at their site. But, we had to be very cautious because they asked a lot of questions and if we wanted to be honest, we could not answer all of these questions because it was important for us that each vendor receive the same information when they replied to the RFP.

> So, we went to their site, but it was made very clear that we were not there to give them information, that we were there only to collect some information about their package and about their company. They had the opportunity to show us many things. I think that we surprised them in the sense that they expected to receive some VPs or people from upper management.

> In a sense, I think that we succeeded because they received more technical people and more end-users, people who knew exactly what our needs were and what they were looking for. We were not there to listen to their marketing speech. What we wanted to see was the concept behind their package.

14.1.3 Establishing Evaluation Criteria

This was very important to the Acquisition process and much time and effort went into establishing the evaluation criteria for the technological solution. Telecom International established evaluation and selection criteria for three distinct areas as stated by Telecom International's Project Manager–Technical:

> The three major categories that we always have are: (1) the functionality, (2) the vendors, and (3) the technological part of the package.

Vendor evaluation criteria included size, financial stability, reputation of the vendor, etc. Functional criteria dealt with the features of the software and included functionalities specific to front-end interfaces, user-friendliness, and so on. Technical criteria dealt with the specifics of systems architecture, performance, security, etc. Telecom International established all of the evaluation criteria (with very few exceptions) for all three areas early in the Acquisition process because the majority of it was needed for incorporation into the RFP and RFQ that would be sent to the vendors. These documents would be used to inform the vendors of the criteria against which their companies and their software solutions were to be evaluated.

A relevant note about Telecom International's evaluation criteria for vendors: Since Telecom International is ISO-certified, they have minimum standards in place that set forth the minimum requirements that they are to look for when considering a vendor-supplier. However, because the Contract Administrator was not involved in the Acquisition process until after the information search was completed and vendors were already contacted, the Acquisition Team was not aware of these minimum standards regarding the vendors. As per the Contract Administrator:

> We're ISO certified, so all the suppliers are required to be ISO certified as well, and this type of check should be done very early in the stages. Unfortunately, this was not done originally. While the companies that were eventually short-listed were very renowned companies—although, it comes to mind that one of them was rather small and there was a risk, and this came out more at the request for quote stage, but it could have been identified as early as the RFI stage if Procurement had been involved a little earlier. (Contract Administrator)

Consequently, this acquisition did not conform to these standards:

> I cannot say that it fully complied or followed our normal practices. It did partly, actually largely I would say, but I do not think that we can say that is was fully accomplished in accordance with the normalized rules that we follow. (Contract Administrator)

14.1.4   Establishing Requirements

Telecom International had to determine exactly what requirements would need to be met by the technology as well as what its own business requirements would be, both current and future.

We talked about what we wanted as our business processes; we talked about exactly what our requirements would be. The key people of our company were responsible to provide us with the information about what they were searching for, what they wanted in this package. It was the same thing with the vendors—we put the criteria that were important for us. We decided if we wanted to deal with someone who was in Canada or in the U.S.A. or in Europe. (Project Manager–Technical)

As part of their assessment, the Acquisition Team needed to consider the international context in which the software was to be used and the requirements that this would impose. They also looked at their current resources—what they had and what they lacked. They looked at what they wanted that was not being met by their current systems. According to the Project Manager–Technical:

We studied what we had already done. Since we already own some in-house legacy billing systems, we studied their weaknesses and their strengths. Briefly, we studied our own actual situation concerning the billing software and our billing needs.

This was also supported by the CIO who stated:

First, of course, you have to define the requirements and come up with your own RFI and RFP. You have to write specifications as detailed as possible. Usually, you deal with the marketers, the finance people, and ask them what they want. What type of services do we want to offer? What are the volumes involved? What type of invoices do you want—do you want them on a monthly basis? What kind of changes, modifications—everything. So you define the specs.

14.1.5   Contingencies

There was full intention on the part of the Acquisition Team to complete the Acquisition process and choose a software solution. Hence, there was no contingency plan per se. It was only when the decision was made to abort the process that Telecom International resorted to an "unwritten" contingent alternative, that being to develop a solution in-house. According to the Project Leader (U.S.):

The only alternative left to us was to develop internally . . . the reason that they stopped there was because the cost was determined to be too high, and so our direction then was to do internal development.

Present Status Assessment

As has already been presented, Telecom International did examine their existing status prior to the acquisition. It was unclear in this case, however, whether Telecom International had determined the staffing requirements that would be needed in order to successfully complete the Acquisition process. As to their information technology requirements (i.e., their infrastructure from both a software and hardware perspective), they studied their present system, identified its strengths and weaknesses, and assessed what would be needed to support (and interface with) the new technology.

14.1.6   Recap of the Planning Process

Planning was valuable in implementing the other stages of the Acquisition process. The acquisition strategies helped guide the Information Search and the Selection processes. With the requirements and the evaluation and selection criteria established, Telecom International was able to proceed to using this information, in part, for narrowing their list of vendors and constructing the RFP, doing evaluations of the vendors' RFI responses, and subsequently, the vendors' RFP and RFQ responses. Certain of these elements or tasks worked hand-in-hand, such as those for selecting and narrowing the list of vendors—Telecom International gathered information from all sources, internal and external, including information obtained from professional research groups and information determined in establishing evaluation criteria requirements. This was also the case for the evaluation of the functional and technical aspects of the software. Several deliverables arose as a result of the Planning Process, some of which include:

- RFI, RFP, and RFQ
- Long-list of vendors
- Determination of the selection and evaluation criteria
- Formation of the Acquisition Team
- Determination of acquisition strategies

14.2   INFORMATION SEARCH PROCESS

For internal information sources, Telecom International gathered information from various sources within the organization that included individual users and team members. These internal sources provided information primarily on the organization's existing requirements at all of the levels and in all of the areas that the technology would impact.

As for external sources, these were sought to provide information about software solutions that might best meet their needs. According to the Project Manager–Technical, Telecom International engaged the services of a professional research group, TRI, to conduct a marketplace search:

> We bought a study by a company called TRI. This company asked us to answer several questions about our billing—our process, our systems, and so on, after which they put together a study of all the major telecommunication companies and about the way TRI works with their customers, their business processes, and their software. We obtained a lot of information from that report. We did not, however, rely only on the information from this report. We also referred to other sources of information such as magazines and so on.

In addition to the TRI report, Telecom International also gathered information from such varied sources as publications, trade shows, conferences, references and site visits, the Internet, and professional research services such as Gartner Group and Meta Group.

> We have dealt with Meta Group before and also the Gartner Group. In this case, we also had other sources. I have other contacts and also articles in various business journals, finance journals—we also some of that to work with as well—of course, the Internet is a big one. (Senior Adviser–Information Systems)

One particularly interesting source of information that Telecom International used was their competitors. Even though this was somewhat difficult for them to do, Telecom International found them to be a useful source:

> You can also call some of your competitors and speak with them, like we did with BT (Bell Telephone) or Sprint. It's not always easy, for obvious reasons, because there are secrets between competitors, but I found out that there is also a need to talk with competitors that everyone has and it is a good source of information also. People from various companies who have experience came up with some good information. (Project Manager–Technical)

Telecom International also used the RFI to obtain information from the vendors. In addition, Telecom International used the RFI as a means of narrowing their list of vendors. Following the review of the responses that they had received from the 40 or so vendors to whom they had sent their RFI, Telecom

International's Acquisition Team was able to eliminate many vendors from further consideration.

As yet another source of information, the Acquisition Team did visits to the vendors' offices, and this is discussed relative to the RFPs that were sent out as part of the Selection process.

It is important to note that the credibility of the sources of information was an important factor in the search process. To Telecom International, the credibility of the source of information was important considering the amount of readily available and often, unreliable information that one has access to. As such, they found TRI to be a credible source of information and, according to Telecom International's Project Manager–Technical, they found the TRI report to be a valuable source of information:

> TRI's report . . . was a very good source of information. Every major vendor was on this report with a lot of details about their revenues, their major customers, what they had done in the past, where they were going. This report was a very good source of information.

14.3   SELECTION PROCESS

Several iterations of screenings were done by Telecom International's Acquisition Team during the Information Search process prior to arriving at a shorter long-list of vendors. To determine which vendors could supply the type of software solution that Telecom International was seeking, information on both the vendors and their technologies was screened using selection and evaluation criteria.

According to the Director–Billing Services and Outsourcing, Telecom International's Selection process was conducted in two phases—the first upon receipt of the RFIs from the vendors and the second with the RFP. With the RFI, an evaluation was done based on a set of high-level criteria that were established a priori in the Planning process. The RFP, on the other hand, contained more refined criteria and was used to arrive at their short-list of vendors.

> It happened in two stages, one was the RFI process and then the RFP process. In the RFI, we did have a list of criteria to evaluate the vendors, and this was at a relatively high level versus the RFP. (Project Leader [US])

According to the Project Manager–Technical, the objective of the Selection process was to create a short-list of vendors (based on the evaluation of the vendors' RFP responses) to whom would be sent the RFQ:

> Individually, we evaluated the RFI [and RFP] responses according to our grids. We then met to compare our responses and to challenge ourselves. We came to a decision and we built a short-list. We presented this short-list to our upper management and they gave us the approval to continue. . . . We showed them exactly what our processes were and they agreed that we should continue in that direction. After that, we built the RFQ . . . and we sent it to our short-listed vendors.

Additional information was gathered on some of the vendors and their software solutions (functional and technical aspects) by means of site visits to certain vendors' offices. The visits coincided with the sending of the RFP (but preceded the return of the RFP responses from the vendors) and provided the Acquisition Team with additional information for their evaluations.

Telecom International reviewed the RFI responses from the group of 40 vendors that were sent the RFI, then narrowed that list of possible candidates to considerably fewer vendors. From among those, they were able to single out the vendors whose software solutions could most likely and best suit Telecom International's needs, and these were visited for more information. As related by Telecom International's Project Manager:

> From here, we built an RFI. . . . Once completed, we sent the RFI to about 40 vendors who responded to it. . . . We studied the responses that we received from the vendors. . . . Following this, we selected some vendors and met with them. We went to their sites to see what they were doing and what they could do for us. We asked them questions but we did not answer any of their questions to us. . . . We asked the same questions to all of the vendors. We did not give them too much information, just the basics. . . . In parallel, we sent an RFP with many questions, though more complex, more detailed. . . . So, then they needed to reply to the RFP. By the time we received the responses to the RFP, we already had a good idea of what they could do for us.

The Selection process began when Telecom International received the RFI and, subsequent to that, the RFP responses back from the vendors. With the RFI and RFP responses in hand, Telecom International then proceeded with the paper evaluation of the vendors' packages. According to the Project Manager–Technical, once this was accomplished, they presented their results to Upper

Management for authorization to proceed with the process. It was at this point that Upper Management requested the Acquisition Team to conduct site visits of the short-listed vendors:

> We presented this short-list to our upper management and they gave us the approval to continue in the direction we were pursuing . . . it was at the request of our upper management that we decided to go on site. (Project Manager–Technical)

Telecom International did perform early high-level screenings of information to narrow the field of possible vendors/solutions. Telecom International's Project Manager–Technical, Senior Adviser–Information Systems, and Director–Billing Services and Outsourcing all provided examples of this activity:

> The first one was to select the right vendors to whom we wanted to send the RFI. With all of the information that we had, and knowing exactly what our needs were, this step was somewhat easy. Even so, we finished with 40 vendors, which is quite a few. (Project Manager–Technical)

> In terms of information for the RFI, we sorted all the players there that we needed. We had representatives from each of the major business areas, and I guess it was just a matter of deciding what information we wanted to include and how we wanted to include it. (Senior Adviser– Information Systems)

> In the RFI, we did have a list of criteria to evaluate the vendors, and this was at a relatively high level versus the RFP. (Director–Billing Services and Outsourcing)

14.4   EVALUATION PROCESS

There were three distinct types of evaluation conducted by Telecom International: vendor, functionality, and technical. Evaluation criteria for all three types were developed in the Planning phase of the Acquisition process.

As part of the Vendor evaluation, each of the vendors was evaluated in terms of their financial stability, certification, etc., based on reports from D&B and TRI as well as other information. According to the Contract Administrator, the vendors were asked to complete a detailed questionnaire that would determine if the vendor could be considered a certified supplier:

> We have here a procedure whereby a supplier becomes a "privileged" supplier or a certified supplier. Once he's got that certification, he's listed on our formal bidders list. The way we do that is as follows. We have several criteria. One of them is, "Have we worked with this company before?" . . . We also have a very detailed questionnaire that we forward to the supplier. We asked him to respond to it and then we evaluate that. Depending on his answers, on his financial profile, and so forth, we determine whether he can be a certified supplier.

While the evaluation of each vendor's financial stability rested with the Contract Administrator, other aspects of the Vendor evaluation rested with the team members who evaluated the various responses to the RFI and who had met with some of the different vendors. In addition to the quantifiable factors such as sales volume and the size of the company ("If you have some companies with two people and they've only been around a year, that has a part in it as well."), according to the Senior Adviser–Information Systems, consideration was also given to qualitative factors such as the "quality of the response, the appropriateness of the response to your particular requirements," as well as the impressions made during face-to-face meetings with the vendors:

> There were also visits from the vendors. You get a very good feel face-to-face which you do not always get in an RFI. Some vendors are very, very good at responding, but face-to-face when you're dealing with them, you may find out that perhaps there are certain things you do not like about that vendor, not quite so much that you do not like, but that are not appropriate or makes them inappropriate for your particular need.

Although Telecom International had planned to conduct extensive functional and technical evaluations of the software (during in-house product demonstrations), this stage of the Acquisition process was never reached. However, Telecom International did conduct progressively refined, albeit higher level, evaluations of the software packages in addition to the evaluations they conducted on the vendors themselves. Telecom International developed a "fast-track grid" (Project Manager–Technical) for evaluating the RFI and it was used during the Selection process to reduce the long-list of vendors to a shorter long-list. This grid contained very high-level criteria for evaluating the vendors and the functional and technical aspects of the software packages. For their evaluation of the RFP responses, the Acquisition Team further refined the criteria to a more detailed level and these were reflected in the functional and technical evaluation matrices that they developed.

Coupled with the matrices that were developed to evaluate the RFP responses, Telecom International used their vendor site visits as another means to evaluate the vendors and their software. In accordance with a suggestion from Telecom International's CIO, the Acquisition Team spent a full day with certain vendors. The Team was accompanied by "three or four guys from IT, one specializing in hardware, another one in software, another one in architecture, and another one in databases or something similar" (CIO). The Team was then to

> . . . compare what they tell you and show you to what you have on paper to see if it's the real thing. (CIO)

For the final RFQ, the criteria were even further refined and the evaluation matrix reflected this as well. Other tools that Telecom International developed to assist them in their Evaluation process were questionnaires and comparative lists.

As a last stage to the Evaluation process, Telecom International had planned to have the short-listed vendors conduct extensive in-house demonstrations of their software packages. However, an Upper Management decision aborted the process just prior to this stage. As per the Project Manager–Technical:

> After that, we asked for a demo only from those who were on our short-list . . . we were ready to contact the vendors again for demonstrations [in-house] and for going into more details in certain areas. However, at this point, upper management told us not to continue with the project for the billing package. So, at that point, we stopped the project.

During the Planning process, in preparation for the different stages of the Evaluation process, Telecom International developed evaluation matrices and assigned weights and scores to the various areas of evaluation. The Project Manager–Technical describes what they did:

> We assigned weights to everything—weight on criteria, weight on the items. The grids needed to represent exactly what our needs were, and so we put a lot of effort into them." Telecom International's Director–Billing Services and Outsourcing added: "We had come up with a weighting mechanism for each of the functional requirements and a scoring mechanism for each item.

14.5   CHOICE PROCESS

Although Telecom International did not complete the Acquisition process, according to the Project Manager–Technical, they had gotten to the point where "we were ready to give our recommendation." Unfortunately, though, the process was halted at this point. As per the Contract Administrator:

> The project got as far as a short-list, doing an internal evaluation (commercial, contractual, financial, and technical) and recommendations were about to be formulated, but the project was put on hold for other considerations.

Among the reasons that were given for the project being put on hold were ownership of code, the cost of the software, and other contractual obligations which were not to Telecom International's liking.

> One of the reasons was that it would be too expensive over a three-year period. Other reasons included that one of our requirements was that we own the code and no vendor wanted to give us the code, at least not too much of it; and then there were also some contractual obligations that we did not like. (CIO)

It was made clear to us, however, by both the Project Manager–Technical and the Director–Billing Services and Outsourcing that regarding a final choice, the Team had indeed narrowed their scope to the point that if they had to make a recommendation, they knew who they would be looking at—"we now know exactly who the best vendor was" (Project Manager–Technical).

14.6   NEGOTIATION PROCESS

Since Telecom International did not reach closure in the Acquisition process, they did not settle on a final choice nor were legal contract negotiations finalized. During the Planning process, preparations had been made for the final part of the Acquisition process, that is, the Legal Negotiations, and according to the Project Manager–Technical:

> [The Contract Administrator] was our person responsible for that and we built a strategy together. We had a few meetings, myself, [the Contract Administrator], the [MIS Director], and we prepared ourselves for negotiation. It was very important the way we were going to negotiate. We made preparations.

The following quotation from the Director–Billing Services and Outsourcing is also relevant to the Legal Negotiations that would have been completed had the acquisition been finalized:

> We had initiated talks with the top vendor—while their product did win out overall, we wanted to explore the areas where they did fall short, what type of customized development they could or would be willing to do for us and we were working to get a cost and time frame for that. Now the . . . not quite contract negotiations but pre-contract negotiations to really understand if they were to implement what we needed, what were we talking in terms of time and cost? If the decision was positive and we moved forward, we would have entered into contract negotiations.

Telecom International used these less formal negotiations to discuss all issues of concern with the short-listed vendors. According to the Project Manager–Technical:

> You see, we have to remember, that every time you talk with the vendors, when you say to them that they were on the short-list, you can say that you have already started your negotiations with them. You have to keep in mind that you will try to build some kind of business relationship with them.

It was during the informal Business Negotiations, however, that an impasse was reached. For issues that included cost and ownership of code, among others, Telecom International aborted the Acquisition process and the purchase was never finalized.

14.7   INFLUENCES

Several influences were noted in the case of Telecom International. They are categorized here according to their effects on the Acquisition process or the Acquisition Team.

14.7.1   Influences on the Acquisition Process

The following items had varying influences on Telecom International's ES Acquisition Process:

- Geographically dispersed team members
- New management

- Economic factors
- Ownership of code
- Software support for geographically dispersed global operations

Geographically Dispersed Team Members

The relatively new phenomenon of international teams or geographical separation between team members also had an impact on the process. As explained by Telecom International's Contract Administrator:

> Another factor that played an influence is the fact that this relationship [Telecom International–Telecom Inc.] is relatively new and working together is still on the learning curve. There are still some adjustments to be made. So, that also played a role.

New Management

New management, in the form of a new CIO, was another influence that played an important part in Telecom International's Acquisition process. The CIO influenced upper management's decision not to proceed with the acquisition and consequently, the outcome of the process. This influence may be attributed to the CIO's extensive experience in developing similar systems for other organizations within the telecommunication industry:

> At Sprint, we designed and . . . built for $6 million, a network management system, fully integrated.

Although the CIO was new to the organization, he allowed the Acquisition Team to continue with the process without impeding it. He did, however, guide the team, offering suggestions at various stages of the process.

> Let's do a genuine, very sincere, non-biased study of the market [speaking to upper management]. That was why I did not interfere with the Team. I just gave them some guidance so that they did not go completely astray and in the wrong direction, but I let them do it. (CIO)

The final decision, however, came from upper management (Telecom International's President) to put the project on hold and eventually, abort it.

Economic Factors

The costs associated with the packaged software influenced Telecom International's decision process.

Ownership of Code

The issue of code ownership also influenced the decision process. According to Director–Billing Services and Outsourcing:

> . . . the cost factor as well as having full control and ownership of the software. Had we purchased "off-the-shelf," you do not have the control of the software, you are dependent to some extent on an outside vendor.

Also, according to the CIO:

> When you buy a software from a vendor, if you are trying on this software and you can own the code, wherever the software comes from—India, Pakistan, Taiwan, France, who cares as long as you have the documentation, you understand what it is, and . . . you own it.

Given the importance of source code ownership to Telecom International, the impasse that was reached on this issue during the negotiations was one of the reasons that the process was aborted.

Software Support for Geographically Dispersed Global Operations

It was of major importance to Telecom International that the vendor be capable of supporting the software in Telecom International's geographically dispersed global operations. As one of Telecom International's criteria for the evaluation of the vendors, this factor influenced their selection process.

> As to influences, physical location—the ability of the vendor to support [Telecom International] in multiple locations in North America as well as overseas, this had some influence as well. . . . I think a vendor was liable to support those locations. (Director–Billing Services and Outsourcing)

14.7.2   Influences on the Acquisition Team

The following items had varying influences on Telecom International's Acquisition Team:

- Acquisition Team composition
- New management
- Final authority outside the Acquisition Team

Acquisition Team Composition

The composition of the Acquisition Team influenced the Acquisition process. Many of the individuals involved on the Team had prior experience with different parts of the process and had also worked together before on projects. According to the Senior Advisor–Information Systems, these two factors influenced the process:

> The team was very experienced in this area in terms of the whole RFI process. We had worked together before, so we had that going for us as well.

New Management

As previously mentioned, new management had an impact on Telecom International's Acquisition Team.

Final Authority Outside the Acquisition Team

Another influencing factor was that the final authority rested outside the Acquisition Team. This was visible within the case and it was from this authority that the decision came not to proceed with the acquisition.

14.8   SUMMARY

The Acquisition process for complex packaged software of this magnitude was a new experience for Telecom International. Working with project management techniques and tools, Telecom International's Acquisition Team created and structured a rigorous and formal process that would have led to the acquisition of a software solution.

Yes, there was a global plan and at every phase, we reviewed it. We tried to follow it. It was very aggressive and we realized, at one point, that it was perhaps a little too aggressive, . . . At this point, we reviewed our schedule . . . and we changed our time frame a little bit. . . . We also had some milestones in the plan and at every milestone, we reviewed our progress. Even before that, every week we had a little review, but at the milestone, we would review our progress and see if we had to change our plan. (Project Manager–Technical)

One of the Team's objectives throughout the process was to set the foundation for a long-term relationship with the primary vendor. This relationship was considered by Telecom International to be important to the long-term success of the acquisition.

You have to keep in mind that you will try to build some kind of business relationship with them. (Project Manager–Technical)

In spite of these efforts and the diligence of the Team, a successful conclusion to the Acquisition process was not reached. Because of the outcome, or rather, the manner in which the process was terminated, an unpleasant feeling of dissatisfaction still remained with the Team members. This feeling can be attributed to the lack of closure they experienced as a result of the decision by Telecom International's upper management to halt the process before the Team could submit their final recommendation. With little doubt, past experience (as in the case of International Air) will be an influencing factor for individuals involved in the next software Acquisition process that is undertaken by Telecom International.

15 Choice and Negotiations

Well, you're nearly there. By this point in the Acquisition process, the majority of the work will have been done, leaving only the final choice of vendor/solution to be made and the negotiations to be completed.

In this chapter, we will begin by presenting what each of the cases did for the Choice process and the tools and techniques that they used to arrive at their final choices. Then we will present the Negotiations process and the issues and factors that should be considered when negotiating with vendors.

15.1 CHOICE PROCESS

The Choice process consists of the final choice of vendor/solution and represents the culmination of all of the activities and processes that were discussed in the preceding chapters. It is also a process that is pretty straightforward. What complicates it, though, is the number of issues, criteria, opinions/perspectives, etc. that need to be factored into the final choice. By this point, however, these will or should have all been considered and documented or scored in some manner. All that now remains is to aggregate them and do a final tabulation. "No problem," you say, but as we have noted from at least one of the cases, this was not as easy a task to accomplish as one might think. Once the final calculation is done, though, the Acquisition Team has its final answer.

To arrive at their choice, each of the acquisition teams used various methodologies. In the case of International Air, the Acquisition Team used a software tool ("Decision Pad") that enabled it to do a pair-wise comparison of the following six evaluation categories that were weighted relative to each other:

- Functional
- Technical
- Implementation
- BPR
- Risks
- Price

While it was noted by the Project Control Officer that the requirements of other types of projects (hardware acquisitions, for example) are usually few enough to use a spreadsheet, such was not the case with this software acquisition project. Moreover, with "so many people involved who all wanted their views known, in terms of the evaluations," that there probably would have been "a hundred views of the spreadsheet and the best I could have done was some sort of arithmetic," the Decision Pad software helped to simplify the task of arriving at a final decision.

First, managers and/or key users from three different areas (organizational/management, technical, and functional) went through each of the categories and assigned weights according to their perspectives. So, for example, from management, the Project Director and the Director of Enterprise Systems/IT could have determined for "Global Requirements" versus "Cost," on a scale of 1 to 10, that they would give "Cost" 7 of the 10 points in comparison to "Global Requirements." In this same manner, each of the other criteria were addressed, compared, and weighted. Management's "organizational" perspective resulted in the International Air or "business" view. Similarly, and again for all of the criteria, a technical view was obtained from International Air's Technical Team and a functional view from two of International Air's project managers for this project. In all, three weighted models were developed to reflect each of the different perspectives (a business view, a functional view, and a technical view). Then, following the functional and technical demonstrations, calculations were done of the scores assessed for all of the evaluation criteria against each of the weighted models to arrive at the final results. Although some skewing was possible, as observed by the Project Control Officer, such as when an evaluation resulted in a strongly technical view, it was not enough to significantly change the overall ranking of the vendors.

As for ESC, they used a scoring matrix which included their main evaluation categories of functionality, cost, integration with other applications, ability to implement quickly and effectively, and vendor strength (see Table 15–1). The weights for each category were first determined by the Acquisition Team. Then, in order to make certain that the Team's expectations in terms of these weightings were consistent with ESC's executives, the Project Manager–Financial System also had the executives go through the same exercise of determining the weights. Although the executives put a little more weight on the "Cost" and a little bit less on "Functionality," for the most part, the weightings by both the

Team and the executives were quite close. Separate scorings were then done for each of the main categories. For example, to determine the final choice for "functionality," a calculation was done of the scores from the Acquisition Team's evaluations of the 2-day scripted demonstrations and the users evaluations. Approximately 50 users were involved in each of the demonstrations, each of which filled out a matrix, scoring each item under evaluation on a scale of 1 to 5. To arrive at the final choice for "cost," information from the top two vendors' cost proposals was reviewed and scored. So it was that each of the main categories received final scorings. Then, through a series of multi-voting techniques, where every member of the project team had an equal vote, on each of the main categories, a final choice of vendor/solution was arrived at. User evaluation scores were also factored into the final choice.

The final results for ESC were as follows: Oracle won out for "Integration" and "Vendor Strength" whereas PeopleSoft won out for "Ease of Implementation" and "Cost."

Table 15–1   Example of Choice or Recommendation Matrix

	Functionality	Cost	Integration with Other Applications	Ability to Implement Quickly and Effectively	Vendor Strength	Sum	Percentage of Total	Other Considerations
Functionality	X	10	10	5	0.2	25.20	39.7%	Reference checks
Cost	0.1	X	0.2	0.2	0.2	0.70	1.1%	Training
Integration with other applications	0.1	5	X	1	5	11.10	17.5%	Technical assistance
Ability to implement quickly and effectively	0.2	5	1	X	10	16.20	25.5%	Technical architecture
Sum	5	5	0.2	0.1	X	10.30	16.2%	
	5.40	25.00	11.40	6.30	15.40	63.50	100.0%	

Rating Scale: 10 = Significantly more important; 5 = more important; 1 = About the same importance; 1/5 = less important; 1/10 = Significantly less important.

Directions: Begin with the first row (Functionality). Compare this criterion against the other four using the rating scale. Enter the appropriate score into the cell, then enter the reciprocal score into the reciprocal cell.

As for Telecom International, they used an evaluation grid that comprised several evaluation criteria for each of their main categories: functionality, technical performance, and vendor's general characteristics.

Keller, by comparison, invited their top vendor candidate back to do an intensive 2-day "scripted" demonstration as the means of confirming their choice. During this demonstration, they tracked the outcome of simulations using a basic evaluation form (used by the members of the Selection Team, the Supervisors, and the EAC). Following the demonstration, they had all participants complete a qualitative survey to gather feedback and impressions about the software.

Once determined, the Acquisition Team's final choice was presented as a "recommendation" to a Steering Committee or Board of Directors for approval, and this was noted in three of the cases (International Air, ESC, and Keller). With the final choice of vendor and solution being made and approval having been received, formal negotiations were initiated with the vendor-of-choice.

Before we proceed to the next section, we want to take a moment to discuss a human factor that is involved in all types of decision situations. No matter how much time and effort will be poured into this project by the Acquisition Team members, let them be assured of at least one thing—in the end, not everybody is going to be happy with the final choice. While most people will be, there will always be one or a few individuals who won't. That's just the way it is. The goal, though, is to minimize the number of disgruntled users in your organization who are dissatisfied with the final choice. So, what is important to remember is that if the users are made to feel like their input is being seriously considered (and not just paid "lip service" to) throughout the course of the Acquisition process, then overall acceptance of the final choice of solution will be greater. In addition to this, we will discuss in Chapter 16 how user acceptance of the final choice from the Acquisition process plays a critical role in the successful implementation of the technology.

15.2   NEGOTIATION PROCESS

When most people think about "negotiations," they normally think of them as occurring when they are close to making a final choice, or only after their final choice has been made. But what if they were to look at negotiations in a different light—what if we were to suggest to you that your negotiations with a vendor really start from the moment you first make contact with them? Would that change how you deal with them? We think it would.

First of all, this change in perspective entails a "shift" in consciousness and takes those who participate in the process from a more "passive" role to a more "active" role in their exchanges with vendors. This does not mean, however, that you need to become more outwardly aggressive or controlling in your interactions with the vendors. What this does mean is that instead of waiting until the end of the Acquisition process to "take hold of the reins," so-to-speak, during final contract negotiations with the primary vendor-of-choice, you would be assuming more of an active role right from the start of the process. In practical terms, this means that your "listening" would become sharper—you'd pick up on those smaller, seemingly insignificant yet important details that are often "dropped" by vendors in conversation, and make note of them; your requests/questions would become more precise, and so on. It also means that you should "talk" less. Extra care needs to be taken to disclose as little private information about your plans as possible—don't show all your cards. While you would want to disclose that you have an approved and adequate budget, for example, you would not necessarily tell vendors your budgetary upper limit, since knowing this figure could discourage vendors from giving larger discounts later in the final negotiations. Your disclosures, therefore, need to be balanced in your efforts to gain credibility with the vendors as a "serious" buyer. Also, encourage all staff who are involved in the Acquisition process to show similar discretion.

Further, we believe that looking at negotiations from this perspective could also inject a little extra "zeal"—like a psychological boost—into the Acquisition Team's efforts for the entire Acquisition process. It could also turn out to be that extra "edge" the Team is looking for in its dealings with the vendors.

> - Negotiations begin with first contact with vendors
> - Assume a more active role
> - Listen attentively
> - Monitor what you say, what you disclose
> - Ask pointed questions
> - Take notes

As to the negotiations themselves, we believe that this process actually consists of two distinct processes, Business (informal) and Legal (formal), and this belief is supported by each of the cases. Moreover, the cases show that the Business Negotiations are continuous throughout most of the ES Acquisition Process, beginning first with "casual" (yet purposeful) exchanges and progressing to more "serious" interactions as the Acquisition Teams draw closer to their final choices.

15.2.1 Business Negotiations

One of the objectives (though not directly implied) of the Business Negotiations is to lay the foundation, through ongoing discussions and the exchange of information, for the eventual long-term relationship between the organization and the vendor-of-choice. The character of the relationships that develop between the vendors and the organization unfolds as the Business Negotiations progress (concurrent with other Acquisition processes) and enables both parties to determine whether a long-term relationship is possible.

One question that was raised in this regard by all of the Teams was, "Can we [our organization] work with them [the vendor]?" The vendor-of-choice, in all of the cases presented here, satisfied this compatibility requirement. The long-term relationship with the vendor was also viewed as a factor that could not be overlooked during the Acquisition process.

The main purpose of the Business Negotiations is to work out all of the terms and conditions that are critical to the business side of the project, which includes everything from product support to user training to pricing to other key terms and conditions. As alluded to at the beginning of this section, we have the following view regarding Business Negotiations: From the moment an organization makes contact with a vendor, negotiations have begun. Why? Because each interaction with a vendor, however casual, paves the way for the next and each is cumulative. Each interaction with a vendor also entails an exchange of some sort of information. As we see them, the Business Negotiations begin right from the initial contact that is made with a vendor, and so, in effect, when several vendors are contacted, you will be in Business Negotiations with each of them. Beginning first with simple requests for information and some back and forth discussions, enough information will be collected to enable you to eliminate vendors who are either unlikely or unable to meet your organization's needs. Remember, you will be assessing, with each interaction with the different vendors, just how flexible each vendor is and the changes (if any) that they will be able and willing to make to their solutions in order to fit them to your needs. You will be negotiating or "bartering" on the price (as we saw in the case of Keller) for those modifications, and/or for support, upgrades, modules, number of licenses, training, etc.—in short, everything that will or should eventually end up in your final contract. As the issues are discussed, make note of what is said and informally agreed to. The goal is that difficult issues are broached with the vendors *prior* to the Acquisition Team arriving at its final choice.

For example, as we saw in the case of Telecom International, the issue of "code ownership" should have been broached with each of the vendors prior to when it was finally raised; that is, late in the Acquisition process. If it had been, the Acquisition Team would have been aware of the vendors (if any, among those it had short-listed) who were agreeable on that issue and could have possibly avoided the outcome that they experienced.

Also, don't take anything for granted or make assumptions, because you may end up paying dearly for it later on (i.e., either during the course of the implementation or afterward). Question everything and be willing to ask the seemingly "stupid" or "obvious" questions. Yes, ask questions. If, for example, a question pops into your head and it's in some way related to the acquisition or the ES's implementation, ask it. That's your instinct telling you that the question needs to be asked, so don't discount it. You might be surprised if the answer you get is not the one you expected. Even if it is, the answer will simply confirm what you thought it was—no harm done. Remember, this is not the time to start putting on airs and pretending that you know it all. Also, at the other extreme, don't go into this process naively thinking and hoping that the vendor is going to offer you everything "on a silver platter" and tell you everything you need to know, without you having to break a sweat. That is the "bury your head in the sand" or the "pipe dream" approach to negotiations. You have to be prepared. You have to ask questions. After all, your organization is investing a lot of time and money into this effort, and so, it is in your best interest not to leave any stone unturned. Make sure that your "due diligence" is indeed diligent!

Finally, while your most serious Business Negotiations are underway with the primary vendor-candidate, they could and even should also be transpiring with your secondary vendor-candidate. In the event that Business Negotiations do not go as expected with the primary vendor-candidate, you will have your secondary vendor-candidate to fall back on. Otherwise, you will be left with returning again to other parts of the Acquisition process to identify one or more suitable vendors/solutions. A secondary choice also ensures you are not placing the primary vendor-candidate in a monopolistic pricing position.

Business Negotiations

- Begin with first contacts with all vendors
- Lay the foundation for the long-term relationship with the vendor
- Enable a determination of your compatibility with the vendor
- Question everything as it relates to acquisition and the implementation
- Begin casually and progressively become more serious
- Most serious Business Negotiations occur with the primary and secondary vendor-candidates concurrently
- Opportunity to work out all critical terms and conditions

In each of the cases, it could be seen that the Acquisition Teams entered a Business Negotiation phase with each of the vendors that concluded with their choice or recommendation of a preferred vendor solution. Each of the cases, with the exception of Telecom International, concluded this phase successfully and proceeded to the Legal Negotiations.

For Telecom International, it was during the Business Negotiations that discussions with their vendor-of-choice broke down—an impasse was reached on issues of cost and code ownership that caused the negotiations to fail. For International Air, the objective of the Business Negotiations was to produce a final revised proposal, which they called a "business understanding document," that detailed everything that had been negotiated (final price, milestones, implementation issues, and terms and conditions, among others) throughout the process. This document, which included the Acquisition Team's recommendation of their preferred vendor solution (based on the results of their Evaluation process), was presented to the Steering Committee for approval. Following approval by the Steering Committee of the recommended vendor solution, this document, which also had the same purpose as a letter of intent, was presented to International Air's vendor-of-choice and marked the starting point of the Legal Negotiations.

15.2.2   Legal Negotiations

As rigorous as the Business Negotiations are, the Legal Negotiations are always even more so. It is the Legal Negotiations that lead to the finalized formal contract. The issues that are dealt with in the Legal Negotiations include all of those that were included in the RFP as well as others, most of which are listed next. Many of these issues were also raised in the 1995 SIM[1] study on software contracting practices.

- Data ownership
- Time-dependent keys
- Software license assignment to a new corporate entity
- Software usage by a business unit formerly within the corporate organization which has been sold
- The right to re-assign software licenses within the corporate entity
- Contingencies for what would occur regarding support, upgrades, etc., should the organization acquire another company or divest or spin-off a division, or if the vendor goes bankrupt, or other similar situations arise

---

1. The Society of Information Management: Working Group on Information Technology Procurement. (1995). *Current practices in software contracting.* School of Information Studies, Syracuse University.

- Duplication and distribution (i.e., software license re-assignment)
- Development and ownership of derivative works (i.e., code changes, translations, adaptations) of the software
- Source Code ownership
- Maintenance costs, e.g., increases to support fees
- Other costs
- Support
- Training
- Upgrades
- Escrow Agreements (i.e., source code agreement)
- Non-performance Clauses (i.e., response time)
- Assurances (i.e., forward compatibility of the software)
- Indemnification
- Intellectual and industrial property:
  - License for any third-party software application used under this contract: The vendor guarantees that the organization may use such software application without infringing upon any third-party intellectual property rights
  - The vendor warrants that the services provided to the organization shall not infringe upon any patent, trademark, trade secret, copyright, or any other right relating to intellectual property rights in force, recorded, or recognized
  - The vendor accepts to indemnify the organization for all losses, damages, or all liabilities arising from the infringement or alleged infringement of such patents, trademarks, trade secrets, copyrights, or any other pertaining to intellectual property rights
- Warranties, liabilities (i.e., viruses)
- Insurance: The vendor agrees to acquire and keep in force at its expense insurance such as programmers errors and omissions insurance, comprehensive general liability insurance, and workers compensation insurance, and to provide evidence of such insurance
- Termination for convenience
- Termination for cause
- Acceptance procedure
- Clauses subsisting beyond termination
- Subcontractors
- Arbitration

The following example speaks to the issue of "Development and ownership of derivative works (i.e., code changes, translations, adaptations) of the software" as presented in the above listing of contractual issues. We present it also as a "what if" scenario for your organization to think about—this actually happened to two organizations (that shall remain anonymous) that we know of.

> **You have decided to acquire an ES solution from your vendor-of-choice and you ask the vendor to either customize the solution or create a new module (because the vendor is unable or unwilling to modify any of their existing modules with the particular functionalities that your organization needs).**

The questions that we raise to you from this "what if" situation are:

- Who has ownership of the customized solution or new module?
- Will this "new" solution help you to gain a competitive advantage?
- Does the vendor have the right to sell this solution to your competitors?
- If not, would you want them to? If so, would you be entitled to compensation?
- What if the vendor asks your permission to add the new functionalities or module to their product line, do you do it with or without compensation?
- Also, do you wish to keep the rights to the technology?

If this type of situation arises for your organization, these questions may need to be raised during the Business Negotiations and carried into the Legal Negotiations process. Also, your organization's legal experts may be better able to deal with these issues.

As a final point, our philosophy is that, if you do not ask, you will not know, and if you ask, all that can happen is that the vendor might say "no." After all, the objective of this whole process is to avoid not knowing and getting bitten for it later.

16

Influences, Critical Success Factors, and Lessons Learned

In this chapter is a discussion of the influences, CSFs, and lessons that were learned as a result of the ES Acquisition Process. Our goal in presenting these to you is to make you aware, first of all, that there will be influences that affect the Acquisition process; second, there are certain factors that are considered "critical" for the success of this type of project; and finally, there were some interesting lessons that all of the organizations learned from going through this process.

16.1 INFLUENCES

No matter how diligent the Acquisition Team is about trying to make the Acquisition process as objective and "matter of fact" as it can possibly be, the process is still going to be influenced and shaped by various factors. It is important, therefore, that the Acquisition Team be aware of this, and in as much as the Team members are aware that influences can affect the Acquisition process, then the next step is knowing what kinds of influences there are.

There are many different types of influences that can and will affect the process. These will be discussed shortly. While some of these factors may influence your Acquisition process, others may not. The influence that any one factor or element may have on the process will vary according to the specific dynamics of your organization, so it is impossible to say whether a given influence will or will not affect your Acquisition process. Some influences, though, will be the same regardless of the organization. Consider Y2K, for instance. Y2K is an example of a factor that had a definite impact on the Acquisition process of two of the cases. In one case, ESC, Y2K was the principal reason for the hastened time frame of their acquisition project.

- **Influences that you need to adapt to:** When, as in the preceding example, you can identify the specific influence, and the influence is immutable (as the coming of Y2K was), then you at least know why adjustments have to be made to the process, and you make them accordingly. In some instances, though, immutable influences might also have to be accounted for as criteria in the selection of the software solution. Such an example comes from the case of International Air where organizational culture was an influence and also a factor in the selection of their software.
- **Influences that can be minimized:** If, however, the influence is not immutable, then steps can be taken to minimize its effect. One of the ways to minimize the subjective element during the Evaluation process, for example, is with the scoring matrix that your Acquisition Team could develop for making the final choice of software solution. As ESC's Project Manager–Financial System explained:

> We probably had 50 people in each of these demos and they filled out scores of 1 to 5—a subjective process and all you're doing is you're aggregating a bunch of very subjective opinions by people and then trying to put a kind of notion of objectivity on it. That's what we were trying to do, just make it as objective as possible, [without] making it overly scientific.

Regardless of the nature of the influences (whether minimizable or immutable), it is simply important that the Acquisition Team be aware of the potential impact that influences can have on the Acquisition process. As you probably already know, some influences in an organization are very subtle yet they have the potential of undermining even the best efforts of the Acquisition Team and can (to the detriment of the organization) derail an acquisition project or affect its outcome. Our hope, therefore, in sharing this information is to help you either minimize their impact on your Acquisition process or, at the very least, show you how other organizations have dealt with them.

16.1.1   Influences on the Acquisition Process

Many influences that were noted from the cases affected the ES Acquisition Process. These included:

- Physical location of the vendor (geographical)
- Y2K (for replacing obsolete systems)

- Performance
- Ownership of code

Physical Location of the Vendor

In the cases of International Air and Telecom International, the capability of the vendor to support their geographically dispersed operations within North America and abroad was an important factor in each of their decision processes. Also of concern for Telecom International, besides the geographical location of the vendor, was the geographical location of their own primary customer for the new system, which is based in the United States (another influence on their decision process). Although Telecom International's procurement activities were done by the Canadian operations, the new software solution would be run in Canada, the United States, and elsewhere, with the primary users being based in the United States. There was, consequently, concern that their primary users would not receive the support they would need from the vendor and, perhaps even, from Telecom International Canada. Since the geographical boundary that exists between Telecom International Canada and Telecom International is a relatively new phenomenon for this organization (since Telecom International is a relatively new subsidiary of Telecom Inc.), their relationship, at the time the ES Acquisition Process occurred, was still on a learning curve (which, in and of itself, seemed to have an influence on the ES Acquisition Process because it presented some uncertainties that could only be resolved with time).

Y2K

Technological determinants were present in three of the cases. International Air, ESC, and Keller were replacing obsolete systems with new technology and also changing to a client-server environment. For both International Air and ESC, Y2K was a determinant factor in their decisions to replace their systems. Although Keller did not mention this factor as being determinant, it would most certainly have arisen given that they were running on an old AS400 system.

Performance

Another technological factor that influenced International Air's ES Acquisition Process arose out of International Air's Information Search process and was subsequently brought into their Technical Evaluation process—it had to do with the performance of the software solution on a WAN. This factor was considered important enough to include as a clause in the final contract and was a factor in the final Legal Negotiations.

Ownership of Code

Of the four cases, the legal issue of ownership of code was a determinant factor in the Acquisition process only for Telecom International. Given the central and strategic nature of this new system acquisition to their organization, Telecom International felt it important to have ownership of the code. Since Telecom International could not reach an agreement with their vendor-of-choice on this issue (this was the second major reason why Telecom International did not proceed with the acquisition), the Acquisition process was halted.

Other influences that were noted arose out of the nature of the organization, with "nature" being defined and circumscribed by the vision, policies, and even attitudes of upper management and reflected in the organization's populace. While some organizational influences can be minimized or even ignored (as in the case of external references from outside organizations), others may need to be accounted for during the Acquisition process.

Of the organizational influences that were apparent from the cases, the following were the most notable for their impact on the Acquisition process:

- Organizational culture
- External references (from other organizations)
- Final authority
- New management

Organizational Culture

Organizational culture also stood out as an important influence on the Acquisition process, especially in the case of International Air. As stated earlier, users at International Air had "a lot of power in determining their functionality." Although International Air had included BPR as a criterion for the desired packaged solution, it would have been very difficult for International Air's management to implement a significant amount of organizational change. International Air's upper management and Acquisition Team seemed to be aware of the amount of change that International Air's user community would be willing to accept. If International Air had selected SAP as their primary choice, the Acquisition Team admitted that it would have been a very difficult internal sell to the users. According to the IT Director:

> SAP is sold as is. You do not change SAP. The organization has to change its processes to accommodate SAP. If you do not want to change your processes, then you do not buy SAP. If you want the best practices as per SAP and you want a new software, then you buy SAP.

> Management's feeling is that it is a lot harder to change a process than to change software, and users at International Air want us to change the software because they do not want to change their processes.

International Air's management felt that it would have been difficult to do process redesign in their organization mainly because of their culture, where the users have a lot of say and whose buy-in carries a lot of weight in the Acquisition process. Hence, in International Air's case, the final recommendation of the Acquisition Team was influenced by this factor.

External References

As to external references from other organizations, these were obtained from the vendors and other information sources such as professional research groups. The feedback provided by these references (which lends to a vendor/product's reputation) was an important influence on the Selection process and was one of the factors considered in narrowing the long-list of candidates to a short-list of two or three vendors. Of the four cases, external references appeared to have the most influence in both Keller's and ESC's cases, but not greatly influential in Telecom International's case.

Final Authority

In all of the cases, the final authority for the purchase rested outside the Acquisition Team with either the Board of Directors (International Air) or the Steering Committee (Telecom International, ESC, and Keller[1]). This is due to two main factors:

1. The strategic nature of the acquisition and its impact enterprise-wide
2. The cost of the acquisition on all levels (financial, human and technical resources, etc.)

New Management

The Telecom International case incurred another influence that was not present in the other three cases. At Telecom International, the data revealed the subtle influence that new management had on the Acquisition process. In the

---

1. At Keller, the Steering Committee (which they referred to as their "Selection Team") was involved in the ES Acquisition Process, directing the activities of the Acquisition Team, as well as performing the activities of the Information Search and Selection processes, contacting references, and being involved with the Evaluation process. The VP of IS (who was also the leader of the Selection Team) was the primary negotiator, and the final authority rested with him as well. This is unusual, as compared to the other cases where the final authority rested entirely with a body separate from the Acquisition Team, but this can be attributed mainly to the size of the organization.

middle of the process, a new CIO came on board who had prior experiences involving the same type of "acquisition versus internal development" scenarios as were experienced by Telecom International prior to their initial decision to buy a packaged software solution. As described earlier, the CIO provided some input into the process. His influence could also be seen in the final choice. Based on his past experiences, and after reviewing the cost and code ownership issues with senior management (Telecom International's Steering Committee), the decision was made to halt the Acquisition process and to develop the system in-house.

The following is a summary listing of all the influences on the ES Acquisition Process that were noted from the cases:

- Obsolete or aging systems
- Y2K
- Technical aspects of the ES
- User community
- User participation
- Organizational culture
- Strong management commitment
- Final authority (outside the Acquisition Teams)
- Well-known issues that arise during implementation
- Organizational IT objective
- Business and technological reasons
- Economic factors
- Outside consultants
- Geographically dispersed team members
- New management
- Ownership of code
- Performance
- Financing

16.1.2   Influences on the Final Choice

Many influences that were noted from the cases affected the final choice of packaged ES solution. These included:

- User buy-in
- Integrated single-vendor solution
- Economic factors

User Buy-In

In all of the cases except Telecom International, the buy-in from users was an important factor in the decision process. This factor weighed heavily in the outcome of the Acquisition process and, in and of itself, was an important influence.

Integrated Single-Vendor Solution

In each of these three cases (International Air, ESC, and Keller), the importance of buying an integrated solution from a single vendor was also mentioned; however, the importance of this factor was stressed more so by International Air and Keller. Telecom International also was looking for a solution from a single vendor that integrated billing with accounts payable, etc., but since they could not find one for a reasonable cost, they opted to develop the solution themselves.

Economic Factors

In all of the cases, economic factors also played their part in influencing the process. None was more apparent, though, than with Keller, especially given the size of their organization. Consequently, Keller was limited to seeking technological solutions from smaller vendors. According to Keller's VP of IS, when he contacted SAP to inquire about their product, in no uncertain terms SAP rejected them based solely on the size of their organization.

> The person from SAP asked him, "Sir, do you know which car lot you're in [with reference to SAP]?" to which he replied, "No." The person from SAP then continued to explain that [with this call] he was currently looking at Rolls Royces, when actually, what he should be looking at, was in the lot across the street—the one that sold compacts.

Cost was a determinant factor for Telecom International as well and it was one of the primary reasons why they did not proceed with their acquisition. According to Telecom International's CIO, since "we did not find any vendor who could have provided us with the perfect global billing system at a reasonable cost, we decided to build it ourselves."

The following list summarizes all of the influences on the final choice:

- Economic factors
- Support for geographically dispersed global operations
- Single-vendor solution
- Integrated packaged software solution

- Business process reengineering
- Vendor demonstrations
- User buy-in
- Capped budget
- Ease of adaptability of the ES system
- Technological preference
- New management
- External references
- Marketplace analysis

16.1.3   Influences on the Acquisition Team

The Acquisition Teams were also subjected to several influences, among which were:

- Influences arising from the nature of its constituent members
  - Interdisciplinary and/or interdepartmental and/or cross-functional skills
  - Leadership
- Past experience
- Steering Committee or Board of Directors (final authorization)

Acquisition Team Composition

In each of the cases, the composition of the Acquisition Teams was either interdisciplinary, with team members coming from various departments, and/or cross-functional with each member contributing knowledge and/or skills required to meet the demands of the acquisition task. As such, each individual team member influenced the process to a greater or lesser extent.

Leadership

In particular, leadership by either the project manager or project director was a factor that influenced the process. This factor had an impact on the level of satisfaction that other team members experienced, not only with regard to the outcome of the process, but also with regard to the manner in which the Acquisition process was organized and carried out. Whether the Acquisition Team leader had technical expertise with systems or not (as was the case for ESC and Keller) did not seem to influence the process as much as their ability to assemble their Acquisition Team, to organize and carry through the process, and, on a more personal level, the respect that people had for them.

Past Experience

Another factor was past experience (either positive or negative) and this factor had a noticeable influence on the Acquisition process. In International Air's case, several of their Acquisition Team members were on an earlier version of this same project in the early 1990s when International Air had decided that they would develop the systems in-house. For several reasons, this project was abandoned, and the stigma of this past experience weighed heavily on these members throughout the Acquisition process. As expressed by one of the team members who was brought in (as a consultant) to participate in this acquisition:

> People would bring bad history with them and you always had to work at saying, "That was the last time. We are not going to make that mistake this time." . . . That was very much an influence that I noticed. . . . People were nervous, they did not want to have the same thing happen again. (Project Control Officer)

Hence, it can easily be stated that the memory of the past "failure" was a motivating and, thus, influencing factor on the process.

Steering Committee

As a group, the Board of Directors or the Steering Committee had an influence on and played an important role in overseeing the process. This was especially apparent in Keller's case where the Steering Committee had a more active role in the Acquisition process.

Following is a list summarizing all of the influences that were noted on the Acquisition Teams:

- Acquisition Team composition
- Interdisciplinary nature of the Acquisition Team
- Cohesiveness of the Acquisition Team
- Leadership
- Competency
- Past experience
- User participation
- New management
- Final authority outside the Acquisition Team
- Steering Committee
- Y2K

16.2 CRITICAL SUCCESS FACTORS (CSFS)

No one CSF, alone, is going to make the ES Acquisition Process a success. It is, rather, the combination of several critical factors that will result in its successful outcome. This section covers the CSFs that were noted in the cases:

- **Planning:** Planning is highly critical to the ES Acquisition Process. With there being so many activities and issues that need to be considered, the odds of having a successful acquisition will be greatly increased the more care that is taken to do this activity well. Also, since many of the factors that need to be accounted for during the Acquisition process are the same as those that need to be considered for the software's implementation, it stands to reason that if the necessary attention and care are given to dealing with them at the acquisition stage, there will be fewer issues and problems (surprises) that will arise during the implementation stage. Hence, a good job in Planning for the acquisition could mean fewer problems come the implementation.

- **Cross-over of Acquisition Team members to the Implementation project:** The Acquisition Team was formed with an eye toward the implementation of the ES. In the case of International Air, the objective when forming the Acquisition Team was to bring together users and project people who would not only be part of the Acquisition process, but who would also be involved with the subsequent implementation of the ES system. This was done to avoid potential conflict and assure the success of the entire ES project. Only certain key users and MIS individuals remained with the project throughout the entire Acquisition process and on into the implementation. They provided "project memory" (comparable to organizational memory) and continuity during the implementation stage.

- **Careful selection of the Acquisition Team members:** While the careful selection of team members is critical for any project, it is especially so for the acquisition of ES. Since this type of technological solution is so complex and diverse in nature, the Acquisition Team needs to be equally diverse in the skills that are required of its team members. Hence, each individual team member needs to have the appropriate skills necessary for the completion of specific sets of tasks or responsibilities within the project. Moreover, each individual team member needs to be selected to perform a functional and/or advisory role based on his/her abilities or past experiences.

- **Clear and unambiguous authority:** Any ambiguity in authority tends to diffuse accountability and increase the possibility of the process being diverted, or unduly shortened or abbreviated, or of conflict arising not only on complex issues but on minor ones as well. Hence, a "clear authority" for the Acquisition process stands out as a CSF. This "authority" or "project leader/manager/director" need not be an individual from the IT department, but should be someone with strong leadership skills and a good sense of objectivity.
- **User participation:** User participation in the process and at the vendor demonstrations was also considered very important.
- **Accurate information:** Since the entire Acquisition process is fueled by information, it is absolutely imperative that the information be accurate and reliable. Hence, it is necessary that information sources be verified and cross-checked as to the quality of the information that they provide. While reputation and credibility may speak to the accuracy and reliability of the information that is obtained, these also should be double checked. As was seen in the case of ESC, although one of the consultants that had supplied the Acquisition Team with information was from a reputable consulting firm, the consultant's former ties with one of the ES vendors biased the information that he provided to ESC's Acquisition Team and resulted in ESC dropping the vendor from their long-list. Although ESC later chose the ES from that vendor, the biased information from that consultant could have resulted in ESC settling on the "wrong" or less than optimal ES solution for its needs—misinformation could have been very costly to ESC.
- **Definition of all requirements:** It is of critical importance that the Acquisition Team thoroughly assess and define all of the current and desired requirements that are relevant to the packaged ES. This means defining the organization's needs at all of its different levels and in all of the functional areas that the ES will have a direct or indirect impact on. It is critical that this activity be completed **before** contacting vendors or doing the Marketplace Analysis.
- **Establishment of selection and evaluation criteria:** As with the definition of all organizational requirements, it is important and critical that the Team establish its selection and evaluation criteria **prior** to contacting any vendor or looking at ES solutions.
- **Structured process:** Structure is also a critical factor for the success of the process. Since a poorly defined structure can hinder, even cripple, the timetable and budget of an ES acquisition project, it is a good idea to define the structure and the techniques that will be used to

manage the process at the very beginning of the Planning phase of the Acquisition process. A well-defined structure for the Acquisition process presupposes the need, also, for a clear authority for the process.

- **Rigorous process:** Rigor is another characteristic that defines the Acquisition process as it was carried out by the Acquisition Teams. This can be a critical factor in the success of the process. If the Acquisition Team is lax in carrying out any part of the Acquisition process, the results are likely to show in the final choice of ES solution for the organization. Moreover, since much of the preliminary work that is done during the Acquisition process (i.e., definition of requirements and addressing of issues regarding process reengineering or redesign, etc.) could be used during the implementation, the more rigorous the Acquisition process is carried out, the better it will become the implementation.

- **Partnership approach:** Another characteristic of the Acquisition process, which was also noted as a CSF, was the "partnership" approach that was adopted by all of the teams with their vendors-of-choice. While this approach was also adopted by all of the teams with their organizations' user communities, none was more strongly emphasized and evidenced than by the teams from International Air and Keller. International Air's Project Director stated that the creation of a "partnership approach (internally) with the various user communities, letting them come up with a recommendation that they felt comfortable with," led to the users giving their full buy-in to the acquisition. International Air used this approach similarly with their Purchasing department. In all of the cases, this approach was used to establish a more open working relationship with the vendors with the objective of avoiding conflictual situations. The following statement by International Air's Project Director expresses the same sentiment as that which came through in the other three cases:

  > This was a very difficult thing to do because we wanted, on the one hand, to get the very best deal, but on the other hand, this first series of working discussions that we were going to have with the vendor would take us from now to years to come.

- **User buy-in:** In all of the cases, but especially for International Air and Keller, user buy-in was a critical factor in the success of the Acquisition process. While much has already been presented on the importance of this factor in the process, let us add simply that user buy-in on the final choice will undoubtedly result in user acceptance of the software following implementation. This was evident in the case of Keller. User buy-in of the choice of technology and even excitement and enthusiasm about its prospects for the organization translated into an open acceptance by the users of the software following implementation. We might also add that this openness to the technology could translate into a shortened learning curve. This would mean that the organization, as a whole, could derive benefits a lot sooner, that is, a return to pre-implementation production levels, or as is hoped with the new ES, better production levels. So, there can be several advantages to getting the users involved and obtaining their buy-in.

- **Vendor relationship:** In all of the cases, the long-term relationship with the prospective vendor was mentioned as being very important. The question that was frequently asked by all concerned was, "Can we work with them?" In the words of International Air's Project Director:

> If this is the vendor that you are going to deal with for the next five to ten years, you had better make sure that you can do business with those people and when it gets tough, that you can resolve those things.

The element of trust factored into this characteristic and all parties felt the need to create an atmosphere of trust right from the start of their dealings with the vendors.

The following list summarizes all of the critical success factors for the ES Acquisition Process:

- Planning
- Cross-over of Acquisition Team members to the Implementation project
- Careful selection of the Acquisition Team members
- Interdisciplinary nature of the Acquisition Team
- Competency/skills of the Acquisition Team members
- Leadership
- Clear and unambiguous authority
- Accountability
- Strong management commitment
- Definition of the requirements
- Establishing selection and evaluation criteria
- Evaluations—Vendor, Functional, and Technical

- Formal process
- Structured process
- Rigorous
- User-driven
- Internal partnership with the various user communities
- Partnership/relationship with the vendor
- User participation
- User buy-in

16.3   LESSONS LEARNED

A few important lessons were learned by the organizations in the course of the Acquisition process:

- New procedures had to be developed for dealing with ES acquisitions.
- Standard purchasing practices had to be modified for the ES acquisition.
- The ES Acquisition Process is very complex.
- Past experience had to be accounted for in the process.

1. **New procedures had to be developed.** Since there were no formalized processes in place in any of the four organizations for the acquisition of packaged software, not to mention ES, the Acquisition Teams constructed the Acquisition process for ES. To do so, they created a structure in which the general process could evolve, with the goal of giving it a sense of order, structure, control, and direction. With the use of project management techniques, each of the teams laid out timetables, tasks, milestones, etc., for certain parts of the process and incorporated various other tools (questionnaires, matrices, etc.), modifying and adjusting as needed, to meet the needs of other parts of the process. As a result, the ES Acquisition Process evolved over the course of the acquisition into what has been shown here. As stated by International Air's Project Director:

> Other than formal RFP guidelines, . . . the rest of the process was essentially put together by the project team.

2. **Existing purchasing procedures had to be modified.** Standard or formalized purchasing practices did not fit the acquisition of the packaged ES. In all cases, they needed to be modified to suit the complexity of this

acquisition. As stated by the Purchasing Manager of Telecom
International:

> I cannot say that it fully complied or followed our normal practices
> . . . or that it [the Acquisition process] was fully accomplished in
> accordance with the normalized rules that we usually follow.

Similarly, International Air's Project Director reported:

> There is a formal process at International Air. If you go through
> Purchasing, they would be the ones to manage the process. So, they
> do provide you with a framework, and essentially, they have RFP
> guidelines, but not much more than that. Then there was their expe-
> rience and you give them your views on what you think is a good
> approach. You can bounce it off them and they give you some sug-
> gestions of their own and provide some guidance. But, other than
> the formal RFP guidelines, I do not think the rest of the processes
> that were described were standard.

3. **The ES Acquisition Process is very complex.** As noted by the Technical
Team Leader–Financial System:

> Even with all the variables known, the magnitude of a project like
> this is complex. There is no way around it.

The Project Manager–Financial System added the following comments on
what he discovered about the complexity of this type of decision process:

> It was a lot more complex than I ever would have imagined. You
> know, there are a lot of things that have changed in terms of the
> way we view what the vendor told us in the pre-sales or sales cycle
> going to the implementation, just because I don't think you ever
> have enough time. It's like so many things—you never have enough
> time, you just have to make a decision based on gut feel sometimes
> and just go with it based on the information that you've got, and we
> did that.

> I'm sure that, you know, we could have . . . spent a year and a mil-
> lion dollars and probably been no closer than we are today, but
> might have uncovered some things. At least we would know a little
> bit more about what we were dealing with going in. But, I'm not
> convinced there's enough benefit in spending that sort of time and
> money.

As you know, my background is in accounting and auditing, and I have always worked around these kinds of implementations. I had a number of clients when I was in the auditing business that implemented packaged software, but I never really understood the complexity of the software or the complexity of the decision until going through what I'm going through right now.

4. **They had to take into account past experience.** Though intangible, past experience was a factor that the Acquisition Team members at International Air learned to deal with during this experience.

Lastly, all of the Teams took extra care to formally document the process. Since this was a new learning experience for all of them, the Teams wanted to leave behind some documentation explaining the rationale that was used and the decisions that were made for choosing one packaged ES over another. As a result, the Teams contributed a documented history of what transpired during the Acquisition process to the organizational memory.

17 Conclusion

While there is much to be digested from this book, there are certain messages that we would like you to retain.

First, an ES project is not so much about the technology as it is about people. This, then, entails an explicit need to understand the organization. The understanding should not be limited to a narrow business focus, but should encompass the organization as a whole—its purpose, its people, and its tools. Hence, the ES project will need to take into account the organization's culture and how the new technology will affect it. It will also be necessary, therefore, to remember that organizations are cross-functional units and that all decisions that are made regarding new technology will have an impact on many, if not all, areas of the organization. Although we have the tendency, as individuals, to believe that our actions do not impact others, history and experience tell us otherwise. Vigilance, care, and due regard for the consequences of our information technology choices are therefore required.

Second, the decision process to acquire an ES solution is an organizational one. The implication here is that it no longer rests solely with one individual, as do many organizational decisions, but rather, that it is the responsibility of each and every member of the organization. The decision to acquire Enterprise Software or any other type of information technology should be based on a consensus among the individuals from the sectors of the organization that will be affected by the new technology. This could mean individuals from sectors that would be directly impacted by the new technology as well as individuals from those sectors where the technology's impact might not be directly felt. Why? Because, when individuals from other organizational units are aware of what is happening within the organization as it pertains to new technology, they will be better equipped to address their own sectors' concerns. These individuals might also be able to provide insights into other areas (outsiders' perceptions, impressions, etc.) or be aware of opportunities that might exist within the organization where similar technology could be of benefit. For example, during the ES Acquisition Process, the involvement of individuals from organizational units not directly impacted by the immediate acquisition might lead to the identification of a need (current or future) that will not be met by the current acquisition. Upon inquiry to the vendor, this need might be met with an additional module that would not significantly add to the cost of the current acquisition.

Third, the ES Acquisition Process provides a means for reducing the risk and uncertainty associated with an ES purchase. Because a wrong decision with regard to an ES solution could adversely affect the organization as a whole and not only the sector where the technology would be applied, every available means to reduce the chance of making a wrong decision should be used. While there is nothing that can predict 100% the successful outcome of anything, the decision process that has been introduced here should help to minimize the level of risk and uncertainty that are inherent to the acquisition of ES, and increase the likelihood of acquiring the best possible solution for the organization's needs.

Fourth, the ES Acquisition Process provides the framework within which the requisite care and attention can be focused on the task of finding the right fit of ES solution for the organization *prior* to its implementation.

Fifth, proper planning and preparation are essential to the success of the ES Acquisition Process and to finding the right fit of ES solution for the organization.

Sixth, the ES Acquisition Process helps to reduce the number of "surprises" that are likely to crop up later during the implementation. There are, after all, enough technical quirks and snags (both software and hardware related) that arise during an implementation. As for situations that are avoidable, foresight in planning and preparation during the Acquisition process could eliminate, and if not eliminate, then at least bring to the organization's awareness problematic situations with the ES that would need to be dealt with during its implementation. These situations, too, could then be included among the evaluation factors for the ES and could be enough to disqualify an ES from further consideration. If, however, these situations are not overly problematic or costly to remedy, and the ES is chosen, then the problems could be factored into the implementation schedule ahead of time. Hence, there will be fewer surprises, potentially fewer delays, and fewer cost overruns.

Finally, this "new" perspective on the Acquisition process for ES, in practical terms, could translate into substantial savings for the organization in terms of actual costs, time, and improved administrative procedures. Other benefits that the organization could realize as a result of this newly gained understanding might also include the development of new purchasing procedures specifically geared for the acquisition of ES, a better handle on the issues that factor into the negotiations for this type of software, and better preparedness for ES implementations.

We hope that you have gained a new awareness of the multitude of issues that are inherent to the acquisition of Enterprise Software solutions. Let our book serve you well. Now go to it!

Index

| Back | Forward | Home | Reload | Images | Open | Print | Find | Stop |

`http://www.phptr.com/`

| What's New? | What's Cool? | Destinations | Net Search | People | Software |

P R E N T I C E   H A L L

Professional Technical Reference
Tomorrow's Solutions for Today's Professionals

DATE DUE

PALCI-YUL065		
Due 2-17-03		
GAYLORD		PRINTED IN U.S.A.

...ith

...1e!

...ppening in
...ere's a bit of what

@ ...ook series, software,
...ful information to

☞ ...ction for the latest
...ers.

$ ...bookseller near you
...a Magnet bookstore

! ...oks for the professional
...vention schedule, join
...leases on topics of

✉ **...ail newsletter!**

...st? Choose a targeted
...ed of the latest PH PTR
products, author events, reviews and conferences in your interest area.

Visit our mailroom to subscribe today! **http://www.phptr.com/mail_lists**

www.phptr.com